Benjamin Franklin

(John S. C. Abbott)

KARTINDO PUBLISHING HOUSE (Kartindo.Com)

PREFACE

Next to George Washington, we must write, upon the Catalogue of American Patriots, the name of Benjamin Franklin. He had so many virtues that there is no need of exaggerating them; so few imperfections that they need not be concealed. The writer has endeavored to give a perfectly accurate view of his character, and of that great struggle, in which he took so conspicuous a part, which secured the Independence of the United States. Probably there can no where be found, within the same limits, so vivid a picture of Life in America, one hundred years ago, as the career of Franklin presents.

This volume is the twelfth of the Library Series of Pioneers and Patriots. The series presents a graphic history of our country from its discovery.

1. *Christopher Columbus* reveals to us the West Indies, and gives a narrative of wonders unsurpassed in fact or fable.

2. *De Soto* conducts us to Florida, and leads us through scenes of romance, crime, blood and woe--through many Indian tribes, across the continent, to the Mississippi, where he finds his melancholy grave.

3. *La Salle*, and his heroic companions, traversed thousands of miles of majestic lakes and unknown rivers, and introduces us to innumerable barbaric tribes. There is no other writer, who, from his own personal observation, can give one so vivid an idea of Life in the Indian village and wigwam.

4. *Miles Standish* was the Captain of the Pilgrims. He conducts us in the May Flower, across the Atlantic, lands us at Plymouth, and tells the never to be forgotten story of the heroism of our fathers in laying the foundations of this great republic.

5. *Captain Kidd*, and the Buccaneers, reveal to us the awful condition of North and South America, when there was no protecting law here, and when pirates swept sea and land, inflicting atrocities, the narrative of which causes the ear which hears it to tingle.

6. *Peter Stuyvesant* takes us by the hand, and introduces us to the Dutch settlement at the mouth of the Hudson, conveys us, in his schooner, up the

KARTINDO PUBLISHING HOUSE (Kartindo.Com)

solitary river, along whose forest-covered banks Indian villages were scattered; and reveals to us all the struggles, by which the Dutch New Amsterdam was converted into the English New York.

7. *Benjamin Franklin* should chronologically take his place here. There is probably not, in the compass of all literature, a biography more full of entertainment and valuable thought, than a truthful sketch of the career of Benjamin Franklin. He leads us to Philadelphia, one hundred and fifty years ago, and makes us perfectly familiar with life there and then. He conducts us across the Atlantic to the Court of St. James, and the Court of Versailles. There is no writer, French or English, who has given such vivid sketches of the scenes which were witnessed there, as came from the pen of Benjamin Franklin. For half a century Franklin moved amid the most stupendous events, a graphic history of which his pen has recorded.

8. *George Washington* has no superior. Humanity is proud of his name. He seems to have approached as near perfection as any man who ever lived. In his wonderful career we became familiar with all the struggles of the American Revolution. With a feeble soldiery, collected from a population of less than three millions of people, he baffled all the efforts of the fleets and armies of Great Britain, the most powerful empire upon this globe.

9. *Daniel Boone* was the Cowper of the wilderness; a solitary man loving the silent companionship of the woods. He leads us across the Alleghanies to the fields of Kentucky, before any white man's foot had traversed those magnificent realms. No tale of romance could ever surpass his adventures with the Indians.

10. *Kit Carson* was the child of the wilderness. He was by nature a gentleman, and one of the most lovable of men. His weird-like life passed rapidly away, before the introduction of railroads and steamboats. His strange, heroic adventures are ever read with astonishment, and they invariably secure for him the respect and affection of all who become familiar with his name.

11. *Paul Jones* was one of the purest patriots, and perhaps the most heroic naval hero, to whom any country has given birth. He has been so traduced, by the Tory press of Great Britain, that even the Americans have not yet done him full justice. This narrative of his astonishing achievements will, it is hoped, give him rank, in the opinion of every reader, with Washington, Franklin, Jefferson and Lafayette.

KARTINDO PUBLISHING HOUSE (Kartindo.Com)

12. *David Crockett* was a unique man. There is no one like him. Under no institutions but ours could such a character be formed. From a log hut, more comfortless than the wigwam of the savage, and without being able either to read or write, he enters legislative halls, takes his seat in Congress, and makes the tour of our great cities, attracting crowds to hear him speak. His life is a wild romance of undoubted truth.

Such is the character of this little library of twelve volumes. The writer, who has now entered the evening of life, affectionately commends them to the young men of America, upon whose footsteps their morning sun is now rising. The life of each one, if prolonged to three score years and ten, will surely prove a stormy scene. But it may end in a serene and tranquil evening, ushering in the glories of an immortal day.

JOHN S. C. ABBOTT.

KARTINDO PUBLISHING HOUSE (Kartindo.Com)

CONTENTS

KARTINDO PUBLISHING HOUSE (Kartindo.Com)

CHAPTER IV.

Mental and Moral Conflicts.

Faithfulness to work--Neglect of Deborah Read--Treatise on Liberty and Necessity--Skill in swimming--Return to America--Marriage of Miss Read--Severe sickness--Death of Mr. Denham--Returns to Keimer's employ--The Junto--His Epitaph--Reformation of his treatise on Liberty and Necessity--Franklin's creed.

CHAPTER V.

The Dawn of Prosperity.

Franklin takes a house--His first job--His industry--Plans a Newspaper--Enters the list as a writer--Advocates a Paper currency--Purchases Keimer's paper--Character of Meredith--Struggles of the firm--Unexpected assistance--Dissolves partnership with Meredith--Franklin's energetic conduct--His courtship, and marriage--Character of Mrs. Franklin--Increase of luxury--Plans for a library--Prosperity of Pennsylvania--Customs in Philadelphia--Style of dress in 1726--Franklin's social position in Philadelphia--His success--A hard student.

CHAPTER VI.

Religious and Philosophic Views.

Studious habits--New religion--Personal habits--Church of the Free and Easy--His many accomplishments--The career of Hemphall--Birth and Death of Franklin's son--The Ministry of Whitefield--Remarkable friendship between the philosopher and the preacher--Prosperity of Franklin--His convivial habits--The defense of Philadelphia--Birth of a daughter--The Philadelphia Academy.

CHAPTER VII.

The Tradesman becomes a Philosopher.

KARTINDO PUBLISHING HOUSE (Kartindo.Com)

CHAPTER VIII.

The Rising Storms of War.

CHAPTER IX.

Franklin's Mission to England.

KARTINDO PUBLISHING HOUSE (Kartindo.Com)

CHAPTER X.

Franklin's Second Mission to England.

Fiendish conduct of John Penn--Petition to the crown--Debt of England--Two causes of conflict--Franklin sent to England--His embarkation--Wise counsel to his daughter--The stamp act--American resolves--Edmund Burke--Examination of Franklin--Words of Lord Chatham--Dangers to English operatives--Repeal of the stamp act--Joy in America--Ross Mackay--New taxes levied--Character of George III--Accumulation of honors to Franklin--Warlike preparations--Human conscientiousness--Unpopularity of William Franklin--Marriage of Sarah Franklin--Franklin's varied investigations--Efforts to civilize the Sandwich Islands.

CHAPTER XI.

The Intolerance of King and Court.

Parties in England--Franklin the favorite of the opposition--Plans of the Tories--Christian III--Letter of Franklin--Dr. Priestley--Parisian courtesy--Louis XV--Visit to Ireland--Attempted alteration of the Prayer Book--Letter to his son--Astounding letters from America--Words of John Adams--Petition of the Assembly--Violent conspiracy against Franklin--His bearing in the court-room--Wedderburn's infamous charges--Letter of Franklin--Bitter words of Dr. Johnson--Morals of English lords--Commercial value of the Colonies--Dangers threatening Franklin.

CHAPTER XII.

The Bloodhounds of War Unleashed.

The mission of Josiah Quincy--Love of England by the Americans--Petition to the king--Sickness and death of Mrs. Franklin--Lord Chatham--His speech in favor of the colonists--Lord Howe--His interview with Franklin--Firmness of Franklin--His indignation--His mirth--Franklin's fable--He embarks for Philadelphia--Feeble condition of the colonies--England's expressions of contempt--Franklin's reception at Philadelphia--His letter to Edmund Burke--

KARTINDO PUBLISHING HOUSE (Kartindo.Com)

KARTINDO PUBLISHING HOUSE (Kartindo.Com)

CHAPTER I

Parentage and Early Life

The parentage of Franklin--His parents emigrate to America--Character of his father--Abiah Folger, his mother--Birth and baptism--Influence of his Uncle Strong--Of the Whistle--Childish exploits--Uncongenial employment--Skill in swimming.--Early reading--Boston at that time--An indentured apprentice--Form of Indenture--Enters a printing office--Fondness for reading--Anecdotes--Habits of study--Fondness for argument--Adopts a vegetable diet--The two creeds.

About the year 1685, Josiah Franklin, with his wife and three children, emigrated from Banbury, England, to seek his fortune in this new world. He was in all respects a very worthy man, intelligent, industrious, and influenced to conduct by high moral and religious principles. Several of Josiah Franklin's neighbors accompanied him in his removal.

Boston was then a straggling village, of five or six thousand inhabitants. In front spread out its magnificent bay, with its beautiful islands. In the rear the primeval forest extended, almost unbroken, through unexplored wilds to the Pacific. His trade was that of a dyer. Finding, however, but little employment in that business, he set up as a tallow chandler and soap boiler. Four years of life's usual joys and sorrows passed away when Mrs. Franklin died, leaving six children. The eldest was but eleven years of age. This motherless little family needed a maternal guardian. Within the year, Mr. Franklin married Abiah Folger, of Nantucket. She was the youngest daughter of Peter Folger, a man illustrious for many virtues, and of whom it has been well said, that "he was worthy to be the grandfather of Benjamin Franklin." She proved to be a noble woman, and was all that either husband or children could wish for. Ten children were the fruit of this union. Benjamin was born on the sixth of January, (O. S.) 1706.

He was born in the morning of a Sabbath day. His father then resided directly opposite the Old South Church, in Milk street. The same day, the babe, whose renown it was then little imagined would subsequently fill the civilized world, was wrapped in blankets, and carried by his father across the street through the wintry air, to the Old South Church, where he was baptized by the Rev. Dr. Willard. He was named Benjamin, after a much beloved uncle then residing in England. This uncle was a man of some property, of decided literary tastes, and

KARTINDO PUBLISHING HOUSE (Kartindo.Com)

of the simple, fervent piety, which characterized the best people of those days. He took an ever increasing interest in Benjamin. He eventually came over to this country, and exerted a powerful influence in moulding the character of his nephew, whose brilliant intellect he appreciated.

Soon after the birth of Benjamin, his father removed to a humble but comfortable dwelling at the corner of Hanover and Union streets. Here he passed the remainder of his days. When Franklin had attained the age of five years, a terrible conflagration took place, since known as the Great Boston Fire. Just as the cold blasts of winter began to sweep the streets, this great calamity occurred. The whole heart of the thriving little town was laid in ashes. Over a hundred families found themselves in destitution in the streets.

An incident took place when Franklin was about seven years of age, which left so indelible an impression upon his mind, that it cannot be omitted in any faithful record of his life. He gave the following account of the event in his autobiography, written after the lapse of sixty-six years:

"My friends, on a holiday, filled my pockets with coppers. I went directly to a shop where they sold toys for children; and being charmed with the sound of a whistle that I met by the way in the hands of another boy, I voluntarily gave all my money for one. I then came home and went whistling all over the house, much pleased with my whistle, but disturbing all the family. My brothers and sisters and cousins, understanding the bargain I had made, told me that I had given four times as much for it as it was worth; put me in mind what good things I might have bought with the rest of the money; and laughed at me so much for my folly, that I cried with vexation; and the reflection gave me more chagrin than the whistle gave me pleasure."

This story, as published by Franklin, with his keen practical reflections, has become as a household word in all the families of England and America; and has been translated into nearly all the languages of modern Europe.

From early childhood Franklin was celebrated for his physical beauty, his athletic vigor and his imperturbable good nature. His companions invariably recognized him as their natural leader. He was in no respect what would be called a religious boy, but in many things he had a high sense of honor.

There was a marsh, flooded at high tides, where the boys used to fish for minnows. Much trampling had converted the spot into a quagmire. A man was about to build a house near by, and had carted a large quantity of stones for the cellar. Franklin called the boys together and suggested that they should go in the evening, take those stones, and build a wharf upon which they could stand with dry feet. It was done. And under the skilful engineering of the youthful Franklin, it was quite scientifically done. Complaints and detection followed. Josiah Franklin severely reproved Benjamin for the dishonest act, but it does not appear that the conscience of the precocious boy was much troubled. He argued very forcibly that the utility of the measure proved its necessity.

At the age of eight years, Benjamin entered the Boston Grammar School. His progress was very rapid, and at the close of the year he was at the head of his class. The father had hoped to give his promising boy a liberal education; but his large family and straitened circumstances rendered it necessary for him to abandon the plan. At the age of ten years his school life was completed, and he was taken into his father's shop to run of errands, and to attend to the details of candle-making, cutting wicks, filling moulds, and waiting upon customers. He could write a good hand, could read fluently, could express himself with ease on paper, but in all arithmetical studies was very backward.

There is scarcely any sport which has such a charm for boys as swimming. Franklin excelled all his companions. It is reported that his skill was wonderful; and that at any time between his twelfth and sixtieth year, he could with ease have swum across the Hellespont. In his earliest years, in all his amusements and employments, his inventive genius was at work in searching out expedients. To facilitate rapidity in swimming he formed two oval pallets, much resembling those used by painters, about ten inches long, and six broad. A hole was cut for the thumb and they were bound fast to the palm of the hand. Sandals of a somewhat similar construction were bound to the soles of the feet. With these appliances Franklin found that he could swim more rapidly, but his wrists soon became greatly fatigued. The sandals also he found of little avail, as in swimming, the propelling stroke is partly given by the inside of the feet and ankles, and not entirely by the soles of the feet.

In the vicinity of Boston there was a pond a mile wide. Franklin made a large paper kite, and when the wind blew strongly across the pond, he raised it, and entering the water and throwing himself upon his back was borne rapidly to the opposite shore. "The motion," he says, "was exceedingly agreeable." A boy carried his clothes around. Subsequently he wrote to M. Dubourg,

"I have never since that time practiced this singular mode of swimming; though I think it not impossible to cross in this manner from Dover to Calais. The packet boat, however, is still preferable."[1]

[Footnote 1: Sparks' Life and Works of Franklin, Vol. 6, p. 291.]

The taste for reading of this wonderful boy was insatiable. He had access, comparatively, to few books, but those he devoured with the utmost eagerness. Bunyan's Pilgrim's Progress was, so to speak, his first love. Having read and re-read it until his whole spirit was incorporated with its nature, he sold the volume and purchased Burton's Historical Collections. This consisted of quite a series of anecdotes and adventures, written in an attractive style, and published at a low price. In those early years he read another book which exerted a powerful influence in the formation of his character. When eighty years of age he alludes as follows to this work in a letter to Mr. Samuel Mather, who was son of the author, Cotton Mather,

"When I was a boy I met with a book entitled 'Essays to do Good,' which I think was written by your father. It had been so little regarded by a former possessor that several leaves of it were torn out; but the remainder gave me such a turn of thinking, as to have an influence on my conduct through life; for I have always set a greater value on the character of a doer of good, than on any other kind of a reputation; and if I have been, as you seem to think, a useful citizen, the public owe the advantage of it to that book."[2]

[Footnote 2: This volume has been republished by the Mass. S. S. Society.]

When Franklin was twelve years of age, the population of Boston had increased to about ten thousand. An incident is recorded of Franklin at this time, which strikingly illustrates the peculiarity of his mental structure and the want of reverence with which he gradually accustomed himself to regard religious things. His father's habit, in the long graces which preceded each meal, rather wearied the temper of his son. The precocious young skeptic, with characteristic irreverence, ventured to say,

"I think, father, that if you were to say grace over the whole cask, once for all, it would save time."[3]

[Footnote 3: Works of Dr. Franklin by W. Temple Franklin. Vol. I, p. 447.]

This was the remark of a boy but twelve years of age. Though it does not

KARTINDO PUBLISHING HOUSE (Kartindo.Com)

indicate a very devout spirit, it certainly gives evidence of an intellect of unusual acuteness.

Franklin ever spoke of his boyhood as the very happy period of a remarkably happy life. His peculiar temperament enabled him to be happy under circumstances in which others would have been very miserable. His affections in after years ever yearned toward Boston; he was accustomed to speak of it as "that beloved place." In one of his letters to John Lathrop he wrote,

"The Boston manner, the turn of phrase, and even tone of voice and accent in pronunciation, all please and seem to revive and refresh me."

For two years Benjamin continued to assist his father in the business of soap and candle making. He was continually looking for an opportunity to escape the drudgery of that employment and enter upon some more congenial business. Like most adventurous boys, he thought much of the romance of a sea-life. An elder brother had run away, had gone to sea, and for years had not been heard from. Benjamin's father became very anxious as he witnessed the discontent of his son. This anxiety was increased when an elder brother married, removed to Rhode Island, and set up a soap and candle establishment for himself. This seemed to Benjamin to rivet the chains which bound him at home. Apparently his father could not spare him from the business. Thus he seemed doomed to spend the remainder of his days in employment which proved to him increasingly uncongenial.

The judicious father, apprehensive that his son might be lured secretly to embark for some distant voyage, visited with his son all the varied workshops of Boston, that he might select that trade which to him would seem most desirable. Benjamin examined all these workshops with intensest interest. He selected the employment of a cutler, and entered upon the business for a few days; but at that time a boy who was about to learn a trade was apprenticed to a master. As a premium for learning the business he usually had to pay about one hundred dollars. Then after a series of years, during which he worked for nothing, he was entitled for a time to receive journeyman's wages. But his father, Josiah Franklin, was unable to settle satisfactorily the terms of indenture, and the cutlery trade was given up.

We have mentioned that Franklin was one of a large family of children. By the two marriages of his father, there were sixteen sons and daughters around the family hearth. One of the sons, James, had been sent to London to learn the

KARTINDO PUBLISHING HOUSE (Kartindo.Com)

trade of a printer. He returned to Boston and set up business on his own account, when Benjamin was eleven years of age. It was decided to bind Benjamin to this business. Reluctantly Benjamin consented to place himself in such subordination to his brother. He was, however, bound to him for a period of nine years, from twelve to twenty-one. During the last year he was to receive a journeyman's wages. The following extract from this form of indenture of apprenticeship, which was in common use in the reign of George the First, will be read with interest.

"He shall neither buy nor sell without his master's license. Taverns, inns, or ale-houses he shall not haunt. At cards, dice, tables, or any other unlawful game he shall not play. Matrimony he shall not contract; nor from the service of his said master day nor night absent himself, but in all things, as an honest and faithful apprentice, shall and will demean and behave himself towards his said master and all his, during said term. And the said James Franklin, the master, for and in consideration of the sum of ten pounds of lawful British money to him in hand paid by the said Josiah Franklin, the father, the receipt of which is hereby acknowledged, the said apprentice in the art of a printer which he now useth, shall teach and instruct or cause to be taught and instructed the best way and manner that he can, finding and allowing unto the said apprentice, meat, drink, washing, lodging and all other necessaries during the said term."

Benjamin devoted himself with great assiduity to learn the trade of a printer. The office in which he worked, stood at the corner of Franklin avenue and Court street. For three years, Franklin was thus employed, apparently never seeking recreation, and never having a moment of leisure save such as he could rescue from sleep or from his meals. There were at that time several bookstores in Boston. The eminent men of that province had brought with them to the New World, literary and scientific tastes of a high order. Even then the axe of the settler had been heard but at a short distance in the primeval forests, which still encircled all the large towns. Bears were not unfrequently shot from Long Wharf, as they swam from island to island, or endeavored to cross the solitary bay. It is said that at that time twenty bears were often shot in a week.

Benjamin Franklin, inspired by his love of reading, cultivated friendly relations with the clerks in the bookstores. From them he borrowed interesting volumes, which he took home in the evening with the utmost care, and having spent most of the night in reading, would return them at an early hour in the morning, before the master of the shop had time to miss them.

Something in the demeanor of Franklin attracted the attention of a merchant in

Boston by the name of Matthew Adams. He invited him to his library and loaned him books. The lad's Uncle Benjamin, in England, who was very fond of composing rhymes which he called poetry, sent many of his effusions to his favorite nephew, and opened quite a brisk correspondence with him. Thus Benjamin soon became a fluent rhymester, and wrote sundry ballads which were sold in the streets and became quite popular. There was a great demand at that time for narratives of the exploits of pirates, the doom of murderers, and wild love adventures. It is said that one of the Boston publishers, in the sale of ballads alone, found a very lucrative business. Benjamin, who found it very easy to write doggerel verse, wrote one ballad called "The Light-house Tragedy." It was a graphic, and what would be called at the present day, a sensational account of a shipwreck, in which the captain and his two daughters perished. He wrote another which was still more captivating, and which in all its main features was historically true. It was an account of the world-renowned pirate, Edward Teach, usually called Blackbeard. The reader will find a minute narrative of the career of that monster in the volume of this series of Pioneers and Patriots entitled "Captain Kidd; or the early American Buccaneers." One stanza has descended to us which it is said composed a portion of this ballad, and which is certainly a fair specimen of the popular style then in vogue.

"Come all you jolly sailors You all so stout and brave, Come hearken and I'll tell you, What happened on the wave. Oh 'tis of that bloody Blackbeard I'm going now for to tell And as how by gallant Maynard He soon was sent to Hell. With a down, down, derry down."

This was indeed wretched stuff, as Franklin afterwards admitted; but it is to be remembered he was then but a boy of fifteen. Having composed the ballad and set in type and printed it, he was then sent to hawk it through the streets. This was certainly a remarkable achievement for a lad of his years. The eagerness with which both of the ballads were seized by the public must have greatly gratified the self-esteem of the young writer.

Addison was a bungler in talk, but every sentence from his pen was elegant. He once said, "I carry no loose change in my pocket, but I can draw for a thousand pounds." Burke said of Goldsmith, "He writes like an angel, but he talks like poor Poll." Franklin was by no means a bungler in his speech, but he was not fluent. He hesitated, and was at a loss for words, but whatever he wrote had a wonderful flow of harmony. The right word was always in the right place. Doubtless had he devoted as much attention to the acquirement of conversational ease, as he did to skill in writing, he would have been as successful in the one art as in the other. From early life it was his great

KARTINDO PUBLISHING HOUSE (Kartindo.Com)

ambition to be not merely a fine but a forcible writer. He did not seek splendor of diction, but that perspicuity, that transparency of expression which would convey the thought most directly to the mind.

An odd volume of the Spectator fell in his way. He was charmed with the style. Selecting some interesting incident, he would read it with the closest care; he would then close the book, endeavoring to retain the thought only without regard to the expression. Then with pen, in hand, he would sit down and relate the anecdote or the incident in the most forceful and graphic words his vocabulary would afford. This he would correct and re-correct, minutely attending to the capitals and the punctuation until he had made it in all respects as perfect as it was in his power. He then compared his narrative with that in the Spectator. Of course he usually found many faults which he had committed, but occasionally he could not but admit he had improved upon his original. This encouraged him with the hope that by long continued practice, he might become an able writer of the English language. This practice he continued for months, varying it in many ways. He continued to rhyme, though he admitted that there was little poetry in his verse. The exercise, however, he thought useful in giving him a mastery of language.

Though Franklin wrote ballads, he seemed to be mainly interested in reading books of the most elevated and instructive character. Locke's "Essay on the Human Understanding," he studied thoroughly. "The Art of Thinking," by the Messrs. de Port Royal, engrossed all his energies. But perhaps there was no book, at that time, which produced so deep and abiding impression on his mind as the "Memorabilia of Socrates," by Xenophon.

Franklin was fond of arguing; he was naturally disputatious. With his keen intellect, he was pretty sure to come off as victor, at least in his own judgment, in discussions with his associates. But the Socratic method of argumentation, so different from that in which he had been accustomed to indulge, at once secured his approval and admiration. Socrates was never guilty of the discourtesy of assailing an opponent with flat contradiction or positive assertion. With a politeness which never failed him, and a modesty of demeanor which won the regard of all others, he would lead his fellow disputant, by a series of questions, to assent to the views which he advocated. Franklin immediately commenced practicing upon this newly discovered art. He was remarkably successful, and became one of the most agreeable and beloved of companions. But ere long he became satisfied of the folly of these disputations, in which each party struggles, not for truth, but for victory. It is simply an exercise of intellectual gladiatorship, in which the man who has the most skill and muscle discomfits his antagonist. Jefferson warned his nephew to avoid disputation. He says, "I have never known, during my long life, any persons' engage in a dispute in which they did not separate, each more firmly convinced than before of the correctness of his own views."

Franklin enjoyed marvellous health. His digestive powers were perfect. He could live upon any thing and almost upon nothing without experiencing any inconvenience. A book advocating purely vegetable diet accidentally fell into his hands. It urged the pecuniary economy and the saving of time in adopting a vegetarian diet. Eagerly he adopted the views presented. He could safely do so, had the author advocated raw onions and carrots. The stomach of Franklin would have received them and assimilated them without any remonstrance. He succeeded in inducing his brother to relinquish one half of his board and allow him to board himself. Benjamin found that in this way, he saved much time and much money. A handful of raisins, a roll of bread, and a glass of water afforded him a dinner. This he could dispose of in from five to ten minutes, and have the remainder of the dinner hour for reading.

The hours of the night were his own. He often sat up late and rose early, his soul all absorbed in intellectual vigils.

There are two platforms of morality, in some respects inseparably blended, in others quite distinctly separated from each other. The one of these platforms constitutes the low standard of mere worldly morality. It says,

You must not kill, you must not steal, you must not lie, you must not slander your neighbor, you must not cheat him in a bargain.

But there is another platform which not only includes all this, but which introduces principles of an infinitely higher grade. It is the platform enforced by Jesus Christ as essential to a life which shall be pleasing to our Heavenly Father. Our Saviour says, You must love God in whom you live and move and have your being: you must daily pray to him with gratitude for the favors you receive. In the great conflict, raging here below, between sin and holiness, your whole heart must yearn with the desire that God's "kingdom may come and that His will may be done on earth as in Heaven." Imitating the example of your Saviour, who was God manifest in the flesh that by His life He might show men how to live, you must do everything in your power to lead your neighbors and friends to love God, to avoid everything in thought, word, or deed, which you think will be displeasing to Him; and you must do all in your power to

KARTINDO PUBLISHING HOUSE (Kartindo.Com)

prepare your heart for that world of purity and love where the spirits of the just are made perfect. No one can be blind to the fact that these principles are infinitely above the principles of mere worldly morality. They are not a substitute for those principles, but an addition to them.

At the age of sixteen, Franklin was disposed to adopt the lower of these creeds as his rule of life; at times affirming that it was superior to the teachings of Jesus Christ; while again there would be the very clear and inconsistent avowal that, in this wicked world, something more was needed than teachings which he could plainly see seldom, if ever influenced a lost and degraded man, to be changed from a Saul of Tarsus to a Paul the Apostle. No one can understand the peculiar religious and moral character of Benjamin Franklin, without bearing in mind these distinctions.

KARTINDO PUBLISHING HOUSE (Kartindo.Com)

CHAPTER II

Developments of Character

Views of the Sabbath--Writings of Collins and Shaftsbury--The creed of Collins--Franklin at sixteen--The Courant--Denunciations of the paper--Franklin's mode of acquiring the art of composition--His success as a writer--The Editor prosecuted--Benjamin becomes Editor and Publisher--Jealousy of his brother--The runaway apprentice--The voyage to New York--Great disappointment--Eventful Journey to Philadelphia--Gloomy prospects--The dawn of brighter days.

Franklin was never scrupulous in the observance of the Sabbath. Still, though he but occasionally attended church, he at times very earnestly urged that duty upon his young friends. It is not probable that the preaching he heard in those days, was calculated to interest him. While a child under the parental roof, he ordinarily accompanied his parents, and seemed to regard it as his duty to do so.

He now, however, with an increasing sense of independence, very much preferred to spend his precious hours in his chamber, reading books which engrossed his most intense interest. Unfortunately many treatises fell into his hands in which unchristian sentiments were conveyed to his mind, by men of the highest intellectual character, and whose writings were invested with the most fascinating charms of eloquence.

Robert Boyle, an Irish nobleman of wealth and fervent piety, had established at Oxford a lectureship, the object of which was to prove the truth of the Christian religion. These lectures had found their way in tracts to the little library of Franklin's father. When but fifteen years of age the boy read them, with a far keener relish than most school-boys now read the flashy novels of the day. In order to refute the arguments of the deists, the lecturers were bound to produce those arguments fairly and forcibly. But to this young boy's piercing mind, the arguments against Christianity seemed stronger than those which were brought forward to refute them. Thus the lad became, not a positive unbeliever, but an honest doubter. He now sought earnestly for other works upon that all-important subject.

KARTINDO PUBLISHING HOUSE (Kartindo.Com)

The two most important, influential and popular writers of that day were perhaps Anthony Collins and the Earl of Shaftsbury. These were both men of fortune, of polished education, and of great rhetorical and argumentative skill. Their influence over young minds was greatly increased by the courtesy and candor which pervaded all their writings. They ever wrote like gentlemen addressing gentlemen; and the views they urged were presented with the modesty of men who were earnestly seeking for the truth.

The main attack of both of these men was directed against the miracles of the Bible. It was very evident that, the Divine authority of the Bible being overthrown, the whole structure of the Christian religion and morality must pass away. Mr. Parton, in his admirable Life of Franklin, says,

"Any one who will turn over an edition of Shaftsbury, and try to read it with the mind of this merry and receptive printer's boy, will perceive how entirely captivating it must have been to him. The raillery that was always the raillery of a gentleman; the irony so delicate as really to deceive some men who passed for acute; the fine urbanity that pervades even the passages called severe; the genuine reverence of the author for virtue; the spectacle revealed of a man uniting in himself all that is good in sense, with all that is agreeable in the man of the world,--how pleasing it must all have been to our inky apprentice as he munched his noon-day crust."

The practical creed of Collins and Shaftsbury, so far as it can be gleaned from the obscurity of their brilliant pages, consisted in the entire renunciation of all that is deemed the spirituality of the Christian creed, and the simple enforcement of the ordinary principles of morality in man's intercourse with his brother man. In substance they said,

"Be truthful and honest. Do not openly oppose the institutions of Christianity, for that will render you obnoxious to your neighbors. Conform to the ordinary usages of the society in the midst of which you move; and as to creeds, let them alone as unworthy of a moment's thought."

Franklin, at sixteen years of age, became a thorough convert to these views. He was virtually without any God. He had no rule of life but his own instincts; but those instincts were of a high order, emboldening his character and restraining him from all vulgar vice. Thus he wandered for many years; though there are many indications of an occasionally troubled mind, and though he at times struggled with great eagerness to obtain a higher state of moral perfection, he

KARTINDO PUBLISHING HOUSE (Kartindo.Com)

certainly never developed the character of a warm-hearted and devoted follower of Jesus.[4]

[Footnote 4: "For some years he wandered in heathenish darkness. He forsook the safe and good though narrow way of his forefathers, and of his father and mother, and his gentle Uncle Benjamin, without finding better and larger ways of his own. He was in danger of becoming a castaway or a commonplace successful man of the world. He found in due time, after many trials, and much suffering and many grievous errors, that the soul of a man does not thrive upon negations, and that, in very truth a man must *believe* in order that he may be saved."--*Parton's Life of Franklin, Vol. I, p. 71.*]

James Franklin was prosperous in his business. On the 17th of August, 1721, he issued the first number of a newspaper entitled "The New England Courant." Benjamin set the type, struck off the impression of two or three hundred, with a hand-press, and then traversed the streets, carrying the diminutive sheet to the homes of the subscribers. The Courant soon attracted attention. A knot of sparkling writers began to contribute to its columns, and while the paper was with increasing eagerness sought for, a clamor was soon raised against it. It was denounced as radical in its political tendencies, and as speaking contemptuously of the institutions of religion. Cotton Mather, even, launched one of his thunderbolts against it. He wrote,

"We find a notorious, scandalous paper called 'The Courant' full freighted with nonsense, unmanliness, raillery, profaneness, immorality, arrogance, calumnies, lies, contradictions and what not, all tending to quarrels and divisions, and to debauch and corrupt the mind and manners of New England."

Increase Mather also denounced the paper, in terms still more emphatic.

At this time a strong antipathy was springing up between James, and his apprentice brother. James assumed the airs of a master, and was arrogant and domineering, at times in his anger proceeding even to blows. Benjamin was opinionated, headstrong and very unwilling to yield to another's guidance. As Benjamin compared his own compositions with those which were sent to the Courant, he was convinced that he could write as well, if not better, than others. He, therefore, one evening prepared an article, before he was sixteen years of age, which, with the greatest care, was written in pure Addisonian diction. Disguising his hand, he slipped this at night under the door of the printing office. The next morning several contributors were chatting together in the editorial office, as Benjamin stood at the printing case setting his types. The anonymous article was read and freely commented upon. The young writer was delighted in finding it highly commended, and in their guesses for the author, the names of the most distinguished men in Boston were mentioned.

The singular nom de plume he assumed was "Silence Dogood." Over that signature he wrote many articles before it was ascertained that he was the author. These articles attracted so much attention that young Benjamin could not refrain from claiming their paternity. This led his brother and others to regard him with far more respect than heretofore.

But the Courant, while popular with the masses, became unpopular with the governmental authorities and with the religious community. As a slap in the face of the government, a fictitious letter was written, professedly from Newport, stating that a piratic ship had appeared off the coast, plundering, burning, and destroying. It was then stated that the government of Massachusetts was fitting out an armed vessel to attack the pirate, and that, wind and weather permitting, the vessel would sail from Boston sometime during the month.

This reflection upon the dilatoriness of government gave great offence. The members of the Council summoned Franklin before them to answer for the libel. He admitted that he was the publisher of the paper, but refused to give the name of the writer. The Council decided that the paragraph was a high affront to the government, and ordered his imprisonment in the Boston jail. Here he was incarcerated for a week. Crushed by his misfortunes he wrote a very humble letter stating that his close confinement endangered his life, and begging that he might enjoy the liberty of the jail-yard. His request was granted, and for three weeks more he remained a prisoner, though with daily permission to leave his cell.

During this time Benjamin conducted the paper, editing it, setting the type, printing the sheets and distributing the copies to the subscribers. He was still but a boy of sixteen. James was eventually released from prison, but the general character of the Courant remained unchanged. Unworthy professors of Christianity were incessantly assailed. The virtues of true Christians--of the multitudes of the disciples of Jesus, who were mothers in Israel, or who were Israelites indeed in whom there was no guile, were forgotten; while every mean and contemptible act of hypocrites and apostates was proclaimed with trumpet resonance.

KARTINDO PUBLISHING HOUSE (Kartindo.Com)

At length the Council declared in reference to a peculiarly obnoxious copy of the paper, that the Courant of that date contained many passages perverting the Holy Scriptures, and slandering the civil government, the ministers, and the good people of the land. A committee of three was appointed to report upon the matter. After two days they brought in the following decision:

"We are humbly of opinion that the tendency of said paper, is to mock religion and bring it into contempt; that the Holy Scriptures are therein profanely abused; that the revered and faithful ministers of the Gospel are ignominiously reflected on; and that His Majesty's government is affronted; and the peace and good order of His Majesty's subjects of this province disturbed by this said Courant."

The committee, therefore, proposed that James Franklin should be strictly forbidden to print or publish the Courant, or any other paper of the like nature, unless it were supervised by the secretary of the province.

James Franklin and his friends, after this decision, met in the office of the Courant, and adroitly decided to evade the mandate by canceling the indentures of apprenticeship of Benjamin, and constituting him the editor and publisher of the journal. This precocious lad prepared his inaugural. It contained the following sentiments:

"Long has the press groaned in bringing forth a hateful brood of pamphlets, malicious scribbles, and billingsgate ribaldry. No generous and impartial person then can blame the present undertaking which is designed purely for the diversion and merriment of the reader. Pieces of pleasantry and mirth have a secret charm in them to allay the heats and tumults of our spirits, and to make a man forget his restless resentment. The main design of this weekly paper will be to entertain the town with the most comical and diverting incidents of human life, which in so large a place as Boston will not fail of a universal exemplification. Nor shall we be wanting to fill up these papers with a grateful interspersion of more serious morals which may be drawn from the most ludicrous and odd parts of life."

It cannot be denied that Franklin aimed his keen shafts at many of the best of men who were consecrating all their energies to the promotion of the physical, moral, and religious welfare of their fellow creatures. He had a keen eye to search out their frailties; and though he seldom if ever, dipped his pen in gall, he did at times succeed in making them the song of the drunkard, and in turning against them the derision of all the lewd fellows of the baser sort.

Benjamin, elated by flattery and success, admits that at seventeen years of age he became in his treatment of his brother "saucy and provoking." James was increasingly jealous and exacting. At length a very violent quarrel arose between them. The elder brother even undertook to chastise his younger brother, whom he still affected to regard as his apprentice. The canceling of the terms of indenture, he regarded as a secret act, intended merely to outwit his opponent. Franklin, burning with indignation, resolved no longer to continue in his brother's employment, and went to several other printers in Boston, hoping to enter into a new engagement. But his brother had preceded him, giving his own version of the story, and even declaring his brilliant brother to be an infidel and an atheist.

Benjamin resolved to run away; for he still felt the binding obligation of his apprenticeship, while he tried to satisfy his mind that the unjust conduct of James entitled him to violate the obligation. There was a vessel about to sail for New York. He sold some of his books to pay his passage; and going on board secretly at night, he solicited the captain to aid him in concealing him, with the *false* statement that he had become involved in a love adventure with a young girl; that she had subsequently proved to be a bad character; that her friends insisted on his marrying her; and that his only refuge was to be found in flight.

His passage to New York was swift and pleasant. It is said that having adopted the vegetarian diet, he doubted our right to deprive an animal of life for our own gratification in eating. The sloop was one day becalmed off Block Island. The crew found it splendid fishing ground; the deck was soon covered with cod and haddock. Franklin denounced catching the fishes, as murderous, as no one could affirm that these fishes, so happy in the water, had ever conferred any injury upon their captors. But Benjamin was blessed with a voracious appetite. The frying pan was busy, and the odor from the fresh fish was exceedingly alluring. As he watched a sailor cutting open a fish, he observed in its stomach a smaller fish, which the cod had evidently eaten.

"Ah!" he exclaimed, "if you can eat one another, I surely have a right to eat you."

All his scruples vanished. He sat down with the rest to the sumptuous repast, and never after seemed to have any hesitancy in gratifying his appetite.

KARTINDO PUBLISHING HOUSE (Kartindo.Com)

Benjamin tells this story in his autobiography, and shrewdly adds, quoting from some one else,

"So convenient a thing it is to be a *reasonable* creature, since it enables one to find or make a reason for everything one has a mind to do."

It was in the beautiful month of October, 1723, when Benjamin landed on the wharves of New York. He was not quite eighteen years of age; had but little money in his purse; and was without any letter of recommendation or any acquaintance in the town. The place consisted of but seven or eight thousand inhabitants. The streets were the crooked lanes which we still find in the vicinity of the Battery. Some of the most important were uncomfortably paved with cobble stones. Most of the inhabitants were Dutch, reading and speaking only the Dutch language. There was at that time indeed, but little encouragement for an English printer. There was but one bookstore then in New York; and but one printing office, which was conducted by William Bradford.

The runaway apprentice could find no employment. But William Bradford had a son in Philadelphia who was also a printer. He said to Benjamin,

"He may employ you, as he has recently lost an apprentice by death."

Leaving his chest of clothes to go round by sea to Philadelphia, Benjamin took passage in a small dilapidated shore boat which crept along the coast to Amboy. A drunken Dutchman was his only fellow passenger. The gloom of the primeval forest overshadowed Governor's Island: not a single cabin as yet had been reared in its solitudes. A squall struck the boat, split its sail, and pitched the Dutchman overboard. Franklin caught him by the hair and saved him from drowning. The sudden tempest increased into a storm, and the boat was driven fiercely before the gale. The surf dashed so violently upon the shore that they could not venture to land. Night approached. Exhausted, drenched and hungry, they cast anchor near the Long Island shore, where a bend in the land afforded them slight protection while still they were in great danger. There were one or two log cabins in the vicinity. Several of the men came to the shore, but could afford them no relief. They had no provision on board excepting a single bottle of bad rum. All night long the tempest beat upon them. In the morning the wind had so far lulled that they were enabled to repair their sail, and to work their way on to Amboy.

KARTINDO PUBLISHING HOUSE (Kartindo.Com)

It was late in the afternoon when they reached the port. For thirty hours they had been without food or water. Such were the perils of a passage from New York to Philadelphia in the year 1723.

Franklin, in the enjoyment of magnificent health, slept quietly that night in an humble inn, and awoke in the morning with all his accustomed vigor. There were still fifty miles of land travel before him, ere he could cross the forest covered plains of New Jersey to Burlington, on the banks of the Delaware, which were seventeen miles above Philadelphia. There was neither railroad, stage-coach nor cart to convey him through the wilderness. Indeed it was thirty-three years after this before the first line of stages across New Jersey was established. There was a rude path, probably following an ancient Indian trail, along which our solitary adventurer trudged on foot. It rained; but still Benjamin found it necessary, having so slender a purse, to press on regardless of discomfort.

Early in the afternoon he came to a hamlet, by the roadside, where he found himself so exhausted by the unaccustomed toil of walking, and by exposure to the rain and the miry roads, that he felt it necessary to remain until the next morning. The aspect he presented was shabby and dilapidated in the extreme; for he was in his working dress, which by the wear and tear of travel had become greatly soiled and tattered. He was not a little mortified to find that the inhabitants of the cabin, while they treated him kindly, evidently regarded him with suspicion as a runaway apprentice.

In the gloom of that night, poor Benjamin bitterly repented the step he had taken, and earnestly wished himself back again in the home which he had forsaken. Clouds and darkness had gathered around his path and he could see but little bright beyond. Early the next morning he resumed his travels, pressing vigorously along all day. When the shades of night enveloped him he had reached a point within ten miles of Burlington. He passed the night comfortably in a settler's cabin, and early the next morning pressed on to the little village of Burlington, from which he was informed that a boat started every Saturday, to descend the still silent and almost unfrequented shores of the Delaware to Philadelphia. Much to his disappointment he reached Burlington just after the regular Saturday boat had gone, and was informed that there was no other boat to leave until the next Tuesday. He made his united breakfast and dinner upon gingerbread, which he bought in the street of an old woman.

Burlington was on the east side of the river, Philadelphia was on the west. There was no road between the two places, the communication being by the

KARTINDO PUBLISHING HOUSE (Kartindo.Com)

river only. It seemed impossible for Benjamin to toil that distance through the pathless, tangled forest. He had but five shillings in his pocket. With the utmost economy that would not defray his expenses at Burlington, for three days, and leave a sufficient sum to pay his passage down the river.

In his distress and perplexity, our young philosopher, whose renown for wisdom subsequently filled all Christian lands, turned back to the poor, aged woman of whom he had bought his gingerbread and solicited her advice. The good old soul, not insensible to the charms of the frank and manly looking boy, with motherly tenderness insisted on his going to her own humble home. Gladly he accepted the invitation. The dinner consisted of what is called ox-cheek; Franklin contributed a pot of beer.

Walking out early in the evening upon the banks of the river, he found, to his great joy, a chance boat had come along, bound to Philadelphia and containing many passengers. Eagerly Franklin joined them, and bidding adieu to his kind entertainer, was soon drifting slowly down the stream. The night was dark, there was no wind, and no cheerful gleam from the white man's cabin or the Indian's wigwam met the eye. It was necessary to resort to rowing. At length, a little after midnight, several of the passengers insisted that they must have passed Philadelphia without seeing it, and refused to row any farther. They therefore ran the boat into a little creek, built a rousing fire, for the night was damp and chill, and ranging themselves around its genial warmth awaited the dawn of the morning. The light revealed to them Philadelphia but a few miles below them. It was Sunday morning. At nine o'clock the boat was made fast at Market street wharf, and Franklin, with one silver dollar and one shilling in copper coin in his pocket, stepped on shore. All his copper coin he paid for his passage.

Such was the introduction of the future Governor of Pennsylvania to the realm over which he was eventually to preside as Governor, and of which he became its most illustrious citizen.

He was unquestionably dressed in the peculiar and picturesque costume of the times. He wore knee breeches of buckskin, and a voluminous overcoat, lined with pockets of astonishing capacity, which pockets were crammed with shirts and stockings. A low, battered, broad-brimmed hat covered his clustering ringlets. His coarse woolen stockings displayed to advantage the admirably moulded calves of his legs. Every article of this costume was draggled, shabby, soiled, and much of it tattered.

KARTINDO PUBLISHING HOUSE (Kartindo.Com)

With an indescribable feeling of loneliness, exhausted with the toilsome and sleepless night, and with the cravings of hunger, he sauntered up into the town. Coming across a baker's shop, he stepped in, and called for three pennyworth of bread. In Philadelphia, food was abundant and bread was cheap. To his surprise three long rolls were given to him. He took one under each arm, and in his hunger the homeless boy walked along devouring the other. Philadelphia was then a village widely spread out, with surrounding vegetable gardens, and containing a population of about seven thousand inhabitants.

Benjamin walked listlessly along as far as Fourth street. He chanced to pass the house of a Mr. Read, whose very pretty daughter, Deborah, was standing at the front door. She was eighteen years of age, and was much amused at the comical appearance which the young man presented as he passed by.

[Illustration]

It is not easy to imagine in these days, the state of society in these early settlements, hewn out from the forests on the river's banks, and with the unexplored wilderness spreading out to unimagined regions in the interior. At night, even from the houses of the village, the howling of the wolves could be heard as they rushed after their prey. Bears and deers were shot in abundance. And Indian bands, painted and plumed, were ever swarming through the streets.

Franklin walked along, devouring his rolls, and returned to the river for a drink of water. Such was his first breakfast in Philadelphia. In the boat was a poor woman with her child. Franklin gave to her the two remaining rolls, which he could not conveniently carry about with him.

Not knowing what to do, and led by curiosity to explore the town, he returned to Market street, then one of the chief avenues of the city. It was a little after ten o'clock in the morning. The street was crowded with well-dressed people, pressing along to church. There was one important edifice called the "Great Meeting House" of the Quakers. It stood at the corner of Second and Market streets.

Franklin joined the crowd, and took his seat with the vast assembly. He soon fell soundly asleep. The hour passed away. The congregation dispersed, and Benjamin was left still asleep. Some one then kindly awoke the tired traveler, and he again stepped out into the streets so lonely, where there was not an individual whom he knew, and where almost without money he could find no refuge which he could call a home.

As he walked toward the river, he met a young Quaker whose countenance pleased him. Of him he inquired where he could find a respectable and comfortable lodging. The friendly Quaker led him to a tavern, near Chestnut street, called the "Crooked Billet." Franklin ordered a frugal dinner, threw himself upon the bed, and slept till supper time, and immediately after supper went to bed and slept soundly till the morning.

He had now been from home eleven days. His money was nearly expended. His clothes were worn; and almost the only hope remaining was the very visionary one that Mr. Bradford's son might possibly have some employment for him. Early in the morning he carefully brushed his travel-worn clothes, his shoes, his hat, and making himself as respectable in appearance as possible, went to the house of the printer, Andrew Bradford. To his surprise and gratification he found the father there, who had just arrived, having traveled from New York to Philadelphia on horseback.

Benjamin met with a courteous reception, was invited to breakfast. He was, however, greatly disappointed in being informed that Andrew Bradford had just engaged another apprentice to take the place of the one who was lost. Mr. Bradford, however, stated that there was a man, by the name of Keimer, who had recently commenced the printing business in the town, and might have employment for him. The old gentleman kindly offered to go to the office with Benjamin, and introduce him to Keimer.

They found Keimer a very eccentric looking individual, in a small office, with an old dilapidated press, and with a few worn-out types. He asked the young man a few questions, put a composing stick into his hands, and professed himself satisfied with his work. He then told Franklin that he could find no work for him immediately, but he thought ere long he could employ him. It seems, however, that at once Benjamin went to work, repairing the dilapidated old press, while he continued to board at Mr. Bradford's, paying for his board by the work which he performed.

KARTINDO PUBLISHING HOUSE (Kartindo.Com)

CHAPTER III

Excursion to England

Attention to dress--Receives a visit from Gov. Keith--His visit to Boston--Collins returns to Philadelphia with him--Sir William Keith's aid--Excursions on the Sabbath--Difficulty with Collins--Spending Mr. Vernon's money--His three friends--Engagement with Deborah Read--Voyage to England--Keith's deceit--Ralph--Franklin enters a printing house in London.

The eccentric Keimer soon found that Franklin was a workman whose services would be invaluable to him. He had no home of his own, but became very unwilling that Benjamin, while in his employ, should board in the family of a rival printer. He therefore made arrangements for him to board at Mr. Read's, whose pretty daughter, Deborah, had made herself merry but a few days before in view of his uncouth appearance.

Fortunately for the young man, who was never regardless of the advantages of a genteel dress, his chest had arrived bringing his clothing. He was thus able to present himself before the young lady in attractive costume. And his address was always that of an accomplished gentleman. As we have mentioned, he was ever in his youth, middle life, and old age, remarkable for his personal beauty.

Bright and sunny days now dawned upon Franklin. His employer appreciated his varied and wonderful merits. He received good wages. The family in which he resided was highly attractive, and he there found a home congenial with his pure and refined tastes. Several months passed away before he heard from the friends he had left in Boston. The tyranny of his brother had so greatly offended him, that for a time he endeavored to exclude from his mind all thoughts of his home. He heard, however, that one of his sisters had married Captain Robert Holmes, the captain of a vessel sailing between Boston and the ports on the Delaware.

In those piratical days, when the master of a ship was compelled to sail with guns loaded to the muzzle, and with sharpened sabres, he was deemed a personage of great importance. No weak or ordinary man could discharge the responsibilities of such a post. Captain Holmes, influenced by the love of his wife, wrote to Benjamin informing him of the grief his departure had caused the family, entreating him to return, and assuring him that all the past should be forgotten.

Benjamin, in his reply, wrote with such precision and force of logic, that Captain Holmes became satisfied that he was by no means so much in the wrong as he had supposed. It so chanced that when the captain received this letter, he was in company with Sir William Keith, then the Governor of Pennsylvania. He read the letter to the Governor. Sir William was charmed with its literary and rhetorical ability; and could scarcely believe that the writer was but eighteen years of age.

"The Philadelphia printers," said he, "are wretched ones. Keimer is a compound of fool and rogue. But this young man is manifestly of great promise and ought to be encouraged."

One day Benjamin and his master were working together, when they saw two well-dressed gentlemen approaching. They proved to be the Governor of Pennsylvania, Sir William Keith, and Franklin's brother-in-law, Captain Holmes, whom he probably had never before seen. Keimer ran down stairs to meet them, supposing, of course, that he must be the man who was entitled to the honor of their visit. To his surprise they inquired for his apprentice, and went up the stairs to the printing office to see him.

Benjamin was quite overwhelmed by the honors with which he was greeted. The Governor paid him many compliments, expressed an earnest desire to make his acquaintance, and politely censured him for not calling at the gubernatorial mansion upon his arrival in Philadelphia. The interview was terminated by taking Franklin with them to a neighboring tavern to dine. There the three met upon apparently perfect social equality, and very freely discussed many important matters as they drank their wine.

The Governor, a very plausible, unreliable man, ever lavish of promises without performance, proposed that Franklin, aided by funds from his father, should open a printing office for himself. He promised to exert his influence to secure for his young protegé the public printing of both the provinces of Pennsylvania and Delaware. When Franklin suggested that he feared his father would be either unable or unwilling to furnish the needed funds, the Governor promised to write to him with his own hand, explaining the advantages of the scheme.

KARTINDO PUBLISHING HOUSE (Kartindo.Com)

During the protracted interview, it was decided that Benjamin should return to Boston by the first vessel. He was to take with him Sir William's letter, and thus aided, endeavor to win over his father to their plans.

A week or two elapsed before there was a vessel ready to sail for Boston. At that time the social rank of a printer was decidedly above that of other mechanic arts. There was something sacred attached to the employment, and it was regarded as near akin to the learned professions. Franklin was frequently invited to dine with the Governor. His perfect self-possession, his careful dress and polished address, united with his wonderful conversational powers, rendered him a great favorite with all the distinguished guests whom he was accustomed to meet at the table of the Governor.

The latter part of April, 1724, Franklin, then eighteen years of age, took passage in a small vessel for Boston. His friends in Philadelphia generally understood that he was going home merely to visit his friends. It was deemed expedient to throw the veil of great secrecy over the enterprise in which he was contemplating to engage.

The voyage was exceedingly tempestuous. The vessel sprang a leak. For some time passengers and crew worked at the pumps night and day. But after being buffeted by winds and waves for fourteen dreary days, the little vessel cast anchor in the harbor of Boston. Franklin had then been absent from home seven months.

His sudden appearance was a great surprise to all the members of the numerous family. It is not surprising that the young man, elated by his brilliant prospects, assumed rather lordly airs. His dress was new and quite elegant. He had purchased a handsome watch, which he was not reluctant to display. He had in his pocket twenty-five dollars of silver coin.

Franklin's brother James, from whom he had run away, was greatly annoyed by the airs of superiority assumed by his old apprentice. With a cold and almost scornful eye, he scanned his person from head to foot, scarcely offering his hand in greeting, and soon coldly and silently returned to his work. But the imperial young man was not thus to be put down. His former acquaintances gathered eagerly around him and listened with intensest interest to the narrative of his adventures. In glowing terms, Benjamin described his new home in Philadelphia, drew out from his pocket handfuls of silver which he exhibited to them, and with quite lordly dignity gave his former fellow-journeymen money to go to the ale-house for a treat.

The candid reader will make some allowances for the conduct of Benjamin, when he remembers that but a few months before, he had run away to escape the cudgel of his brother. He will also feel inclined to make some allowance for James, when informed that he was in adversity, and struggling severely with pecuniary embarrassment. The Courant, deprived of the graphic pen of Franklin, was rapidly losing its subscribers, and soon became extinct.

Benjamin's father Josiah, who needed in his own business every dollar of the funds he could raise, silently and almost without remark, read the letter of Sir William Keith, and listened attentively to the glowing descriptions of his son. Soon after Captain Holmes arrived. The judicious father conversed fully with him, and expressed his opinion that Sir William Keith must be a man of but little discretion to think of setting up independently, in very responsible business, a young man of but eighteen years of age.

Though Captain Holmes earnestly advocated the views of the Governor, Josiah Franklin, after mature deliberation, decisively declined furnishing the necessary funds.

"Benjamin," said he, "is too young to undertake an enterprise so important. I am much gratified that he has been able to secure the approbation of the Governor of Pennsylvania, and that by his industry and fidelity he has been able to attain prosperity so remarkable. If he will return to Philadelphia and work diligently until he is twenty-one, carefully laying up his surplus earnings, I will then do everything in my power to aid him."

The cautious Christian father then gave his son some very salutary advice. He entreated him to be more careful in throwing out his arrows of satire, and to cease presenting, in the aspect of the ridiculous, so many subjects which religious men regarded with veneration. He wrote a very courteous letter to Sir William Keith, thanking him for his kindness to his son, and stating his reasons for declining the proposed aid. Indeed, Josiah Franklin was intellectually, morally, and in all sound judgment, immeasurably the superior of the fickle and shallow royal Governor.

Sixty years after this visit of Franklin to his paternal home, he wrote a letter to the son of the Rev. Cotton Mather, from which we make the following pleasing extract:

KARTINDO PUBLISHING HOUSE (Kartindo.Com)

"The last time I saw your father was in the beginning of 1724, when I visited him after my first trip to Pennsylvania. He received me in his library; and on my taking leave showed me a shorter way out of the house through a narrow passage which was crossed by a beam overhead. We were still talking as I withdrew, he accompanying me behind, and I, turning partly toward him, when he said hastily, *stoop, stoop!* I did not understand him till I felt my head hit against the beam. He was a man that never missed any occasion of giving instruction; and upon this he said to me 'You are young and have the world before you. Stoop as you go through it, and you will miss many hard thumps.' This advice, thus beat into my head, has frequently been of use to me. And I often think of it when I see pride mortified and misfortunes brought upon people by their carrying their heads too high."

There was in Boston a young man by the name of Collins, a reckless, dissipated spendthrift, of very considerable personal attractions. He had been quite an intimate friend of Franklin; and was so pleased with his descriptions of Philadelphia that he decided to remove there. This proved one of the calamities of Franklin's life.

Franklin eventually embarked, in a sloop, for his return. It touched at Newport. His brother John lived there, pursuing the trade of a candle-maker. Benjamin was received by him with great cordiality. At Newport, among the other passengers, two young girls were taken on board for New York. They were showy, voluble, gaudily dressed. All their arts were exerted to secure intimate association with Franklin.

A venerable Quaker lady on board called the inexperienced young man aside, and with motherly tenderness warned him against their wiles. Though he doubted the necessity of this caution, he was put upon his guard. When the girls left at New York, he declined their pressing invitation for him to visit them at their home, and he learned from the captain that they had undoubtedly stolen from him a silver spoon, an article then not often seen in common life, and highly prized. They were charged with the crime, convicted, and it is said that they were publicly whipped in the market place.

Upon Franklin's arrival at New York, Collins, the playmate of his childhood, was one of the first to meet him. In his earlier days he had been sober, industrious, and was highly esteemed for his mental powers and attainments. But he had become intemperate and a gambler, and was every day intoxicated. Reduced almost to beggary, Franklin felt compelled to furnish him with money to save him from starvation. Penniless he had come on board the boat at New

York, and Franklin paid his passage to Philadelphia.

William Burnett was then Governor of New York. He was very fond of books and had collected a large library. Franklin also had the same taste and had a large number of books which he was conveying to Philadelphia. The captain informed the Governor that he had a young man on board fond of books, and of superior literary attainments. The Governor begged the captain to bring young Franklin to see him.

"I waited upon him," wrote Franklin, "and would have taken Collins with me had he been sober. The Governor received me with great civility; and we had a good deal of conversation relative to books and authors. This was the second Governor who had done me the honor to take notice of me, and to a poor boy like me it was very pleasing."

Upon reaching Philadelphia, Franklin presented the letter of his father to Sir William Keith. The Governor, upon reading the letter, said,

"Your father is too prudent. There is a great difference in persons. Discretion does not always accompany years; nor is youth always without it. But since he will not set you up, I will do it myself. Give me an inventory of the things necessary to be had from England, and I will send for them. You shall repay me when you are able. I am resolved to have a good printer here and I am sure you must succeed."

Franklin supposed of course, that he could rely upon the word of the Governor. He drew up an inventory of goods to the amount of about five hundred dollars. The strange Governor, who found it very easy to talk, ran his eye over the list and as if money were a consideration of no moment to him, and suggested that Franklin should go to London in person. Greatly elated at this idea, young Franklin eagerly embraced it, and the Governor directed him to be ready to embark in the London Hope, a ship which sailed regularly between London and Philadelphia, leaving each port once a year.

Several months would elapse before the ship would sail. Sir William enjoined it upon Franklin to keep their plans in the utmost secrecy. Consequently, Franklin continued to work for Keimer, not giving him the slightest intimation that measures were in progress for the establishment in Philadelphia, of a printing house which would entirely overshadow his own. This secrecy which was practiced also prevented any one from informing Franklin of the Governor's

KARTINDO PUBLISHING HOUSE (Kartindo.Com)

real character, as a vain, unreliable, gasconading boaster.

Six months passed away. They were with Franklin happy months. He was in perfect health, greatly enjoyed his own physical and intellectual attributes, was much caressed, and was engaged in lucrative employment. He was highly convivial in his tastes, very fond of social pleasures, of the wine cup and of the song: and on Sundays in particular, the enchanting forests of the Schuylkill resounded with the songs and the shouts of the merry bacchanals, led by Franklin, who was ever recognized as their chief.

There probably never was a young man more skillful than Benjamin Franklin in plucking the rose and avoiding the thorn. In all his festivities he was the thoughtful philosopher. Never did he drink to excess; no money was squandered at the gaming table. Carefully he avoided all views which he deemed vulgar and degrading; and he made it the general rule of his life, to avoid everything which would bring pain to his body, or remorse to his soul.

Still man is born to mourn. Even Franklin could not escape the general lot. The drunken Collins became his constant scourge. Franklin felt constrained to lend his old friend money. He had been entrusted by a family friend, a Mr. Vernon, to collect a debt of about fifty dollars. This money he was to retain till called for. But to meet his own expenses and those of his spendthrift companion, he began to draw upon it, until it all disappeared. He was then troubled with the apprehension that the money might be demanded. Bitter were the quarrels which arose between him and John Collins. His standard of morality which was perhaps not less elevated than that which the majority of imperfect professing Christians practice, was certainly below that which the religion of Jesus Christ enjoins. Had he been a true Christian according to the doctrines and precepts of Jesus, he would have escaped these accumulating sorrows.

[Illustration]

This breaking in upon his friend Vernon's money, and spending it, he pronounces in his autobiography, to have been the *first great error* of his life. Though it so chanced that the money was not required until Franklin was able to pay it, yet for several months he was in the endurance of intense mental anxiety and constant self-reproach.

At length, Collins and Franklin became so antagonistic to each other as to proceed to violence. They were on a pleasure party in a boat down the river.

KARTINDO PUBLISHING HOUSE (Kartindo.Com)

Collins, as usual, was intoxicated. The wrath of the muscular Benjamin was so aroused, by some act of abuse, that he seized the fellow by the collar and pitched him overboard. Collins was a good swimmer. They therefore kept him in the water till he was nearly drowned. When pretty thoroughly humbled, and upon his most solemn promise of good behavior, he was again taken on board. Seldom after this was a word exchanged between them. Collins, deeply indebted to Franklin, accepted of some business offer at Barbadoes. He sailed for that island, and was never heard of more.

Almost every young man has a few particular friends. The three most intimate companions of Benjamin Franklin were young men of his own rank and age, of very dissimilar characters, but having a common taste for business. They were all clerks. One of these, Joseph Watson, was, according to Franklin's description, "a pious, sensible young man of great integrity." It would seem that they were all persons of very estimable character, though some of them had imbibed Franklin's skeptical opinions. They spent many of their Sabbaths, wandering on the banks of the romantic Schuylkill, reading to each other their compositions in prose and verse.

James Ralph, who was very emphatic in his deistical views, in his enthusiasm, decided to devote himself to the art of rhyming. The sensible Franklin tried to dissuade him from his folly, but in vain. On one occasion they all agreed to attempt a version of the Eighteenth Psalm. This sublime production of an inspired pen contains, in fifty verses, imagery as grand and sentiments as beautiful, as perhaps can anywhere else be found, within the same compass, in any language. It certainly speaks well for the intellectual acumen of these young men, and for their devotional instincts, that they should have selected so noble a theme. As their main object was to improve themselves in the command of language, and in the power of expression, they could not have chosen a subject more appropriate, than the Psalmist's description of the descent of God to earth.

"He bowed the heavens also and came down; and darkness was under his feet. And He rode upon a cherub and did fly; Yea he did fly upon the wings of the wind. He made darkness his secret place. His pavilion round about him were dark waters, thick clouds of the skies. At the brightness which was before him his thick clouds passed. Hail stones and coals of fire."[5]

[Footnote 5: The intelligent reader will recall the glowing version of this Psalm, by Steinhold.

KARTINDO PUBLISHING HOUSE (Kartindo.Com)

"The Lord descended from above, And bowed the heavens most high; And underneath his feet he cast The darkness of the sky. On cherub and on cherubim, Full royally he rode; And on the wings of mighty winds, Came flying all abroad."]

Joseph Watson died quite young, in the arms of Franklin. Charles Osborne acquired money and reputation, as a lawyer. Removing to the West Indies, he died, in the prime of life.

Franklin and Osborne entered into the agreement, which has so often been made, that whichever should first die, should, if possible, return to the other and reveal to him the secrets of the spirit land. It is hardly necessary to say that Franklin watched long in vain, for a visit from his departed companion.

Two months before Franklin sailed for London, Mr. Read, with whom he boarded, died. With the father, mother, and very pretty and amiable daughter, Deborah, Franklin had found a happy home. A strong affection apparently sprang up between the two young people. She was seventeen years of age, and Franklin eighteen. Their union would be eminently fitting, as in fortune and position in society, they were on the same level.

Franklin, enjoying the patronage of the governor, and with, as he supposed, very brilliant prospects before him, entered into an engagement with Deborah, and was anxious to be married before he embarked for England, designing to leave his young bride at home with her mother. But Mrs. Read, in consideration of their youth, urged that the nuptials should be postponed until after his return.

Sir William Keith continued to invite Franklin to his house, and lavished commendation and promises upon him. Still he continually postponed giving him any letters of credit with which he could purchase types, paper and press. Though, as the hour for sailing approached, Franklin called again and again to obtain the needful documents, he was continually met with apologies. At length, the day for the ship to weigh anchor arrived. It was about the 5th of November, 1724.

At that late hour the private secretary of the Governor called upon Franklin and informed him that Sir William would meet him at Newcastle, where the vessel was to cast anchor, and would then and there, deliver to him all the important documents. Franklin went on board. The ship dropped down the broad and beautiful Delaware, whose banks were brilliant with foliage in their richest autumnal brilliance, about thirty-two miles below Philadelphia, to Newcastle. To the great disappointment of Franklin, the Governor still did not appear. He however sent his secretary, with a profusion of excuses, and professing to be pressed with business of the utmost importance, promised to send the letters to the captain before the vessel would be permitted to sail.

Franklin, naturally buoyant and hopeful, did not even then, consider it possible that the Governor was intending to deceive him. Neither was it possible to conceive of any motive which would induce Sir William to betray him by so deceptive a game. At length a bag from the Governor, apparently filled with letters and dispatches, was brought on board, and again the vessel unfurled her sails. Franklin, with some solicitude, asked for those which were directed to him. But Captain Annis, all engrossed with the cares of embarkation, said that he was too busy to examine the bag at that time, but that they would, at their leisure, on the voyage select the letters.

On the 10th of November, 1724, the good ship, the London Hope, pushed out from the Delaware upon the broad Atlantic. We know not whether Franklin was surprised to find on board, as one of the passengers, his poetical deistical friend James Ralph. This young man, who had renounced Christianity, in the adoption of principles, which he professed to believe conducive to the formation of a much higher moral character, had deliberately abandoned his wife and child to seek his fortune in London. He had deceived them by the most false representation. Carefully he concealed from Franklin, his unprincipled conduct and visionary schemes.

The voyage was long and rough, as the vessel did not reach London until the twenty-fourth of November. On the passage he very carefully, with the captain, examined the letter-bag. But no letter was found addressed to him. There were several, however, addressed to other persons, with Franklin's name upon the envelope as if they were in his care. As one of these was addressed to the king's printer and another to a stationer in London, the sanguine young man through all the dreary and protracted voyage, clung to the hope that all was right.

Upon arriving in London, Franklin hastened first to the stationer's and presented him with the letter, saying to him, "Here is a letter from Governor Keith, of Pennsylvania." The stationer looked up with surprise and said:

"Governor Keith! I do not know of any such person." Then breaking the seal, and looking at the signature, he said very contemptuously, "Riddlesden. I have lately found him to be a complete rascal. I will have nothing to do with him, nor receive any letters from him."[6]

[Footnote 6: We both of us happen to know, as well as the stationer, that Riddlesden, the attorney, was a very knave. He had half ruined Miss Read's father by persuading him to be bound for him. By his letter it appeared there was a secret scheme on foot to the prejudice of Mr. Hamilton; that Keith was concerned in it with Riddlesden.--Works of Franklin, by Sparks, Vol. i, p. 55.]

So saying he thrust the letter back into Franklin's hand, and turned away to serve a customer. Franklin was almost stunned with this intelligence. He immediately conferred with a Mr. Denham, a judicious friend whose acquaintance he had made on board the ship. They ascertained that the infamous Governor, from motives which it is difficult to comprehend, had not furnished Franklin with a single document. There was not a bill of credit or a single letter of introduction, commending the young adventurer to people in London. Denham then told him that no one who knew Keith had the slightest confidence in his promises. That the idea that he would furnish him with any letters of credit was preposterous, since Sir William had no credit with any body.

And thus Franklin found himself with his companion James Ralph, alone in the great world of London, without any letters of introduction, without any prospect of employment, and almost without money. The virtues of Franklin had exerted a restraining influence upon the unprincipled Ralph, and Franklin had not as yet become acquainted with the true basis of his character. The two young men met together to consult in this dilemma and to examine their finances. It appeared that Ralph had scarcely one penny in his pocket. He had intended to be a hanger-on upon Franklin, in whose ability to take care of himself and others he had the greatest confidence. Franklin's purse contained about fifty dollars.

Again he returned to consult with Mr. Denham. He very wisely advised Franklin to seek employment in some of the printing offices in London. He encouraged him with the thought that thus with a few months' labor, he might not only pay his expenses, but also lay up a sufficient sum to defray his passage home.

Franklin gradually perceived to his dismay, what an old man of the sea he had got upon his shoulders in the person of James Ralph. The following is his calm comment upon the atrocious conduct of Keith:

"What shall we think," he writes, "of a governor playing such pitiful tricks, and imposing so grossly upon a poor ignorant boy? It was a habit he had acquired; he wished to please every body, and having little to give, he gave expectations. He was otherwise an ingenuous, sensible man, a pretty good writer, and a good governor for the people, though not for his constituents the proprietaries. Several of our best laws were of his planning, and passed during his administration."

The entire absence of anger in this statement, has won for Franklin great commendation.

With his dependent protegé Ralph, he took humble lodgings in Little Britain street. Ralph had remarkable powers of conversation, with much more than ordinary literary talent, and could, whenever he wished, make himself very agreeable and almost fascinating as a companion. But he was quite a child as to all ability to take care of himself. Franklin really loved him at that time. He was a very handsome young man, graceful in his demeanor; and those who listened to his eloquent harangues would imagine that he was destined to attain to greatness.

Franklin immediately applied for work at the great printing establishment of Palmer in Bartholomew Close. Fifty journeymen were here employed. He promptly entered into a contract with the proprieter for the remuneration of about six dollars a week. Ralph, characteristically hurried to the theatre to enter upon the profession of a play-actor. Being disappointed in that attempt, his next plan was to edit a newspaper to be called the Spectator. Not being able to find a publisher, he then went the rounds of the law offices, in search of copying, but not even this, could he obtain. In the meantime they were both supported by the purse of Franklin. With fifty dollars in his pocket, and earning six dollars a week, he felt quite easy in his circumstances, and was quite generous in his expenditure for their mutual enjoyment.

CHAPTER IV

Mental and Moral Conflicts

Faithfulness to work--Neglect of Deborah Read--Treatise on Liberty and Necessity--Skill in swimming--Return to America--Marriage of Miss Read--Severe sickness--Death of Mr. Denham--Returns to Keimer's employ--The Junto--His Epitaph--Reformation of his treatise on Liberty and Necessity--Franklin's creed.

Franklin and Ralph were essentially congenial in their tastes. Neither of them were religiously inclined in the ordinary acceptation of those words. But the thoughtful philosophy of Franklin has by many been regarded as the development of an instinctively religious character. They were both exceedingly fond of amusement and especially of pleasure excursions on the Sabbath. Very seldom, did either the intellect or the heart lure them to listen to such teachings as they would hear from the pulpit. It certainly would have been better for them both, had they been church-going young men. There was no pulpit in all London from which they would not hear the reiterated counsel, Cease to do evil; learn to do well.

Franklin was faithful in the highest degree to his employer. Weary with the day's toil, which with his active mind was highly intellectual as well as mechanical, he almost invariably in the evening sought recreation with Ralph in the theatre. It is safe to infer that the best productions of our best dramatists, were those which would most interest the mind of our young philosopher. Ralph was daily gaining an increasing influence over his mind. It is said that we are prone to love more ardently those upon whom we confer favors than those from whom we receive them.

To these two young men the pleasures of London seemed inexhaustible. Franklin began to forget his old home and his friends. He began to think that London was a very pleasant place of residence, and that it was doubtful whether he should ever return to America again. He had constant employment, the prospect of an increasing income, and with his economical habits he had ample funds to relieve himself from all pecuniary embarrassment. With his friend Ralph, he was leading a very jovial life, free from all care.

KARTINDO PUBLISHING HOUSE (Kartindo.Com)

His love for Deborah Read began to vanish away. He thought very seldom of her: seldom could he find time to write to her; and ere long his letters ceased altogether; and she was cruelly left to the uncertainty of whether he was alive or dead. Ralph had entirely forgotten his wife and child, and Franklin had equally forgotten his affianced. In subsequent years the memory of this desertion seems to have weighed heavily on him. He wrote in his advanced life in reference to his treatment of Deborah,

"This was another of the great errors of my life; which I could wish to correct were I to live it over again."

For nearly a year, Franklin thus continued in the employment of Mr. Palmer, receiving good wages and spending them freely. A very highly esteemed clergyman of the Church of England named Wollaston, had written a book entitled, "The Religion of Nature Delineated." It was a work which obtained much celebrity in those days and was published by Mr. Palmer. It was of the general character of Butler's Analogy, and was intended to prove that the morality enjoined by Jesus Christ, was founded in the very nature of man; and that the principles of that morality were immutable, even though deists should succeed in destroying the public faith in the divine authority of Christianity. It was eminently an amiable book, written with great charity and candor, and without any dogmatic assumptions.

It chanced to fall to Franklin to set up the type. As was customary with him, he made himself thoroughly acquainted with the treatise of which he thus became the compositor. His mind was in such a state in reference to the claims of that Christianity which certainly did not commend the mode of life he was living, that it excited not only antagonistic but even angry emotions. So thoroughly were his feelings aroused, that he wrote and published a pamphlet of thirty-two pages, in refutation of the theory of Mr. Wollaston.

Franklin dedicated his work, which was entitled "A dissertation on Liberty and Necessity, Pleasure and Pain," to James Ralph. Fortunately, the treatise has descended to us unmutilated. He commences with the observation:

"I have here given you my present thoughts upon the general state of things in the universe."

The production was certainly a very able one to come from the pen of a young printer of but nineteen years. Mr. Palmer, while recognizing its ability, pronounced its principles to be atrocious and demoralizing. The production of such a work, literary, philosophical and religious, by probably the youngest companion of the journeymen printers, caused them all to open their eyes with astonishment, and he was regarded at once as a great man among them.[7]

[Footnote 7: In this extraordinary document our young deist writes, "There is said to be a first mover, who is called God, who is all wise, all good, all powerful. If he is all good, whatsoever he doeth must be good. If he is all wise, whatever he doeth must be wise. That there are things to which we give the name of *Evil*, is not to be denied--such as theft, murder, etc. But these are not in reality evils. To suppose anything to exist or to be done contrary to the will of the Almighty is to suppose him not Almighty. There is nothing done but God either does or permits. Though a creature may do many actions, which, by his fellow creatures, will be named evil, yet he can not act what will be in itself displeasing to God.

"We will sum up the argument thus, When the Creator first designed the universe, either it was his will that all should exist and be in the manner they are at this time, or it was his will that they should be otherwise. To say it was His will things should be otherwise, is to say that somewhat hath contradicted His will; which is impossible. Therefore we must allow that all things exist now in a manner agreeable to His will; and, in consequence of that, all are equally good and therefore equally esteemed by Him. No condition of life or being is better or preferable to another."

This whole treatise may be found in the appendix to the first volume of Parton's Life of Franklin.]

The deists of London, who had united in a club of merry free-thinkers, holding their meetings at an ale-house, sought out Franklin and drew him into their convivial gatherings. These men had no common principle of belief; they were united only in the negative principle of unbelief in the Christian religion. Ralph had formed a connection with a young milliner, by whom, through his many fascinations, he was mainly supported.

Franklin, with his increasing expenditures, was now disposed to shake off Ralph, as he needed all his money for his own convivial enjoyments. Ralph went into the country and opened a school, where he utterly failed. The unhappy milliner, ruined in character, and with a little child, wrote to Franklin imploring aid. Her letters touched his kindly heart. He could never see sorrow

KARTINDO PUBLISHING HOUSE (Kartindo.Com)

without wishing to relieve it. He furnished her with money, in small sums, to the amount of one hundred and thirty dollars; and worst of all, we regret to say that he commenced treating her with such familiarity, that she, still faithful to Ralph, repulsed him indignantly.[8]

[Footnote 8: Franklin writes in his autobiography, "I grew fond of her company, and being at that time under no religious restraint, and taking advantage of my importance to her, I attempted to take some liberties with her, another *erratum*, which she repulsed with a proper degree of resentment. She wrote to Ralph and acquainted him with my conduct. This occasioned a breach between us; and when he returned to London, he let me know he considered all the obligations he had been under to me as annulled."--Works of Franklin, Vol. i, p. 59.]

Franklin does not conceal these *foibles*, as he regarded them, these *sins* as Christianity pronounces them. He declares this simply to have been another of the great errors of his youth. She informed Ralph of his conduct. He was enraged, broke off all further communication with Franklin, and thirty-five years passed away before they met again. Ralph, goaded to desperation, gained a wretched living in various literary adventures; writing for any body, on any side, and for any price. Indeed he eventually gained quite an ephemeral reputation. He could express himself with vivacity, and several quite prominent politicians sought the aid of his pen.

Franklin, thus relieved from the support of Ralph, soon after entered a more extensive printing house, at Lincoln's Inn Fields. Though he was exceedingly fond of a sparkling glass of wine in his convivial hours, he was too much of a philosopher to stupefy his brain in guzzling beer. His habitual daily beverage was cold water.

"My companion at the press," he wrote, "drank every day a pint before breakfast, a pint at breakfast with his bread and cheese, a pint between breakfast and dinner, a pint at dinner, and another when he had done his day's work. I thought it a detestable custom. But it was necessary, he supposed, to drink strong beer that he might be strong to labor. I endeavored to convince him that the bodily strength afforded by beer could only be in proportion to the grain or the barley dissolved in the water of which it was made; that there was more flour in a pennyworth of bread, and, therefore, if he could eat that with a pint of water, it would give him more strength than a quart of beer. He drank on, however, and had four or five shillings to pay, out of his wages, every Saturday night, for that vile liquor; an expense I was free from; and thus these poor devils keep themselves always under."

Again Franklin wrote in characteristic phrase, in reference to the influence of his example over some of his companions,

"From my example, a great many of them left their muddling breakfast of bread, beer and cheese, finding they could, with me, be supplied from a neighboring house, with a large porringer of hot water gruel, sprinkled with pepper, crumbled with bread and a bit of butter in it, for the price of a pint of beer,--three half-pence. This was a more comfortable, as well as a cheaper breakfast, and kept their heads clearer. Those who continued sotting with their beer all day, were often, by not paying, out of credit at the ale-house; and used to make interest with me to get beer; their *light* as they phrased it being out. I watched the pay table on Saturday night, and collected what I stood engaged for them, having to pay sometimes on their account."

Franklin's skill in swimming, as we have mentioned was very remarkable. At one time he swam from London to Chelsea, a distance of four miles. Several of his companions he taught to swim in two lessons. His celebrity was such that he was urged to open a swimming school.[9] The life of self-indulgence he was now living in London, was not such as even his loose religious principles could approve. He had abandoned the faith of his fathers, and had adopted, for his rule of conduct, the principle, that it was right to yield to any indulgences to which his passions incited him. He became tired of London, and probably found it necessary to break away from the influences and associates with which he had surrounded himself.

[Footnote 9: "On one of these days I was, to my surprise, sent for by a great man I knew only by name, Sir William Wyndham. He had heard of my swimming from Chelsea to Blackfriars and of my teaching Wygate and another young man to swim in a few hours. He had two sons about to set out on their travels. He wished to have them first taught swimming, and proposed to gratify me handsomely if I would teach them. They were not yet come to town, and my stay was uncertain, so I could not undertake it. But from the incident I thought it likely that if I were to remain in England and opened a swimming-school I might get a good deal of money. And it struck me so strongly that had the overture been made me sooner, probably I should not so soon have returned to America."--Autobiography, Vol. I. p. 66.]

Mr. Denham, his companion of voyage, had decided to return to Philadelphia, and open an extensive store. He offered Franklin two hundred and fifty dollars a year as book-keeper. Though this was less than the sum Franklin was then earning, as compositor, there were prospects of his advancement. This consideration, in addition to his desire to escape from London, led him to accept the offer. He was now twenty years of age. It does not appear that he had thus far formed any deliberate plan for his life's work. He floated along as the current of events drifted him.

On the twenty-first of July, 1726, Franklin embarked on board the ship Berkshire for Philadelphia. He had been absent from America but little more than a year and a half. During this time he had not increased his fortune, for he had spent his money as fast as he had earned it. After a voyage of eighty days, the ship cast anchor before Philadelphia. At that time ships were often from three to seven months effecting the passage across the Atlantic.

As usual Franklin kept a diary punctually during his long voyage. Its pages were replete with pithy remarks of wit and wisdom. He was very fond of a game of checkers, and in that amusement beguiled many weary hours. We find the following striking comments upon the diversion in his journal:

"It is a game I much delight in. But it requires a clear head and undisturbed. The persons playing, if they would play well, ought not much to regard the *consequences* of the game; for that diverts and withdraws the mind from the game itself, and makes the player liable to make many false, open moves. I will venture to lay it down for an infallible rule that if two persons equal in judgment, play for a considerable sum, he that loves money most, shall lose. His anxiety for the success of the game confounds him. Courage is almost as requisite for the good conduct of this game as in a real battle; for if the player imagines himself opposed by one that is much his superior in skill, his mind is so intent on the defensive part, that an advantage passes unobserved."

The Governor of the Isle of Wight had died, leaving the reputation of having been one of the most consummate scoundrels who ever exercised despotic power. Franklin, in his treatise upon "Liberty and Necessity," written but a few months before, had assumed that there was no such thing as good and evil; that God ordered and controlled every event; and that consequently every event was in accordance with His will, and alike pleasing in His sight. But now we find the following record in his journal, which most readers will recognize as inconsistent with the young philosopher's theological opinions. He writes:

KARTINDO PUBLISHING HOUSE (Kartindo.Com)

"At the death of this governor, it appeared that he was a great villain, and a great politician. There was no crime so damnable, which he would stick at in the execution of his designs. And yet he had the art of covering all so thick, that with almost all men in general, while he lived he passed for a saint. In short, I believe it is impossible for a man, though he has all the cunning of a devil, to live and die a villain, and yet conceal it so well as to carry the name of an honest fellow to the grave with him, but some one by some accident or other, shall discover him. Truth and sincerity have a certain distinguishing, native lustre about them, which cannot be perfectly counterfeited. They are like fire and flame that cannot be painted."

We should infer, from some intimations in Franklin's diary, that he was troubled by some qualms of conscience, in view of his abandonment of Miss Read, and his irregular life in London. He has left a paper in which he stated that he had never formed any regular plan for the control of his conduct: that he was now about to enter on a new life; and that he was resolved that henceforth he would speak the truth, be industrious in his business, and speak ill of no man. These were rather meagre resolutions for a young man under these circumstances to adopt.

Soon after landing at Philadelphia, Franklin chanced to meet Sir William Keith in the streets. The governor seemed much embarrassed, and passed by without speaking. It does not appear that the acquaintance was ever resumed. The governor lived nearly twenty-five years afterward, a dishonored and ruined man, and died in the extreme of poverty.

Poor Miss Read, heart-broken, and deeming herself forever abandoned, yielded to the importunities of her friends and married a mechanic by the name of Rogers. He proved to be a thoroughly worthless fellow. His unconcealed profligacy, and unfaithfulness to his wife, compelled her, after a few months of wretchedness, to return to her mother, and to resume her maiden name. The profligate husband fled from his creditors to the West Indies. Rumors soon reached Philadelphia of his death, leaving probably another wife.

Franklin entered upon his duties as clerk of Mr. Denham, with his accustomed energy and skill. He carried into his new vocation, all his intellectual sagacity, and speedily won not only the confidence but the affection of his employer. He lived with Mr. Denham, and being always disposed to look upon the bright side of everything, even of his own imperfections, notwithstanding his infidelity to Miss Read, he seems to have been a very happy and even jovial young man.

KARTINDO PUBLISHING HOUSE (Kartindo.Com)

Four months after Franklin had entered upon his mercantile career, both Mr. Denham and Franklin were seized with the pleurisy. Mr. Denham died. Franklin, though brought near to the grave, recovered. He writes:

"I suffered a great deal; gave up the point in my own mind; and was at the time rather disappointed when I found myself recovering; regretting in some degree that I must now, sometime or other, have all that disagreeable work to do over again."

The death of Mr. Denham broke up the establishment, and Franklin was thrown out of employment. Keimer, in whose service he had formerly been engaged, again made him an offer to superintend a printing office. Franklin accepted the proposition. There were five inefficient hands, whom Franklin was expected to transform into accomplished printers. With these, and a few others, he organized a literary club, called the "Junto; or the Leathern Apron Club," as nearly every member was a mechanic.

The club met every Friday evening, and the wine cup, to stimulate conviviality, passed freely among them. There were twenty-four questions, which were every evening read, to which answers were to be returned by any one who could answer them. Between each question, it was expected that each member would fill, and empty, his glass. One would think that the wine must have been very weak, or the heads of these young men very strong, to enable them to quaff twenty-four glasses unharmed. We give a few of the questions as specimens of their general character.

1. "Have you met with anything in the author you last read?

3. "Has any citizen in your knowledge failed, and have you heard the cause?

7. "What unhappy effects of intemperance have you lately observed?

12. "Has any deserving stranger arrived in town since your last meeting?

16. "Has anybody attacked your reputation lately?

23. "Is there any difficulty which you would gladly have discussed at this time?"

Debates, declamation, and the reading of essays added to the entertainment of these gatherings. Stories were told, and bacchanal songs sung. No man could tell a better story, and few men could sing a better song than Benjamin Franklin. No one was deemed a suitable member of the club, who would not contribute his full quota to the entertainment or instruction. The questions proposed by Franklin for discussion, developed the elevated intellectual region his thoughts were accustomed to range. We give a few as specimens.

"Can any one particular form of government suit all mankind?

"Should it be the aim of philosophy to eradicate the passions?

"Is perfection attainable in this life?

"What general conduct of life is most suitable for men in such circumstances as most of the members of the Junto are?"

The Junto was limited to twelve members. It soon became so popular that applications for admission became very frequent. Six months passed rapidly away, when Keimer, who was an exceedingly immoral and worthless man, and was fast going to ruin, in some fit of drunkenness, or ungovernable irritation, entered the office, and assailed Franklin with such abuse, that he took his hat, and repaired to his lodgings, resolved never to return.

Franklin was twenty-one years of age. He had laid up no money. He was still but a journeyman printer. The draft which he had received from Mr. Vernon for fifty dollars had not yet been paid. He was exceedingly mortified when he allowed himself to reflect upon this delinquency which certainly approached dishonesty. In this emergence he conferred with a fellow journeyman by the name of Hugh Meredith, whose father was a gentleman of considerable property. Meredith proposed that they should enter into partnership, he furnishing the funds, and Franklin the business capacity.

At that time Franklin, remembering his narrow escape from the grave by the pleurisy, wrote his own epitaph which has been greatly celebrated. It has generally been admired; but some of more sensitive minds perceive in it a tone which is somewhat repulsive.

"The Body of BENJAMIN FRANKLIN, *Printer*, (Like the cover of an old book, Its contents torn out, And stripped of its lettering and gilding,) Lies here, food for worms. Yet the work itself shall not be lost, For it will, as he believed, appear once more, In a new And more beautiful edition, Corrected and amended By THE AUTHOR."

The excellencies of Franklin did not run in the line of exquisite sensibilities. At the early age of fifteen he began to cast off the restraints of the religion of his father and mother. Nearly all his associates were what were called Free-thinkers. He could not be blind to their moral imperfections. Mr. Parton writes,

"His old friend Collins, he remembered, was a Free-thinker, and Collins had gone astray. Ralph was a Free-thinker, and Ralph was a great sinner. Keith was a Free-thinker, and Keith was the greatest liar in Pennsylvania. Benjamin Franklin was a Free-thinker, and how shamefully he had behaved to Ralph's mistress, to Mr. Vernon and Miss Read, whose young life had been blighted through him."[10]

[Footnote 10: Parton's Life of Franklin, Vol. I, p. 168.]

Franklin's creed thus far, consisted only of negations. He had no belief; he had only unbelief. Indeed he seems to have become quite ashamed of his treatise upon Liberty and Necessity, published in London, and felt constrained to write a refutation of it.[11] As this strange young man in his discontent looked over the religions of the world, he could find no one that met his views. He therefore deliberately and thoughtfully sat down to form a religion of his own. Many such persons have appeared in the lapse of the ages, and almost invariably they have announced their creeds with the words, "Thus saith the Lord." But our young printer of twenty-two years, made no profession whatever, of any divine aid. He simply said, "Thus saith my thoughts." One would think he could not have much confidence in those thoughts, when it is remembered that at this time he was writing a refutation of the opinions, which he had published in London but a few months before.

[Footnote 11: "My arguments perverted some others, especially Collins and Ralph. But each of these having wronged me greatly without the least compunction; and recollecting Keith's conduct towards me, who was another Free-thinker, and my own towards Vernon and Miss Read, which at times gave me great trouble, I began to suspect that this doctrine, though it might be true, was not very useful. My London pamphlet, printed in 1725, and which had for its motto,

"'Whatever is is right,'

and which from the attributes of God, His infinite wisdom, goodness and power, concluded that nothing could possibly be wrong in the world, and that vice and virtue were empty distinctions, no such things existing, appeared now not so clever a performance, as I once thought it; and I doubted whether some error had not insinuated itself unperceived into my argument."

In the year 1779, Dr. Franklin wrote to Dr. Benjamin Vaughn respecting this pamphlet.

"There were only one hundred copies printed, of which I gave a few to friends. Afterwards, disliking the piece, I burnt the rest, except one copy. I was not nineteen years of age when it was written. In 1730, I wrote a piece on the other side of the question, which began with laying for its foundation that almost all men, in all ages and countries, have at times made use of prayer.

"Thence I reasoned that if all things are ordained, prayer must be among the rest ordained; but as prayer can procure no change in things that are ordained, praying must then be useless and an absurdity. God would, therefore, not ordain praying if everything else was ordained. But praying exists, therefore all other things are not ordained. This manuscript was never printed. The great uncertainty I found in metaphysical reasoning disgusted me, and I quitted that kind of reading and study for others more satisfactory."--Autobiography, p. 76.]

The book which Franklin thus prepared was entitled "Articles of Belief, and Acts of Religion." His simple creed was that there was one Supreme God who had created many minor gods; that the supreme God was so great that he did not desire the worship of man but was far above it.

The minor gods are perhaps immortal, and perhaps after the ages lapse they are changed, others supplying their place. Each of these subordinate gods has created for himself a sun with its planetary system, over which he presides and from the inhabitants of which he expects adoration. He writes,

"It is that particular wise and good God, who is the author and owner of our system that I propose for the object of my praise and adoration. It is to be inferred that this God is not above caring for us, is pleased with our praise, and offended when we slight him."

KARTINDO PUBLISHING HOUSE (Kartindo.Com)

He then prepares an invocation to this god of our solar system. It is founded on the style of the Psalms, but is immeasurably inferior to most of those sublime utterances of the Psalmist of Israel. And still the sentiments breathed were ennobling in their character; they proved that Franklin was vastly superior to the thoughtless, reckless deists who surrounded him, and that his soul was reaching forth and yearning for higher and holier attainments. In this invocation, the whole of which we cannot quote, he writes,

"O Creator! O Father! I believe that thou art good; and that thou art pleased with the pleasure of thy children. Praised be thy name forever. By thy power thou hast made the glorious sun with his attending worlds. By thy wisdom thou hast formed all things. Thy wisdom, thy power, and thy goodness are everywhere clearly seen. Thou abhorrest in thy creatures treachery and deceit, malice, revenge, intemperance, and every other hurtful vice. But thou art a lover of justice and sincerity, of friendship and benevolence, and every virtue. Thou art my friend, my father, and my benefactor. Praised be thy name; O God, forever. Amen."

The prayer which followed, doubtless giving utterance to his most inward feelings, is beautiful.

"Inasmuch," he wrote, "as by reason of our ignorance, we cannot be certain that many things, which we often hear mentioned in the petitions of men to the Deity, would prove real goods if they were in our possession, and as I have reason to hope and believe that the goodness of my Heavenly Father will not withhold from me a suitable share of temporal blessings, if by a virtuous and holy life I conciliate his favor and kindness; therefore I presume not to ask such things; but rather humbly and with a sincere heart, express my earnest desire that he would graciously assist my continual endeavors and resolutions of eschewing vice and embracing virtue, which kind of supplication will at the same time remind me in a solemn manner of my extensive duty."

He then added the supplication that he might be preserved from atheism, impiety and profaneness; that he might be loyal to his prince; that he might be gracious to those below him; that he might refrain from calumny and detraction; that he might be sincere in friendship, just in his dealings, grateful to his benefactors, patient in affliction; that he might have tenderness for the weak, and that, rejoicing in the good of others, he might become truly virtuous and magnanimous.

KARTINDO PUBLISHING HOUSE (Kartindo.Com)

It is very evident that some unexplained circumstances had called the attention of Franklin very earnestly to the subject of religion. He wrote very much upon that theme, and published a new version of the Lord's Prayer, and a lecture upon Providence and Predestination. He, however, admits that he very seldom attended any public worship, adding,

"I had still an opinion of its propriety and its utility, when rightly conducted; and I regularly paid my annual subscription for the support of the only Presbyterian minister."

Rumors soon reached Franklin's good father of Boston, of his son's free-thinking, and he wrote to his son in much alarm. In Franklin's reply, he said,

"All that should be expected from me, is to keep my mind open to conviction; to hear patiently and examine attentively whatever is offered me for that end. And if after all I continue in the same errors, I believe your usual charity will induce you rather to pity and excuse, than to blame me. In the meantime, your care and concern for me, is what I am very thankful for. My mother grieves that one of her sons is an Arian, and another an Arminian. What an Arminian or an Arian is, I cannot say that I very well know. The truth is, I make such distinctions very little my study. I think vital religion has always suffered when orthodoxy is more regarded than virtue. And the Scriptures assure me that at the last day we shall not be examined what we thought but what we did."

Franklin, having no revealed religion to guide him, and having no foundation for his faith, but the ever-changing vagaries of his own fantastic imagination, could have no belief to-day, of which he had any certainty that he would hold the same to-morrow. He was continually abandoning one after another of the articles of his fantastical creed, and adopting others in their place. At length he settled down upon the following simple belief, which with very considerable tenacity, but without any attempt to promulgate it, he adhered to for many years. It consisted of the six following articles which we give in briefest language.

1. "There is one God.

2. "He governs the world.

3. "He ought to be worshipped.

KARTINDO PUBLISHING HOUSE (Kartindo.Com)

4. "Doing good is the service most acceptable to him.

5. "Man is immortal.

6. "In the future world the souls of men will be dealt with justly."

It is very evident that Franklin had no great confidence in his theological opinions. He studiously avoided all writing upon the subject, and as far as possible all conversation. Still, with his keen sense of humor, he could not refrain from occasionally plunging a pretty sharp dagger's thrust into the palpable imperfections of the various and contending sects.

There was very little moral power, in the creed he professed, to arrest young men, of glowing passions, and exposed to the most difficult temptations, in their downward career. No voice of Franklin was heard with potency calling upon those who were thronging the broad road. In a lecture upon Providence, to his companions of the Junto, which was subsequently published, and which reflects some considerable honor upon the earnestness of his thoughts, he wrote,

"I am especially discouraged when I reflect that you are all my intimate pot-companions, who have heard me say a thousand silly things in conversation, and therefore have not that laudable partiality and veneration for whatever I shall deliver that good people have for their spiritual guides; that you have no reverence for my habit, nor for the sanctity of my countenance; that you do not believe me inspired, nor divinely assisted; and therefore will think yourself at liberty to assert, or dissert, approve or disapprove of anything I advance, canvassing and sifting it as the private opinion of one of your acquaintance."

Though it was Franklin's assumption that his religion was one of works and not of faith, still it must be admitted that his life was very inconsistent with those principles of purity, moral loveliness and good report which the Gospel enjoins. With his remarkable honesty of mind, in strains which we are constrained, though with regret to record, he writes,

"That hard-to-be governed passion of youth had hurried me frequently into intrigues with low women that fell in my way, which were attended with some expense and great inconvenience, besides a continual risk to my health by distemper, which of all things I dreaded, though by great luck I escaped it."

KARTINDO PUBLISHING HOUSE (Kartindo.Com)

Mr. Parton writes, "It was perhaps owing to his frequent delinquencies in this way, that his liturgy contains no allusion to a vice, which is of all others the most alluring to a youth of Franklin's temperament. He was too sincere and logical a man to go before his God and ask assistance against a fault which he had not fully resolved to overcome, and that immediately. About a year after the date of his liturgy was born his illegitimate son William Franklin, who became Governor of New Jersey. If laws were as easily executed as enacted, Benjamin Franklin would have received, upon this occasion, twenty-one lashings at the public whipping-post of Philadelphia."

CHAPTER V

The Dawn of Prosperity

Franklin takes a house--His first job--His industry--Plans a Newspaper--Enters the list as a writer--Advocates a Paper currency--Purchases Keimer's paper--Character of Meredith--Struggles of the firm--Unexpected assistance--Dissolves partnership with Meredith--Franklin's energetic conduct--His courtship, and marriage--Character of Mrs. Franklin--Increase of luxury--Plans for a library--Prosperity of Pennsylvania--Customs in Philadelphia--Style of dress in 1726--Franklin's social position in Philadelphia--His success--A hard student.

Franklin had now reached the end of life as an apprentice and a journeyman. With his friend Meredith he hired a house in the lower part of Market street, at the rent of about one hundred and twenty dollars a year. A large portion of this house he prudently re-let to another mechanic who was a member of the Junto. It would seem that Meredith was disappointed in the amount of money he expected to raise. Consequently after utterly exhausting their stock of cash, they still found it necessary to run deeply into debt for those appurtenances of a printing office which were absolutely necessary.

Just as they got ready for work, quite to their delight, a countryman came in introduced by one of the Junto, George House, who wanted a five shilling job executed.

"This man's five shillings," writes Franklin, "being our first fruits, and coming so seasonably, gave me more pleasure than any crown I have since earned. And from the gratitude I felt toward House, has made me often more ready, than perhaps I otherwise should have been, to assist young beginners."

The two young men devoted themselves to their work, with assiduity which was a sure precursor of success. Often Franklin was found diligently employed until eleven o'clock at night. His industry and energy soon attracted attention. A gentleman living near the office said to some of his friends:

"The industry of that Franklin is superior to anything I ever saw of the kind. I see him still at work when I go home from the club, and he is at work again before his neighbors are out of bed."

This statement produced such an impression upon a merchant who was present, that he called upon the young men and offered to supply them with stationery on credit. Franklin's literary taste, and his remarkable success as a writer, led him ever to cherish, as a darling project, the idea of the establishing of a newspaper. In a few months he had quite deliberately formed his plan; but in some way Keimer got wind of it, and immediately issued a prospectus for the establishment of a paper of his own. Though he was totally unqualified for the task of editorship, yet his project was quite hurtful to the plans of Franklin.

Very much annoyed by the treachery which had revealed his plans to Keimer, and perceiving that his paper was unpopular and heavy, Franklin very wisely decided to establish his own reputation as a vivacious writer, before entering upon the important undertaking of issuing a journal in his own name. There was a small paper then published in the city called "The Mercury." He commenced writing a series of very witty and satirical articles over the signature of "Busy Body." The first number contained the following sentences as intimations of what was to come.

"It is probable that I may displease a great number of your readers who will not very well like to pay ten shillings a year for being told of their faults, but as most people delight in censure when they themselves are not the object of it, if any are offended at my publicly exposing their private vices, I promise they shall have the satisfaction in a very little time, in seeing their good friends and neighbors in the same circumstances."

These sparkling contributions of Franklin attracted much attention, and created for him a growing literary reputation. The subject of paper money which agitated our country, was then being discussed in Pennsylvania with intense interest. Franklin wrote a carefully studied pamphlet entitled "A Modest Inquiry into the Nature and Necessity of a Paper Currency."

This treatise, written by a young printer of but twenty-three years, upon one of the most difficult questions of finance, displayed great ability. Warmly he advocated a paper currency. His arguments, however, were such as would not now probably exert much influence upon the public mind. The main proposition he endeavored to sustain was, that there was not a sufficiency of gold and silver in Pennsylvania, for carrying on the trade of the province. He therefore argued that all branches of industry must languish unless the currency were increased by an issue of paper.[12]

[Footnote 12: This pamphlet may be found in Sparks' "Works of Franklin," Vol. ii, p. 253.]

It has been suggested that Franklin might have been unconsciously influenced in his views, by the fact that he had been very successful in printing paper money, and that he anticipated still more employment in that line. It is certain that Franklin's pamphlet exerted a powerful influence at the time, and a new issue of paper currency was ordered. Franklin thought that the effect was highly conducive to the prosperity of the province, and he never swerved from the views which he had so earnestly and successfully urged in his pamphlet.

Franklin's sun was rapidly rising. Keimer's was as rapidly sinking. After publishing thirty-nine numbers of the "Universal Instructor" and the subscription list having dwindled to ninety, he gladly sold the paper for a trifle to Franklin and Meredith. The genius of Franklin was immediately displayed in the improved literary character of the paper, and in its mechanical execution. The name was changed to the "Pennsylvania Gazette." The first number issued by him was on Oct. 2, 1729.

The subject of religion was almost entirely ignored. Franklin seems to have become weary of the darkness and the fogs through which his unillumined mind had been so long painfully floundering, without coming to any results upon which he could place reliance. Christianity he generally treated with respect, though he could not refrain from occasionally giving a sly thrust at those imperfections of Christians which were so palpable to his observant mind. And though he never assailed that which was not inherently bad, it cannot be denied that occasionally his keen sarcasms brought Christianity itself into reproach, as if it were a religion which produced no better fruits, perhaps not so good, as no religion at all.

The business of this young firm of Franklin and Meredith, viewed in the light of the grand printing enterprises of the present day, was indeed trivial. The two young men did all the work themselves without even a boy to help them. In fact Meredith, who at the best was a poor workman, and who fell into intemperate habits, neglected his business, frequented the ale-houses, and left all responsibility resting upon the efficient shoulders of his partner.

Franklin, who endeavored to be perfect in every thing he undertook, printed his paper so admirably that it is said that there is probably not a journal now in Philadelphia which is issued in better style than "The Pennsylvania Gazette" of 1729.

For seven years Franklin had been embarrassed by the thought of the fifty dollars which he had received from Mr. Vernon, and which had not yet been repaid. Mr. Vernon wrote him a very gentle intimation, stating that it would be very convenient for him to receive the money. Franklin returned a contrite and magnanimous letter. He made no attempt to extenuate his fault, promised immediately to strain every nerve to meet the debt, and in a few months paid the whole, principal and interest.

Still the infant firm was struggling with adversity. The partners had commenced operations with scarcely any capital excepting promises. Their outfit cost about a thousand dollars. Mr. Meredith had been unfortunate in business, and found himself unable to pay the second instalment promised of five hundred dollars. The stationers who furnished paper began to be uneasy, for they could not but see that Meredith was fast going to ruin.

Franklin was seldom in the habit of dwelling upon his misfortunes. In these dark hours he wrote,

"In this distress two true friends whose kindness I have never forgotten, nor ever shall forget while I can remember anything, came to me separately, unknown to each other, and without any application from me, offered each of them to advance me all the money that should be necessary to take the whole business upon myself; but they did not like my continuing in partnership with Meredith, who, as they said, was often seen drunk in the street, playing at low games in ale-houses, much to our discredit."

Franklin generously was very reluctant to throw aside Meredith. Dissolute as the young man had become, he could not forget that he was the son of a man who had been his friend; but after carefully pondering the question and seeing ruin stare him in the face, he said one day to Meredith,

"Perhaps your father is dissatisfied at the part you have undertaken in this affair of ours; and is unwilling to advance for you and me, what he would for you. If that is the case tell me, and I will resign the whole to you and go about my business."

KARTINDO PUBLISHING HOUSE (Kartindo.Com)

Meredith replied,

"My father has really been disappointed, and is really unable. I am unwilling to distress him further. I see this is a business I am unfit for. I was bred a farmer and it was folly in me to come to town, and put myself at thirty years of age an apprentice to learn a new trade. Many of our Welsh people are going to settle in North Carolina where land is cheap. I am inclined to go with them, and follow my old employment. If you will take the debts of the company upon you, return to my father the hundred pounds he has advanced, pay my little personal debts, and give me thirty pounds and a new saddle, I will relinquish the partnership, and leave the whole in your hands."

These were hard terms; but there was no other way in which Franklin could escape from the embarrassments of this untoward partnership. He accepted the proposal at once; borrowed the needful money of his friends; and became his own sole partner.

True prosperity now began to attend his indomitable industry, frugality, and wisdom. The advance of the young man was necessarily slow, but it was sure. Well aware that his reputation with the community would be invaluable to him, he not only endeavored to be industrious, but to let it be seen by his neighbors that he left no stone unturned to accomplish his purposes.

He would trundle, through the streets of Philadelphia, in a wheel-barrow, the paper which he purchased, by no means seeking by-streets where his more fashionable companions would not see him. He dressed with the utmost simplicity, but always in clean garments, well cut, and which presented his admirable form to great advantage. Never did he allow himself to sink to the vulgarity of a slatternly appearance. He was ever ready, when engaged in the most busy employments of his office, to receive without a blush, any guests, however high, who might chance to call.

The tranquil months glided on. Franklin was prospered in business, paid his debts, and began to accumulate a little property. Our young philosopher was never an impassioned lover. As he would contemplate, in his increasing prosperity, removing to another more commodious office, so he now thought, having reached the age of twenty-four, that it might be expedient for him to have a home of his own, and a wife to take care of his domestic affairs.

He had let a portion of the house which he used for his printing office, to a

KARTINDO PUBLISHING HOUSE (Kartindo.Com)

mechanic of the Junto by the name of Godfrey. He conferred with Mrs. Godfrey upon the subject. She had a relative, a very pretty girl, Miss Godfrey, whom she highly recommended and brought, as it were by accident, to take tea with Franklin. She was graceful, amiable, and a child of parents well to do in the world. Franklin was a remarkably handsome and fascinating young man. The courtship proceeded successfully and rapidly.

The reader will be interested in seeing Franklin's own account of this affair. He writes, in his Autobiography:

"Mrs. Godfrey projected a match with a relation's daughter, took opportunities of bringing us often together, till a serious courtship on my part ensued; the girl being, in herself, very deserving. The old folks encouraged me by continual invitations to supper, and by leaving us together, till at length it was time to explain. Mrs. Godfrey managed our little treaty. I let her know I expected as much money with their daughter as would pay off my remaining debt for the printing house; which I believe was not then above a hundred pounds. She brought me word they had no such sum to spare; I said they might mortgage their house in the loan-office. The answer to this, after some days, was, that they did not approve the match; that, on inquiry of Mr. Bradford, they had been informed the printing business was not a profitable one, the types would soon be worn out, and more wanted; that Keimer and David Harvy had failed one after the other, and I should probably soon follow them; and therefore I was forbidden the house, and the daughter was shut up."

Occasionally Franklin had gone to the home of Mrs. Read, the mother of the unhappy Deborah. His conscience reproached him for his conduct to that good girl. She was always dejected and solitary, and with a broken heart clung to her mother, her only friend. It is doubtful whether she were ever legally married to Rogers. It was rumored that at the time of their marriage, he was the husband of one, if not more wives. If legally married, there was another serious obstacle in her path. Rogers had run away to the West Indies. Rumor alone had announced his death. He might be still living.

Franklin's sympathy gradually became excited in her behalf. And at length he proposed that, regardless of all the risks, they should be married. It seems that he had announced to her very distinctly that he had a living child, and very honorably he had decided that that child of dishonor was to be taken home and trained as his own.

KARTINDO PUBLISHING HOUSE (Kartindo.Com)

These were sad nuptials. The world-weary wife knew not but that she had another husband still living, and a stigma, indelible, rested upon Franklin. The marriage took place on the first of September, 1730. It subsequently appears that Rogers, the potter, was really dead. The child was taken home and reared with all possible tenderness and care. It is a little remarkable that nothing is known of what became of the mother of that child. The boy grew up to manhood, espoused the Tory cause, when the Tories were hunting his father to hang him, and by his ungrateful, rebellious conduct, pierced his heart with a thousand empoisoned daggers.

Mrs. Franklin proved in all respects an excellent woman, and an admirable wife for her calm, philosophic and unimpassioned husband. Franklin never had a journeyman in his office who performed his functions more entirely to his satisfaction, than his wife discharged her responsible duties. She was always amiable, industrious and thrifty.

There was a little shop attached to the printing office which Mrs. Franklin tended. She also aided her husband in folding and distributing the papers, and with a mother's love trained, in the rudiments of education, the child whose mother was lost.

Franklin, in his characteristic, kindly appreciation of the services of all who were faithful in his employ, speaks in the following commendatory terms of the industrial excellencies of his wife. When far away dazzled by the splendors, and bewildered by the flattery of European courts, he wrote to her,

"It was a comfort to me to recollect that I had once been clothed, from head to foot, in woolen and linen of my wife's manufacture, and that I never was prouder of any dress in my life."

In Franklin's Autobiography, as published by Sparks, we read, "We have an English proverb that says, 'He that would thrive, must ask his wife.' It was lucky for me that I had one as much disposed to industry and frugality as myself. She assisted me cheerfully in my business, folding and stitching pamphlets, tending shop, purchasing old linen rags, for the paper-makers, etc. We kept no idle servants; our table was plain and simple, our furniture of the cheapest. For instance, my breakfast was, for a long time, bread and milk, (no tea) and I ate it out of a two-penny earthern porringer, with a pewter-spoon.

"But mark how luxury will enter families, and make a progress in spite of principle. Being called one morning to breakfast, I found it in a china bowl, with a spoon of silver. They had been bought for me without my knowledge, by my wife, and had cost her the enormous sum of three and twenty shillings; for which she had no other excuse or apology to make, but that she thought her husband deserved a silver spoon and china bowl, as well as any of his neighbors. This was the first appearance of plate or china in our house; which afterward, in a course of years, as our wealth increased, augmented gradually to several hundred pounds in value."[13]

[Footnote 13: Life of Franklin, by Sparks, p. 102.]

While thus engaged he conceived the idea of establishing a public subscription library. His knowledge of human nature taught him that if he presented the enterprise as his own, feelings of jealousy might be excited, and it might be imagined that he was influenced by personal ambition. He therefore said that a number of gentlemen had adopted the plan, and had requested him to visit the lovers of books and of reading, and solicit their subscriptions. Each subscriber was to contribute two pounds to start the enterprise, and to pay a yearly assessment of ten shillings.

By the arduous labors of five months, Franklin obtained fifty names. With this the enterprise commenced. Such was the origin of the Philadelphia Library, now one of the most important institutions of the kind in our land. In the year 1861, seventy thousand volumes were reported as on its shelves.

Philadelphia contained a population of nearly ten thousand people. Pennsylvania was decidedly the central point for European emigration. Its climate was delightful; its soil fertile; and William Penn's humane policy with the Indians had secured for the colony peace and friendship with the native inhabitants for more than fifty years.

The white man, on this continent, has told his own story. The Indians have had no historians. But nothing is more clear than that in almost every instance they were goaded to war by the unendurable wrongs which were inflicted upon them.[14] Until Braddock's dreadful defeat, Pennsylvania had scarcely known a single alarm. In the summer of 1749, twelve thousand Germans landed at Philadelphia. This was the average number for many years. The policy of William Penn had been to establish upon the banks of the Delaware, an extended and beautiful village, where every house should have its lawn and its garden for vegetables and flowers. In the year 1732, when Franklin was twenty-six years of age, the dwellings of this village were mostly of brick or stone, and were spread along the banks of the river for the distance of a mile, with streets running back into the interior to the distance of about half a mile.

[Footnote 14: "No other British colony admits of the evidence of an Indian against a white man; nor are the complaints of Indians against white men duly regarded in other colonies; whereby these poor people endure the most cruel treatment from the very worst of our own people, without hope of redress. And all the Indian wars in our colonies were occasioned by such means."

Importance of the British Plantations in America to these Kingdoms, London. 1731.]

The prosperity of Philadelphia, indeed of Pennsylvania, was remarkable. Provisions and the most delicious fruits were in great abundance. Even the pigs were fattened upon the most luscious peaches. Each family in the city kept its cow, which grazed upon the common lands on the outskirts of the town. The Philadelphia of that period was a green village, beautifully shaded by trees, and presenting to every visitor an aspect of rare attractions. Professor Peter Kalm, who published an exceedingly interesting account of his travels in North America between the years 1748 and 1751, writes,

"There were fine orchards all about the city. The country people in Sweden and Finland guard their turnips more carefully than the people here do the most exquisite fruits. A Philadelphian has so much liberty and abundance that he lives in his house like a king."

The Quakers, or as they prefer to be called, the Friends, at that time composed about one-third of the population of Philadelphia, and one-half of the State of Pennsylvania. They were a remarkably intelligent, industrious and worthy people. Probably a better and more thrifty community was never colonized on this globe.

The state of society has greatly changed since that day, and customs, which were then deemed essential, have since become obsolete. For instance, the whipping-post, the pillory, and the stocks, were prominent in the market-place and were in frequent use. There was a public whipper, who, for his repulsive services, received a salary of fifty dollars a year. Until as late as 1760, women were frequently publicly whipped. It is said that a whipping occurred on an average, twice a month.

KARTINDO PUBLISHING HOUSE (Kartindo.Com)

The dress of gentlemen was gaudy and extravagant, unsurpassed by that of French or British courtiers. Immense wigs, with their profusion of waves or curls, were in use by the gentry. Very tight knee-breeches were worn, with silk stockings, and shoes embellished with immense silver buckles, highly polished. Their coats were richly embroidered, often of silk velvet, and their full flow reached below the knees. Ruffled shirts and ruffled wrist-bands of linen, of snowy whiteness, added to the beauty of the dress. A jewelled scabbard containing a polished sword hung by the side. A three-cornered hat completed this showy attire. There is not a Rocky Mountain Indian in his most gorgeous war-dress of paint and plumes, who would attract more attention walking down Broadway, than would Benjamin Franklin as he was painted in 1726.

His portrait was taken when he was in London, working as a journeyman printer. Contrary to the general impression, Franklin was then, and through all his life, fully conscious of the advantages which dress confers. When surrounded by the homage of the court of Versailles, there was no courtier in those magnificent saloons more attentive to his attire than was Benjamin Franklin. His keen sagacity taught him the advantage of appearing in a dress entirely different from that of the splendid assembly around him, and thus he attracted universal observation. But never did he appear in the presence of these lords and ladies but in a costly garb to which he had devoted much attention.

[Illustration]

Mr. Parton, speaking of the portrait which Franklin then had painted in London, says,

"The fair, full, smiling face of Franklin is surrounded in this picture by a vast and stiff horse-hair wig; and his well-developed figure shows imposingly in a voluminous and decorated coat that reaches nearly to his heels. Under his left arm he carries his cocked hat. His manly bosom heaves under snowy ruffles, and his extensive wrist-bands are exposed to view by the shortness of his coat sleeves."

Between the years 1740 and 1775, while abundance reigned in Pennsylvania, and there was peace in all her borders, a more happy and prosperous population could not perhaps be found on this globe. In every home there was comfort. The people generally were highly moral, and knowledge was extensively diffused. Americans, who visited Europe, were deeply impressed by the contrast. In the Old World they saw everywhere indications of poverty and suffering. Franklin wrote, after a tour in Great Britain in 1772,

"Had I never been in the American colonies, but were to form my judgment of civil society by what I have lately seen, I should never advise a nation of savages to admit of civilization. For, I assure you, that in the possession and enjoyment of the various comforts of life, compared with these people, every Indian is a gentleman; and the effect of this kind of civil society seems to be the depressing multitudes below the savage state, that a few may be raised above it."

Yet let it not be supposed that the effects of the fall were not visible here, or that man's inhumanity to man had ceased. There were bickerings, and heart burnings, and intense political struggles, in which the strong endeavored to extend their power, and the weak endeavored to throw off the shackles with which they were bound. William Penn complains of the ambitious politicians who he said thought--"nothing taller than themselves but the trees." John Adams denounced in severest terms the tricks of the petty politicians; and speaking of the more ambitious ones who sought the positions of governor or custom-house officers, he writes:

"These seekers are actuated by a more ravenous sort of ambition and avarice."

For twenty years Franklin continued a prosperous but uneventful life, as an active business man in Philadelphia. His integrity, his sagacity, and his prosperity, rapidly increased the esteem in which he was held. But still he was engaged in business as a printer and a shop-keeper, which would not now give him admission into what he called the higher circles of society.

He not only edited, printed and published his newspaper, but he also kept books for sale and a small quantity of stationery, and also was a binder of books. He made and sold ink; was an extensive dealer in rags; and soap and feathers could be purchased at his shop. We find in his advertisements the announcement of coffee and other groceries for sale.

And still his printing office gradually became the nucleus for the gathering of the most intelligent and influential men. If any important project was on foot, it was deemed essential to consult Benjamin Franklin. His Gazette proved a great success, and was incomparably the ablest paper published in the colonies.[15]

[Footnote 15: Life and Works of John Adams, Vol. ii, p. 165.]

KARTINDO PUBLISHING HOUSE (Kartindo.Com)

Franklin's editorials were very sparkling, and are considered as among the most brilliant of his intellectual efforts. He was almost invariably good natured, and the design of all he wrote, was to promote integrity and kindly feeling. He would write an article, as if from a correspondent, which would give him an opportunity to return an amusing article in the next number. A complete file of the paper is preserved in the Philadelphia Library.

In 1732, Franklin issued the first number of the Almanac, called Poor Richard, which subsequently attained such wide renown. The popularity of the work was astonishing; for twenty-five years it averaged ten thousand copies a year. This was a wonderful sale in those times. Everybody was quoting the pithy sayings of Poor Richard.[16]

[Footnote 16: "And now after the lapse of one hundred and thirty years, we find persons willing to give twenty-five dollars for a single number, and several hundred dollars for a complete set. Nay, the reading matter of several of the numbers, has been republished within these few years, and that republication already begins to command the price of a rarity."--*Parton's Life of Franklin*, Vol. i, p. 231.]

Franklin was an extensive reader. He had a memory almost miraculous; and his mind was so constituted, that it eagerly grasped and retained any sharp or witty sayings. Thus, though many of the maxims of Poor Richard originated with him, others were gleaned from the witticisms of past ages, upon which Franklin placed the imprint of his own peculiar genius. I give a few of those renowned maxims which soon became as household words, in every shop and dwelling of our land.

"There is no little enemy." "Three may keep a secret if two of them are dead." "He is no clown who drives the plough, but he that does clownish things." "Wealth is not his that has it, but his that enjoys it." "The noblest question in the world is, 'what good may I do in it.'" "Keep your eye wide open before marriage; half shut afterward."

Franklin was not a poet. He could scheme easily, but even his rhymes were poor. His sense of delicacy was quite obtuse, but perhaps not more so, than we ought to expect from the unrefined times in which he lived.[17]

[Footnote 17: "Poor Richard, at this day, would be reckoned an indecent production. All great humorists were all indecent, before Charles Dickens.

They used certain words which are now never pronounced by polite persons, and are never printed by respectable printers; and they referred freely to certain subjects which are familiar to every living creature, but which it is now agreed among civilized beings, shall not be topics of conversation. In this respect Poor Richard was no worse, and not much better than other colonial periodicals, some of which contain things incredibly obscene, as much so as the strongest passages of Sterne, Smollet and De Foe."--*Parton.*]

The increasing circulation of the Pennsylvania Gazette, the extensive sale of Poor Richard, and the success of many of the small books which Franklin published, soon placed the finances of Franklin in a very flourishing condition. This enabled him to send for every important work published in England. As he was never an hour in idleness, and seldom entered any place of popular amusement, he found time to study all these solid and useful works. The superior powers with which God had endowed him, enabled him to glean from their pages, and store up in his memory, all that was most valuable. By these indefatigable studies, he was rapidly becoming one of the most learned of men, and was preparing himself for that brilliant career, in which, as a statesman and a philosopher, he stood in the first ranks of those who had been deemed the great men of earth.

His first entrance to public life was as Clerk to the General Assembly, which was then the Legislature of the Pennsylvania Colony. This was an office of but little emolument or honor. His first election was unanimous. The second year, though successful, he was opposed by an influential member.

Franklin, who wished to have every one his friend, was anxious to conciliate him. He accomplished his purpose shrewdly--perhaps cunningly, is not too strong a word to use. Having heard that the gentleman had a very rare and valuable book in his library, he wrote him a very polite and flattering letter, soliciting the loan of it. No man could pen such an epistle more adroitly than Franklin.

After a few days he returned the book with one of his most exquisite notes of thanks. The gentleman was caught in the trap. Charmed with the urbanity Franklin displayed in the correspondence, the next time he met the philosopher, he grasped him cordially by the hand. Though he had never spoken to him before, he invited him to his house.

Franklin, commenting upon this adventure, writes,

KARTINDO PUBLISHING HOUSE (Kartindo.Com)

"He ever after manifested a readiness to serve me on all occasions, so that we became great friends, and our friendship continued to his death. This is another instance of the truth of an old maxim I had learned, which says 'He that hath once done you a kindness will be more ready to do you another than he whom you yourself have obliged,' and it shows how much more profitable it is prudently to remove than to resent, return, and continue inimical proceedings."

There was something in this transaction, an apparent want of sincerity, an approach to trickery, which will impress many readers painfully. It was a shrewd manoeuvre, skillfully contrived, and successfully executed. The perfect sincerity of a friendly and magnanimous mind is the safest guide in all the emergencies of life.

KARTINDO PUBLISHING HOUSE (Kartindo.Com)

CHAPTER VI

Religious and Philosophic Views

Studious habits--New religion--Personal habits--Church of the Free and Easy--His many accomplishments--The career of Hemphall--Birth and Death of Franklin's son--The Ministry of Whitefield--Remarkable friendship between the philosopher and the preacher--Prosperity of Franklin--His convivial habits--The defense of Philadelphia--Birth of a daughter--The Philadelphia Academy.

Franklin was a perservering and laborious student, for whatever he read he studied. With increasing intellectual tastes, he found time every day to devote many hours to his books. His reading was of the most elevated and instructive kind. It consisted almost exclusively of scientific treatises, and of history, biography, voyages and travels.

His mind was still struggling and floundering in the midst of religious and philosophical speculations. He seems, from some unexplained reason, to have been very unwilling to accept the religion of Jesus Christ; and yet he was inspired undeniably by a very noble desire to be a good man, to attain a high position in morality. Earnestly he endeavored to frame for himself some scheme which would enable him to accomplish that purpose.

At this time he wrote,

"Few in public affairs act from a mere view of the good of their country, whatever they may pretend. Fewer still in public affairs act with a view to the good of mankind. There seems to me, at present, great occasion to raise a 'United Party for Virtue,' by forming the virtuous and good of all nations into a regular body, to be governed by suitable good and wise rules, which good and wise men may probably be more unanimous in their obedience to, than common people are to common laws. I at present, think, that whoever attempts this aright, and is well qualified, cannot fail of pleasing God, and of meeting with success."

Influenced by these exalted motives, he concentrated all the energies of his well informed mind to the organization of a new religion. To this church he gave the name of "The Society of the Free and Easy." The members were to be Free

KARTINDO PUBLISHING HOUSE (Kartindo.Com)

from vice, and consequently, Easy in mind. The first article of his creed was that he would have no creed. And yet this religion, which drew an antagonistic distinction between faith and works, denouncing all faith at the same time announced that its fundamental and absolutely essential faith was that piety consisted in cherishing the ordinarily recognized virtues. These were Temperance, Silence, Order, Resolution, Frugality, Industry, Sincerity, Justice, Moderation, Cleanliness, Tranquillity, Charity and Humility.

His ritual consisted in devoting one week to the cultivation of each of these virtues. He had no Sabbath, no preached Gospel, no Sacraments. But his creed, with its corresponding practice, certainly exerted a very powerful influence, and in many respects beneficial, upon his own mind.

With his list of virtues before him, this remarkable young man commenced the effort vigorously to attain perfection. The Christian reader will not be at all surprised to read from Franklin's pen the following account of the result:

"I was surprised to find myself so much fuller of faults than I had imagined. But I had the satisfaction of seeing them diminish. After a while I went through one course only in a year, and afterwards only one in several years; till at length I omitted them entirely, being employed in voyages and business abroad, with a multiplicity of affairs that interfered."

Franklin was a very proud man. He could not but be conscious of his great superiority over most of those with whom he associated. He avows that the virtue of humility he never could attain. The semblance of that virtue he could easily assume, but he says that the pride of his heart was such that had he attained it, he would have been proud of his humility. He adopted the following as the ordinary routine of life.

He rose at five, very carefully performed his ablutions, and then offered a brief prayer to a being whom he called "Powerful Goodness." Why he should have preferred that address to the more simple one of "Our Heavenly Father," we know not. He then laid out the business of the day, and for a short time directed his mind to the especial virtue which he intended that day and week to cherish.[18]

[Footnote 18: "It was about this time I conceived the bold and arduous project of arriving at moral perfection. I wished to live without committing any fault at any time. As I knew, or thought I knew what was right and wrong, I did not see

KARTINDO PUBLISHING HOUSE (Kartindo.Com)

why I might not always do the one and avoid the other. But I soon found that I had undertaken a task of more difficulty than I had imagined."--Autobiography, p. 105.]

In the freshness of all his morning energies he devoted himself to his books for an hour and a half. This brought him to breakfast-time. At eight o'clock he commenced work in his shop, to which he devoted himself assiduously until twelve. An hour was then allowed for dinner and rest. At one he returned to the arduous labors of his shop, labors which engrossed all his energies, and continued the employment until six. His day's hard work was then ordinarily closed. He took his supper, received his friends, or more commonly read and studied until ten o'clock at night, when almost invariably he retired to his bed.

His mind still for a time continued much interested in his plan for the church of the Free and Easy. We find among his papers that he decided that candidates for admission should, after a careful examination, to ascertain that their creed was, to have no creed, and that their faith was, to abjure all faith, be subject to a probation of thirteen weeks. It seems that no candidate ever applied for admission. There were no apostles to wander abroad proclaiming the new gospel. Increasing business absorbed Franklin's time, and the new church was forgotten.

The sole motive which Franklin urged to inspire to action, was self-interest. "You should be honest," he would say, "because it is politic. You abstain from vice for the same reason that you should not drink poison, for it will hurt you." In the enforcement of these views he writes,

"It was my design to explain and enforce this doctrine, *that vicious actions are not hurtful because they are forbidden, but forbidden because they are hurtful*. It was, therefore, every one's interest to be virtuous who wished to be happy in this world. And I should from this circumstance (there being always in the world a number of rich merchants, nobility, states and princes, who have need of honest instruments for the management of their affairs, and such being so rare) have endeavored to convince young persons that no qualities are so likely to make a poor man's fortune as those of probity and integrity."

It may be doubted whether such considerations ever made a truly good man. Virtue must be loved for its own sake. Vice must be deserted for its inherent baseness, even though it may bring a great reward.

KARTINDO PUBLISHING HOUSE (Kartindo.Com)

Franklin, in the prosecution of his studies, devoted himself to French, Spanish, Italian, and even to Latin. In all these he became a proficient. His mind was wonderfully prompt in the acquisition of knowledge. He could hardly have devoted himself more assiduously and successfully to these studies, had some good angel whispered in the ear of the young printer the astounding intelligence, "You are yet to be the ambassador of the United States to European courts. You are to appear in those glittering assemblages as the equal of the highest noble; and are to enjoy the hospitalities of kings and queens. Familiarity with these languages, and the intellectual culture you are thus acquiring will be of more value to you than mines of gold."

This remarkable man prized all branches of knowledge; and seemed to excel in all. He devoted much attention to music. With much skill he played upon the harp, the guitar, the violin, and the violincello.

In the year 1734, a young preacher by the name of Hemphall came to Philadelphia from England. He was deemed by the orthodox clergy, very heterodox in his opinions. Probably suspicions of his orthodoxy were enhanced from the fact that he brought high testimonials of eloquence from several of the most prominent deists and free-thinkers in England. He was very fluent, at times very eloquent, and Franklin was charmed with the man and his doctrines.

Boldly denouncing all creeds, and all religious faith, he announced it as *his* creed and *his* faith that piety consists in conduct alone. Crowds flocked to hear him. One day, after preaching a very eloquent sermon, some one discovered that he had stolen that sermon from Dr. James Foster, the most popular preacher in London. An investigation took place, in which he was compelled to acknowledge that he had stolen every one of his sermons. Franklin writes,

"This detection gave many of our party disgust, who accordingly abandoned his cause, and occasioned our more speedy discomfiture in the synod. I stuck by him, however. I rather approved his giving us good sermons composed by others, than bad ones of his own, though the latter was the practice of our common teachers."

Had the young man said frankly, "I am rehearsing to you the most eloquent sermons of the most eloquent English divines," no one could have found any fault. But for him to assume that the sermons were his own, and that he personally was entitled to the credit of whatever power they exhibited, was certainly practicing deception. It was a gross violation of Franklin's cardinal virtue of sincerity. It was unworthy of Franklin, in his charitable regard for the offender, to gloss over the real criminality of the offence.

A year after Franklin's marriage, a son was born to him, to whom he gave the name of Francis Folger Franklin. All accounts agree in describing the child as endowed with remarkable beauty and intelligence. Probably Franklin never loved any being as he loved that child. In the year 1736, when this wonderful boy was but four years of age, he was seized with the small-pox and died. Even the philosophic Franklin was almost crushed by the terrible calamity. The cheering views of the Christian faith could not sustain him. He had no vivid conception of his cherub boy an angel in Heaven awaiting his father's arrival. He could only say that "I am *inclined to believe* that my child has not passed away into utter annihilation; but who knows? Many of the wisest and best on earth utterly discard the idea of a future existence. They deem the thought the conceit of ignorance and fanaticism."

We read the following epitaph on his little grave-stone with much sympathy for the bereaved father. He could only write

Francis F. Son of Benjamin and Deborah Franklin. Deceased November 12, 1736, Aged four years, one month and one day. The delight of all who knew him.

In the year 1739, Rev. George Whitefield arrived in Philadelphia. It is remarkable that a warm friendship should have sprung up between men so very diverse in character. But Franklin could not be insensible to the wonderful power of this preacher, in promoting public morals, and in transforming the worst of men into valuable citizens, faithfully performing all the duties of life. It is surprising that this effect of the Gospel did not teach him that Christianity is the "wisdom of God, and the power of God to salvation." *Love* was emphatically the message which Whitefield, with tearful eyes and throbbing heart, proclaimed to the wicked and the sorrowing. "God so *loved the world*, that he gave his only begotten son that whosoever believeth in him should not perish but should have everlasting life." Christ "came not into the world to condemn the world, but that the world through him might be saved."

Such were the themes which this apostolic preacher unfolded, and which moved human hearts, in these new colonies as seventeen hundred years ago they were moved by the preaching of our Lord Jesus Christ, and his disciple Paul, upon the plains of Asia.

KARTINDO PUBLISHING HOUSE (Kartindo.Com)

Whitefield taught that *belief* controlled conduct. As a man sincerely believes so will he act. Franklin, with his accustomed candor, in his Autobiography, wrote in the following terms, the effects of the preaching of this remarkable reformer:

"The multitudes of all sects and denominations that attended his sermons were enormous. It was wonderful to see the change soon made in the manners of our inhabitants. From being thoughtless or indifferent about religion, it seemed as if all the world were growing religious; so that one could not walk through the town, in an evening, without hearing psalms sung in different families of every street.

"Mr. Whitefield, on leaving us, went preaching all the way through the colonies to Georgia. The settlement of that province had been lately begun; but instead of being made with hardy, industrious husbandmen, accustomed to labor, the only people fit for such an enterprise, it was with families of broken shop-keepers, and other insolvent debtors; many of indolent and idle habits, taken out of the jails who, being set down in the woods, unqualified for clearing land, and unable to endure the hardships of a new settlement, perished in numbers, leaving many helpless children unprovided for.

"The sight of their miserable situation inspired the benevolent heart of Mr. Whitefield with the idea of building an Orphan House there in which they might be supported and educated. Returning northward, he preached up this charity, and made large collections.

"I did not disapprove of the design; but as Georgia was then destitute of materials and workmen, and it was proposed to send them from Philadelphia at a great expense, I thought it would have been better to have built the house at Philadelphia, and brought the children to it. This I advised. But he was resolute in his first project, rejected my counsel, and I therefore refused to contribute.

"I happened soon after to attend one of his sermons, in the course of which I perceived he intended to finish with a collection, and I silently resolved he should get nothing from me. I had in my pocket a handful of copper money, three or four silver dollars, and five pistoles in gold, (about twenty-five dollars). As he proceeded I began to soften, and concluded to give the copper; another stroke of his oratory made me ashamed of that, and determined me to give the silver; and he finished so admirably that I emptied my pockets wholly into the collector's dish, gold and all.

KARTINDO PUBLISHING HOUSE (Kartindo.Com)

"Some of Mr. Whitefield's enemies affected to suppose that he would apply these collections to his own private emolument. But I, who was intimately acquainted with him, being employed in printing his sermons and journals, never had the least suspicion of his integrity; but am to this day decidedly of the opinion, that he was in all his conduct a perfectly honest man; and methinks my testimony ought have the more weight, as we had no religious connection. He used, indeed, sometimes to pray for my conversion, but never had the satisfaction of believing that his prayers were heard. Ours was a friendship sincere on both sides, and lasted to his death."[19]

[Footnote 19: "Autobiography of Franklin," as given by Sparks, p. 139.]

At one time Franklin wrote to Whitefield, in Boston, inviting him, as he was about to come to Philadelphia, to make his house his home. The devout preacher replied,

"If you make this offer for Christ's sake you will not lose your reward."

Promptly the philosopher rejected any such motive, and rejoined,

"Do not be mistaken. It was not for Christ's sake I invited you, but for your own sake."

In all the numerous letters, essays, and philosophical and religious disquisitions of Franklin, we seldom, I think, find a sentiment indicative of any high appreciation of the character of Jesus Christ; or the debt of gratitude we owe to him, either for his teaching or for his example. As Franklin discarded all idea of the Atonement, he of course could not express any gratitude for that which is, to the Christian, the crowning act even of divine love. This Saviour, to millions who cannot be counted, has proved, even if the comfort be a delusion, in temptation, disappointment, and death, more precious than it is in the power of words to declare.

One article from Franklin's newspaper, published in the year 1740, gives an idea of the extraordinary interest which the preaching of Whitefield excited.

"On Thursday last the Reverend Mr. Whitefield left this city, and was accompanied to Chester by about one hundred and fifty horse; and preached there to about seven thousand people. On Friday he preached twice at Willings

Town to about five thousand. On Saturday, at Newcastle, to about two thousand five hundred; and the same evening at Christiana Bridge to about three thousand; on Sunday at White Clay Creek, he preached twice, resting about half an hour between the sermons, to eight thousand, of whom three thousand, it is computed, came on horseback. It rained most of the time, and yet they stood in the open air."

The keenness of the scrutiny with which Franklin watched all the operations of nature, led him to the discovery of the before unknown fact that the fierce north-east storms which sweep our Atlantic coast invariably begin in the south-west, and move backwards, diminishing in violence as they go. He also, about this time, invented the Franklin stove, which in the day when wood was the only fuel consumed has invested so many firesides with a rare aspect of cheerfulness. He wrote a very ingenious pamphlet, elucidating the philosophy of house-warming.

There is great moral power in prosperity, when wisely accepted and enjoyed. Franklin was now a prosperous man. His income was constantly increasing. His virtues, and they were great ones, proved in all respects promotive of his worldly welfare. His journal was the leading paper, certainly in all that region, and had not its superior in any of the colonies. His renowned almanac, Poor Richard, attained an unexampled sale. The work executed in his printing office was so excellent as to bring in to him many orders even from the other provinces. The various books and pamphlets he had published had all been successful. Philadelphia had already become the chief town of the Colonies.

Notwithstanding Franklin's devotion to books, to business, and to philosophical research, he is represented to have been at this time, a jovial man, very fond of convivial gatherings. He could not only write a good song, but he could sing it, to the acceptance of his companions. One of these songs entitled "The Old Man's Wish" he says he sang over a thousand times. We give the concluding stanza, illustrative of its general character.

"With a courage undaunted, may I face the last day, And when I am gone may the better sort say,-- In the morning when sober, in the evening when mellow, He has gone and not left behind him his fellow, For he governed his passions with absolute sway."

There was, as usual, war in Europe. Enormous armies were burning cities and villages, drenching the trampled harvest fields with blood, and filling the

KARTINDO PUBLISHING HOUSE (Kartindo.Com)

humble hamlets of the poor with misery. There was every reason to fear that these awful storms, raised by the passions of depraved men, would reach the peaceful shores of the Delaware. Philadelphia was entirely undefended. It is said that there was not an available cannon in Pennsylvania.

A well-armed privateer could at any hour, seize and sack the city. Quaker influence so far prevailed that the legislature could not be induced to raise a battery, or purchase a gun. Franklin wrote a very powerful pamphlet, called Plain Truth, urging the necessity of adopting some measures of defence. He showed how the colony could, at any time, be ravaged by a few vessels from any European nation then in conflict with England. I give a few extracts from this admirable pamphlet:

"On the first alarm, terror will spread over all. Many will seek safety by flight. Those that are reputed rich will flee, through fear of torture to make them produce more than they are able. The man that has a wife and children, will find them hanging on his neck, beseeching him to quit the city, and save his life. All will run into confusion, amid cries and lamentations, and the hurry and disorder of departures. The few that remain, will be unable to resist.

"Sacking the city will be the first; and burning it, in all probability, the last act of the enemy. This I believe will be the case, if you have timely notice. But what must be your condition, if suddenly surprised without previous alarm, perhaps in the night. Confined to your houses, you will have nothing to trust but the enemy's mercy. Your best fortune will be to fall under the power of commanders of king's ships, able to control the mariners, and not into the hands of licentious privateers.

"Who can without the utmost horror, conceive the miseries of the latter when your persons, fortunes, wives and daughters, shall be subject to the wanton and unbridled rage, rapine, and lust, of negroes, mulattoes, and others, the vilest and most abandoned of mankind?"

This warning effectually roused the community. A public meeting was summoned, in the immense building erected to accommodate the crowds who flocked to hear Whitefield. Here Franklin harangued the multitude. An Association of Defence was organized. Ten thousand persons enrolled their names. In a few days nearly every man in the province, who was not a Quaker, had joined some military organization. Each man purchased for himself a weapon, and was learning how to use it.

KARTINDO PUBLISHING HOUSE (Kartindo.Com)

Eighty companies were organized and disciplined. The companies in Philadelphia united in a regiment, and chose Franklin their colonel. Wisely he declined the office, "conceiving myself unfit," he says. A battery was thrown up below the town. Some cannon were sent for from Boston. Several eighteen-pounders were obtained in New York, and more were ordered from London. In manning the battery, Franklin took his turn of duty as a common soldier.

There was not a little opposition to these measures, but still the strong current of popular opinion was in their favor. Even the young Quakers, though anxious to avoid wounding the feelings of their parents, secretly gave their influence to these preparations of defence. The peace of Aix la Chapelle in 1748, terminated these alarms. But the wisdom and energy which Franklin had displayed, caused him to be regarded as the most prominent man in Pennsylvania. The masses of the people regarded him with singular homage and confidence.

In 1744, Franklin had a daughter born, to whom he gave the name of Sarah. His motherless son William, who was destined to give his father great trouble, was growing up, stout, idle, and intractable. Early in the war he had run away, and enlisted on board a privateer. With much difficulty his father rescued him from these engagements. Franklin was evidently embarrassed to know what to do with the boy. He allowed him, when but sixteen years of age, to enlist as a soldier in an expedition against Canada.

About this time Franklin wrote to his sister Jane, whose son had also run away to enlist as a privateer. He wished to console her by the assurance that it was not in consequence of unkind treatment, that the boys were induced thus to act. He wrote:

"When boys see prizes brought in, and quantities of money shared among the men, and their gay living, it fills their heads with notions that half distract them; and puts them quite out of conceit with trades and the dull ways of getting money by working. My only son left my house unknown to us all, and got on board a privateer, from whence I fetched him. No one imagined it was hard usage at home that made him do this. Every one that knows me thinks I am too indulgent a parent, as well as master."

The father of Benjamin Franklin died in Boston, at the great age of eighty-nine years. He had secured, in a very high degree, the respect of the people, not only by his irreproachable morals, but by his unfeigned piety. The Boston News Letter, of January 17, 1745, in the following brief obituary, chronicles his death:

"Last night died Mr. Josiah Franklin, tallow chandler, and soap maker. By the force of steady temperance he had made a constitution, none of the strongest, last with comfort to the age of eighty-nine years. And by an entire dependence on his Redeemer, and a constant course of the strictest piety and virtue, he was enabled to die as he lived, with cheerfulness and peace, leaving a numerous posterity the honor of being descended from a person who, through a long life, supported the character of an honest man."

In the year 1743 Franklin drew up a plan for an Academy in Philadelphia. In consequence of the troubled times the tract was not published until the year 1749. It was entitled, "Proposals Relating to the Education of Youth in Pennsylvania." The suggestions he presented indicated a wide acquaintance with the writings of the most eminent philosophers. He marked out minutely, and with great wisdom, the course of study to be pursued. It is pleasant to read the following statement, in this programme. Urging the study of History, he writes,

"History will also afford frequent opportunities of showing the necessity of a *public religion*, from its usefulness to the public; the advantages of a religious character among private persons; the mischiefs of superstition and the excellency of the *Christian religion* above all others, ancient and modern."

Perhaps this tribute to the excellence of Christianity ought in some degree to modify the impression left upon the mind, by Franklin's studious avoidal, in all his writings, of any allusion to the name of Jesus Christ its founder.

Twenty-five thousand dollars were speedily raised for this institution. All the religious sects harmoniously united. One individual from each sect was appointed, to form the corporate body intrusted with the funds. But almost the entire care and trouble of rearing the building, and organizing the institution fell upon Franklin. He was found to be fully adequate to all these responsibilities.

CHAPTER VII

The Tradesman becomes a Philosopher.

Franklin appointed Indian commissioner--Effects of Rum--Indian logic--Accumulating honors--Benevolent enterprises--Franklin's counsel to Tennent--Efforts for city improvement--Anecdotes--Franklin appointed postmaster--Rumors of War--England enlists the Six Nations in her cause--Franklin plans a Confederacy of States--Plans rejected--Electrical experiments--Franklin's increase of income--Fearful experiments--The kite--New honors--Views of the French philosopher--Franklin's Religious views--His counsel to a young pleader--Post-office Reforms.

In the year 1740, Franklin, then forty-four years of age, was appointed on a commission to form a treaty with the Indians at Carlisle. Franklin, knowing the frenzy to which the savages were plunged by intoxication, promised them that, if they would keep entirely sober until the treaty was concluded, they should then have an ample supply of rum. The agreement was made and faithfully kept.

"They then," writes Franklin, "claimed and received the rum. This was in the afternoon. They were near one hundred men, women and children, and were lodged in temporary cabins, built in the form of a square, just without the town. In the evening, hearing a great noise among them, the commissioners walked to see what was the matter.

"We found that they had made a great bonfire in the middle of the square; that they were all drunk, men and women quarreling and fighting. Their dark-colored bodies, half-naked, seen only by the gloomy light of the bonfire, running after and beating one another with firebrands, accompanied by their horrid yellings, formed a scene the most resembling our ideas of hell, that could well be imagined. There was no appeasing the tumult, and we returned to our lodgings. At midnight a number of them came thundering at our door demanding more rum, of which we took no notice.

"The next morning they all seemed very much ashamed of the disgraceful orgies in which they had indulged. There was a law written in their own hearts, which told them that they had done wrong. Three chiefs were appointed to call upon the commissioners with an humble apology. With downcast looks they confessed their fault, and then with logic which more intelligent men sometimes use, endeavored to throw the blame upon God. In remarkable speech one of them said,

"'The Great Spirit, who made all things, made everything for some use. Whatever use he designed anything for, that use it should be always put to. Now, when he made rum, he said, "Let this be for the Indians to get drunk with! and it must be so."'"

The Governor at this time appointed Franklin a Justice of Peace. Franklin says he was much flattered by these accumulating honors. Soon he was elected to a seat, as one of the Legislators in the Assembly. Mainly through his influence, a hospital for the sick was established in Philadelphia. Though the measure encountered much opposition, he carried it; and the institution proved of incalculable benefit.

The Rev. Gilbert Tennent solicited Franklin's aid in raising money for building a Meeting House. As Franklin had been so continually engaged in asking for money for various objects of benevolence, he was afraid he should become obnoxious to his fellow-citizens, and declined. Mr. Tennent then requested him to give him a list of the names of those influential persons upon whom it would be well for him to call. Every Christian minister who reads this, will appreciate the nature of his embarrassment. Franklin says that he thought it would be unbecoming in him, after having emptied the purses of his friends, to send other beggars to them, with renewed importunities. This request he therefore declined. Mr. Tennent then urged him to give him some advice. Franklin replied,

"That I will willingly do. In the first place, I advise you to apply to all those who you know will do something; next, to those who you are uncertain whether they will give anything or not, and show them the list of those who have given; and lastly, do not neglect those who you are sure will give nothing, for in some of them you may be mistaken."

Mr. Tennent laughed heartily, and declared that he would rigorously follow out this advice. He did so. His success was wonderful; a much larger sum was raised than he had anticipated, and soon a capacious and beautiful Meeting House rose in Arch street.

KARTINDO PUBLISHING HOUSE (Kartindo.Com)

The streets of Philadelphia, though laid out with great regularity, were unpaved, and in wet weather were almost impassable quagmires. Franklin, by talking with his friends, and by urging the subject in his paper, at length succeeded in having a sidewalk paved with stone, upon one of the most important streets. It gave great satisfaction, but the rest of the street not being paved, the mud was thrown by passing carriages upon it, and as the city employed no street cleaners, the sidewalk soon ceased to afford a clean passage to pedestrians.

Franklin found an industrious man who was willing to sweep the pavement twice a week, carrying off the dirt from before all the doors, for the sum of sixpence a month, to be paid by each house.

The philosophic Franklin then, having started this enterprise, printed on a sheet of paper the great advantages of keeping the sidewalk clean, and sent one of these papers to each house. He urged that much of the soiling of the interior of the houses would thus be avoided, that an attractive sidewalk would lure passengers to the shops; and that, in windy weather, their goods would be preserved from the dust.

After a few days he called, in person, at each house and shop to see who would subscribe sixpence a month. It was a great success. The cleanliness of the pavement in the important streets surrounding the market, greatly delighted the people, and prepared the way for carrying a bill which Franklin presented to the Assembly for paving and lighting all the important streets of the city.

A gentleman, by the name of John Clifton, had placed a lamp before his door. This suggested the idea. Lamps were sent for from London. Globes were furnished. They were expensive. The smoke circulated in the globe and obstructed the light. They had to be wiped clean each day. An accidental stroke demolished the whole globe. Franklin suggested four flat panes. One might be broken, and easily replaced. Crevices were left below to admit a current of air, and a funnel to draw off the smoke. Thus for a long time the glass remained undimmed.

Wherever Franklin went, he carried with him this spirit of improvement. When in London, he found the streets wretchedly dirty. One morning he found a poor woman at his door in Craven street, sweeping the sidewalk with a wretched broom. Her pallid and exhausted appearance touched the sympathies of Franklin. He asked who employed her. She replied:

"Nobody. I am poor and in distress. I sweeps before gentlefolks's doors, and hopes they will give me something."

Franklin immediately engaged her to sweep the whole street. It was nine o'clock in the morning. She was so languid and debilitated that he thought it would take her nearly all day. But in three hours she came for her shilling. Franklin thought she could not have done her work faithfully. He sent his servant to examine. He reported that the work was thoroughly done. A new problem rose before Franklin: If this feeble woman could in so short a time sweep such a street, a strong man, with a suitable broom, could certainly do it in half of the time. He therefore drew up a plan for cleaning the streets of London and Westminster, which was placed in the hands of one of the most influential of the public-spirited men of London.

Franklin apologizes for speaking in his autobiography of such trifles. Very truly, he says,

"Human felicity is produced not so much by great pieces of good fortune that seldom happen, as by little advantages that occur every day. Thus if you teach a poor young man to shave himself and keep his razor in order, you may contribute more to the happiness of his life than in giving him a thousand guineas. This sum may be soon spent, the regret only remaining of having foolishly consumed it. But in the other case, he escapes the frequent vexation of waiting for barbers, and of their sometimes dirty fingers, offensive breath, and dull razors. He shaves when most convenient to him, and enjoys daily the pleasure of its being done with a good instrument."

Nearly all the important offices in the colonies were filled by appointments from the British Crown. For some time, Franklin had been employed as an assistant to the Postmaster General, in simplifying and bringing regularity into his accounts. Upon the death of the American Postmaster, Franklin, in 1753, was appointed jointly with Sir William Hunter to succeed him. The appointment was made by the Postmaster General in England.

The post-office department had scarcely been self-supporting. It had never paid anything to the crown. The salary offered to the two postmasters was three thousand dollars a year each, if they could save that sum from the profits of the office. Franklin writes,

"To do this a variety of improvements was necessary. Some of these were inevitably, at first, expensive; so that in the first four years, the office became above nine hundred pounds in debt to us. But it soon after began to repay us. And before I was displaced by a freak of the ministers, of which I shall hereafter speak, we had brought it to yield three times as much clear revenue to the crown as the post-office of Ireland. Since that imprudent transaction, they have received from it not one farthing."

Again there were menaces of war, insane and demoniac, to fill the world with tears and woe. As we read the record of these horrid outrages which through all the centuries have desolated this globe, it would seem that there must be a vein of insanity as well as of depravity, in the heart of fallen man. England and France were again marshaling their armies, and accumulating their fleets, for the terrible conflict.

It was certain that France, in Canada, and England, in her colonies, could not live in peace here, while the volcanic throes of war were shaking the island of Great Britain, and the Continent of Europe.

In the heart of New York, then almost an unbroken wilderness, there were six exceedingly fierce and war-like tribes called the Six Nations. Like the wolves they delighted in war. The greatness of a man depended on the number of scalps with which he could fringe his dress. These savage warriors were ready and eager to engage as the allies of those who would pay them the highest price. Mercy was an attribute of which they knew not even the name.

It was not doubted that France would immediately send her emissaries from Canada to enlist these savages on her side. Awful would be the woes with which these demoniac men could sweep our defenceless frontiers; with the tomahawk and the scalping knife, exterminating families, burning villages, and loading their pack-horses with plunder. To forestall the French, and to turn these woes from our own frontier to the humble homes of the Canadian emigrants, the English government appointed a commissioner to visit the chiefs of these tribes in the year 1754.

The all important council was to be held in Albany. Governor Hamilton appointed four commissioners, of whom Franklin was one, to act in behalf of Pennsylvania. They were furnished with rich gifts with which to purchase the favor of the Indians. It was a long and tedious journey from Philadelphia to Albany.

KARTINDO PUBLISHING HOUSE (Kartindo.Com)

Franklin, on this journey, was deeply impressed with the importance of a union of the colonies for self-defence. He therefore drew up a plan for such union. Several gentlemen of the highest intelligence in New York, having examined it, gave it their cordial approval. He accordingly laid it before Congress.

There were several other persons in other colonies who were impressed as deeply as Franklin with a sense of the importance of such a confederacy, and they also sent in their suggestions.

Congress appointed a committee of one from each province, to consider the several plans. The committee approved of Franklin's plan, and reported accordingly. While the commissioners were conferring with the Indians in Albany, Congress was engaged in discussing the plans of a confederacy. Franklin's plan was finally rejected. It did not meet the views either of the Assembly, or of the British Court. And here we see, perhaps the germs of the great conflict which soon culminated in the cruel war of the Revolution.

The Assembly objected to the plan as too aristocratic, conferring too much power upon the crown. The court emphatically rejected it as too democratic, investing the people with too much power. Franklin ever affirmed that his plan was the true medium. Even the royalist governor of Pennsylvania warmly commended the compromise he urged.

In visiting Boston he was shown an electric tube, recently sent from England. With this tube some very surprising electrical experiments were performed, ushering in a new science, of which then but very little was known. Franklin became intensely interested in the subject. Upon his return to Philadelphia, he devoted himself, with great assiduity, to experimenting with electric tubes. At this time he wrote to a friend,

"I never was before engaged in any study that so totally engrossed my attention and my time, as this has lately done; for what with making experiments when I can be alone, and repeating them to my friends and acquaintances, who, from the novelty of the thing, come continually in crowds to see them, I have little leisure for anything else."

This was during the winter of 1746-7. Franklin suggested that the electricity was collected, not created by friction. He also propounded the theory of positive and negative electricity. He was, at this time, comparatively a wealthy man, and consequently could afford to devote his time to philosophical investigation. It is estimated that his income, from his estates, amounted to about seven hundred pounds a year; this was equal to about six or seven thousand dollars at the present time. Mr. Parton writes,

"Besides this independence, Franklin was the holder of two offices, worth together perhaps one hundred and fifty pounds a year. His business, then more flourishing than ever, produced an annual profit, as before computed, of two thousand pounds; bringing up his income to the troublesome and absurd amount of nearly three thousand pounds; three times the revenue of a colonial governor."

Under these prosperous circumstances, Franklin withdrew from active business, became a silent partner in the firm, and devoted nearly all his time to the new science. He wrote, in the autumn of 1748, to his friend Cadwallader Colden of New York,

"I have removed to a more quiet part of the town, where I am settling my old accounts, and hope soon to be quite master of my own time, and no longer, as the song has it, 'at every one's call but my own.'

"Thus you see I am in a fair way of having no other tasks than such as I shall like to give myself, and of enjoying what I look upon as a great happiness, leisure to read, study, make experiments, and converse at large with such ingenious and worthy men, as are pleased to honor me with their friendship or acquaintance, on such points as may produce something for the common benefit of mankind, uninterrupted by the cares and fatigues of business."

He wrote a treatise upon thundergusts, which displayed wonderful sagacity, and which arrested the attention of nearly all the philosophers in Europe and America. The all-important topics of this exceedingly important document, were the power of points to draw off electricity, and also the similarity of electricity and lightning. He therefore urged that metallic rods might be attached to buildings and ships, which, pushing their needle points above roofs and masts, might draw the electric fire harmlessly from the clouds. He confesses that he cannot imagine why the points should possess this curious power, but urges that facts seem to demonstrate it.

One day, for the entertainment of his friends, he had made arrangements to kill a turkey with an electric shock. Two large jars were heavily charged. Incautiously manipulating, he took the shock himself. In the following

KARTINDO PUBLISHING HOUSE (Kartindo.Com)

language, he describes the effect:

"The flash was very great, and the crack was as loud as a pistol; yet my senses being instantly gone, I neither saw the one nor heard the other; nor did I feel the stroke on my hand, though I afterwards found it raised a round swelling where the fire entered, as big as half a pistol bullet.

"I then felt what I know not well how to describe, a universal blow throughout my whole body from head to foot, which seemed within as well as without; after which the first thing I took notice of was a violent, quick shaking of my body, which gradually remitting, my sense as gradually returned, and then, I thought the bottle must be discharged, but could not conceive how, till at last I perceived the chain in my hand, and recollected what I had been about to do.

"That part of my hand and fingers which held the chain, was left white as though the blood had been driven out; and remained so eight or ten minutes after, feeling like dead flesh; and I had numbness in my arms and the back of my neck which continued to the next morning, but wore off."

Franklin was much mortified at his awkwardness in this experiment. He declared it to be a notorious blunder, and compared it with the folly of the Irishman, who wishing to steal some gun-powder, bored a hole through the cask with red hot iron. But notwithstanding this warning, not long afterwards, in endeavoring to give a shock to a paralytic patient, he received the whole charge himself, and was knocked flat and senseless on the floor.

In the spring of 1752, Franklin tried his world renowned experiment with the kite. A June thunder cloud was rising in all its majesty. Franklin, accompanied by his son, repaired to a field secretly, being afraid of the ridicule of the people. Here he raised the kite, made of a large silk handkerchief. The top of the perpendicular stick was pointed with a sharp metallic rod. The string was hemp with the exception of the part held in the hand, which was silk; at the end of the hempen string a common key was suspended. With intense anxiety and no slight apprehension of danger, he held the line. Soon he observed the fibres of the hempen string to rise and separate themselves, as was the case of the hair on the head, when any one was placed on an insulating stool. He applied his knuckle to the key, and received an unmistakable spark. As the story is generally told, with occasionally slight contradictions, he applied his knuckle again and again to the key with a similar result. He charged a Leyden jar with the fluid and both he and his son took a shock. He then drew in his kite, packed up his apparatus and returned to his laboratory probably the most exultant and happy man in this wide world.

Most of the English and many of the French philosophers were very unwilling to believe that an obscure American, in what they deemed the savage and uncultivated wilds of the New World, was outstripping them in philosophical research. They were unwilling to acknowledge the reality of his experiments; but in France, where an American would receive more impartial treatment, three of the most eminent philosophers, Count de Buffon, M. Dalibard and M. de Lor, at different places, raised the apparatus Franklin had recommended to draw electricity from the clouds. Their success was unmistakable; the results of these experiments were proclaimed throughout Europe.

Franklin had now obtained renown. No one could deny that he merited a high position among the most eminent philosophers. The experiments he had suggested were tried by scientists in the philosophical circles of every country in Europe.

Both Yale and Harvard, in this country, conferred upon him the honorary degree of Master of Arts, and the Royal Society, in Europe, by a unanimous vote, elected him a member, remitting the usual initiation fee of five guineas, and the annual charge of two and a half guineas. The next year this Society conferred upon him the Copley medal.

For seven years Franklin continued to devote himself almost exclusively to this science, and he became, without doubt, the most accomplished electrician in the world. At the same time his mind was ever active in devising new schemes for the welfare of humanity. The most trivial events would often suggest to him measures conducive to the most beneficial results. It is said that Franklin saw one day in a ditch the fragments of a basket of yellow willow, in which some foreign commodity had been imported to this country. One of the twigs had sprouted. He planted it; and it became the parent of all the yellow willows in our country.

Franklin was best loved where he was best known. And this was right; for he was ever conferring deeds of kindness upon his neighbors. His religious views excited sorrow among his Christian friends. Others, composing perhaps a majority, cared nothing about what he believed. In conversation he ever frankly avowed himself a deist, though generally he made no attempt to convert others to his views. It is not improbable that he was in some degree influenced by the

KARTINDO PUBLISHING HOUSE (Kartindo.Com)

beneficial effect produced upon the popular mind by the preaching of his friend Mr. Whitefield.

The writer was once, in Paris, conversing with one of the most illustrious of the French philosophers. He said to the philosopher, "I am much interested to ascertain the views of gentlemen of your intellectual position respecting the Christian religion." He with perfect frankness replied, "I think that there are no men of high culture in France, with a few exceptions, who believe in the divine origin of Christianity. But there is no philanthropist who will say so. We have been taught, by the horrors of the French Revolution, that the masses of the people can only be restrained from violence by the superstitious restraints which Christianity presents. We therefore think that every man, who is a gentleman, will do what he can to sustain the church and the clergy. Men of culture and refinement, are governed by principles of honor, and they do not need the superstitious motives of Christianity to influence them."

I may remark, in passing, that this gentlemanly philosopher had abandoned his own wife, and was then living with the wife of another man. It is not improbable that Franklin, as he looked upon the tumultuous and passion-tossed young men of Philadelphia, did not deem it expedient to say to them,

"The Bible is a fable. The Sabbath is no more sacred than any other day. The church is merely a human club without any divine authority. Marriage is an institution which is not founded upon any decree which God has issued, but one of the expediency of which each individual must judge for himself. The Sacraments of Baptism, and the Lord's Supper, are mere human contrivances. The preaching of the Gospel had better be laid aside for literary and scientific disquisitions."

With the eye of a benevolent philosopher, Franklin, as we have seen, had watched the effect of the preaching of Mr. Whitefield, and had candidly acknowledged its power in reforming society. It is improbable that, in his heart, he felt that the preaching of pure deism could ever secure such results. In 1753 he wrote to Mr. Whitefield, in reply to a communication from him upon the Christian faith:

"The faith you mention certainly has its use in the world. I do not desire to see it diminished, nor would I endeavor to lessen it in any man."

Franklin had resolved to decline all office, that he might devote himself to his studies. But his reputation for wisdom was such, that he found it very difficult to persevere in this plan. Menaces of war were continually arising. The majority of the members, in the Assembly, were Quakers. It was a small body consisting of but forty delegates. The Quakers opposed every measure for public defence. Franklin, as we have mentioned, became a Justice of the Peace. Soon after he was an Alderman, and then he took his seat in the General Assembly.

"I was a bad speaker," he writes, "never eloquent; subject to much hesitation in the choice of words; and yet I generally carried my point."

He adds, in language which every young man should treasure up in his memory, "I retained the habit of expressing myself in terms of modest diffidence; never using, when I advanced anything that might possibly be disputed, the words, *certainly*, *undoubtedly*, or any others that give the air of positiveness to an opinion; but rather, I *conceive*, or *apprehend* a thing to be so and so. *It appears to me*, or, *I should not think it so for such and such reasons*, or, *I imagine it to be so*, or, *It is so if I am not mistaken*. This habit, I believe, has been of great advantage to me when I have had occasion to inculcate my opinions; and to persuade men into measures that I have been from time to time proposing."

When Franklin assumed the charge of the post-office, the department was in a feeble and peculiar condition. As late as the year 1757, the mail-bag in Virginia was passed from planter to planter. Each one was required to forward it promptly, under the penalty of forfeiting a hogshead of tobacco. Every man took, from the bag, what belonged to his family, and sent on the rest. The line of post-offices then extended from Boston, Mass., to Charleston, S. C. It was twenty years after this, before any governmental mail penetrated the interior.

In the year 1753, Franklin visited every post-office excepting that of Charleston. His wisdom introduced reforms, some of which have continued to the present day. A newspaper was charged nine pence a year, for a distance of fifty miles, and eighteen pence for one hundred miles or more. In the large towns a penny post was established, and all letters left remaining in the office were advertised.

A mail was conveyed from Philadelphia to New York once a week in summer, and once in two weeks in winter. Franklin started a mail to leave each of these cities three times a week in summer, and twice in winter. It generally required six weeks to obtain an answer from a letter sent to Boston. Most of the roads, into the interior, consisted of narrow passages, cut through the forest, called Bridle Paths, because the pack horses were led through them, in single file by the bridle.

KARTINDO PUBLISHING HOUSE (Kartindo.Com)

CHAPTER VIII

The Rising Storms of War

Aristocracy--Anecdote--Conflicting laws of Nations--Franklin's scheme of colonization--Proposal of the British Court--The foresight of Franklin--Braddock's campaign--Remonstrances of Franklin and Washington--Franklin's interviews with Braddock--Franklin's efficiency--Confidence of Braddock--The conflict with the Proprietaries--The non-resistant Quakers--Fate of the Moravian villages--The winter campaign--The camp of Gaudenhutton--Anecdote--Renewal of the strife with the Proprietaries--Franklin recalled to assist the Assembly--Destruction of the Fort--Claim of the Proprietaries--The great controversy.

With increasing wealth the spirit of aristocratic exclusiveness gained strength in the higher circles of Philadelphia. Some of the more opulent families planned for a series of dancing entertainments during the winter. It was proposed among other rules that no mechanic, or mechanic's wife or daughter, should be invited. The rules were shown to Franklin. He glanced his eye over them and pithily remarked,

"Why these rules would exclude God Almighty!"

"How so?" inquired the manager.

"Because," Franklin replied, "the Almighty, as all know, is the greatest mechanic in the universe. In six days he made all things." The obnoxious article was stricken out.

The following incident, narrated by Franklin, illustrates a very important principle in political economy, which those are apt to ignore, who denounce all the elegancies and luxuries of life.

Mrs. Franklin received some small favor from the captain of a little coaster, which ran between Cape May and Philadelphia. He declined to receive any remuneration for his trifling services. Mrs. Franklin, learning that he had a pretty daughter, sent her a new-fashioned Philadelphia cap or bonnet. Three

KARTINDO PUBLISHING HOUSE (Kartindo.Com)

years after, the captain called again at the house of Mr. Franklin. A very plain but intelligent farmer accompanied him. The captain expressed his thanks to Mrs. Franklin for the gift she had sent his daughter, and rather discourteously added,

"But it proved a dear cap to our congregation. When my daughter appeared with it at meeting, it was so much admired that all the girls resolved to get such caps from Philadelphia. And my wife and I computed that the whole could not have cost less than a hundred pounds."

The farmer, with far higher intelligence, said, "This is true; but you do not tell the whole story. I think the cap was nevertheless an advantage to us. It was the first thing that put our girls upon knitting worsted mittens, for sale at Philadelphia, that they might have wherewithal to buy caps and ribbons there. And you know that that industry has continued and is likely to continue and increase, to a much greater value, and answer better purposes."

"Thus by a profitable exchange, the industrious girls at Cape May had pretty bonnets, and the girls at Philadelphia had warm mittens."

For seventy-five years it had been the constant design of the British government to drive the French from North America. England claimed the whole country, from the Atlantic to the Pacific, because her ships had first sailed along the Atlantic coast. It was one of the recognized laws of nations that a newly discovered region belonged to the nation who had first raised upon it its flag.

France, admitting the claim of England to the Atlantic coast, asserted her right to the great valleys of the interior, those of the Ohio and the Mississippi, because her boatmen had first discovered those magnificent rivers, had explored them throughout, and had established upon them her trading and military posts. It was a recognized law of nations, that the power which discovered, explored, and took possession of a new river, was the rightful possessor of the valley which that river watered. Thus the conflict of claims originated.

To add to the intensity of the insane strife, which caused an amount of blood and misery which no tongue can tell, religious bitterness was aroused, and the French Roman Catholic was arrayed against the British Protestant.

Three wars, bloody and woful, had already ravaged this continent. We have before alluded to the menace of a new war in the year 1754, and to Franklin's mission to Albany to enlist the chiefs of the Six Nations to become allies of the English. We have also alluded to the plan, which Franklin drew up on this journey, for the union of the colonies, and which was rejected. The wisdom of this plan was, however, subsequently developed by the fact that it was remarkably like that by which eventually the colonies were bound together as a nation.

Assuming that the English were right in their claim for the whole continent, Franklin urged the eminently wise measure of establishing strong colonies, in villages of a hundred families each, on the luxuriant banks of the western rivers. But the haughty British government would receive no instructions from American provincials.

Governor Shirley, of Boston, showed Mr. Franklin a plan, drawn up in England, for conducting the war. It developed consummate ignorance of the difficulties of carrying on war in the pathless wilderness; and also a great disregard of the political rights of the American citizens. According to this document, the British court was to originate and execute all the measures for the conduct of the war; and the British Parliament was to assess whatever tax it deemed expedient upon the American people to defray the expenses. The Americans were to have no representation in Parliament, and no voice whatever in deciding upon the sum which they were to pay.

Franklin examined the document carefully, and returned it with his written objections. In this remarkable paper, he anticipated the arguments which our most distinguished statesmen and logicians urged against the Stamp Act-- against Taxation without Representation. A brief extract from this important paper, will give the reader some idea of its character:

"The colonists are Englishmen. The accident of living in a colony deprives them of no right secured by Magna Charta. The people in the colonies, who are to feel the immediate mischiefs of invasion and conquest by an enemy, in the loss of their estates, lives and liberties, are likely to be better judges of the quantity of forces necessary to be raised and maintained, and supported, and of their own ability to bear the expense, than the Parliament of England, at so great a distance. Compelling the colonists to pay money without their consent, would be rather like raising contributions in an enemy's country, than taxing of Englishmen for their own public benefit. It would be treating them as a conquered people, and not as true British subjects."

KARTINDO PUBLISHING HOUSE (Kartindo.Com)

At length the brave, but self-conceited and haughty General Braddock came with his army of British Regulars. Frenchmen, Indians, and Americans, he alike regarded with contempt. His troops were rendezvoused at Fredericktown, in Maryland. A bridle path led through the wilderness to this place, from Philadelphia, a distance of a hundred and twenty miles.

Intelligent American gentlemen were much alarmed, by the reckless and perilous measures which the ignorant British general declared his intention to pursue. He became very angry with Pennsylvanians, because they were so unwilling to fall in with his plans. It was said that, in his anger, he manifested more desire to ravage Pennsylvania than to defeat the French.

The Assembly at Philadelphia appointed a commission, consisting of Benjamin Franklin and his son, a resolute, insubordinate man of thirty years, and of the Governors of New York and Massachusetts, to visit the arrogant British officer, and to endeavor, in some way, to influence him to wiser measures. It was the middle of April, a beautiful season in that climate, of swelling buds, and opening leaves.

Each of the four gentlemen was attended by servants, as was customary in those days. They were all finely mounted. Joyfully they rode along, seeking entertainment each night at the residence of some planter. A courier was always sent forward to announce their coming, and the planter, accompanied by one or two of his servants, would generally ride forward a few miles to meet them, and escort them to his hospitable home.

Franklin was received by Gen. Braddock with the condescension with which, in that day, English gentlemen were ever accustomed to regard Americans of whatever name or note. The little army, which was to march upon Fort Duquesne, was to traverse the dreary and pathless ridges and ravines of the Alleghany mountains, and force their way through a tangled wilderness, for a distance of several hundred miles. During all this march they were hourly exposed to be attacked by an overpowering force of French and Indians. The French could easily descend to the Ohio, in their boats from Canada, and nearly all the Indians of this vast interior, were in alliance with them.

Braddock insisted upon encumbering his march with heavily laden wagons, which were to penetrate savage regions through which he must, every mile, construct his road. There was a young American in the camp by the name of George Washington. He was a man of the highest rank, and of commanding influence, having obtained much experience in Indian warfare. Modestly, but warmly, he remonstrated against this folly. He not only feared, but was fully assured that such a measure would lead to the inevitable destruction of the army. He urged that pack horses only should be employed, and as few of them as possible; and that thus they should hurry along as rapidly and in as compact a mass as they could.

But Braddock was inexorable. He demanded his two hundred and fifty wagons, and a large train of pack horses, to be laden with sumptuous provisions for his officers. The farmers of Maryland and Virginia were reluctant to expose the few wagons and teams they had, to such inevitable destruction. Neither had they any confidence that the British Government would ever remunerate them in case of their loss.

Four-wheeled vehicles were very scarce in the colonies. There were many people who had never seen one. The general, after exhausting all his efforts, could obtain but twenty-four. One day as he was giving vent to his indignation, Franklin suggested that it would probably be much more easy to obtain wagons in the more densely settled parts of Pennsylvania. Braddock immediately urged him to undertake the enterprise. Unwisely, we think, he consented. With his son he hastened to Pennsylvania, and selected Lancaster, York, and Carlisle as his centres of operation.

Whatever Franklin undertook, he was pretty sure to accomplish. In twenty days he obtained one hundred and fifty four-horse wagons, and two hundred and fifty-nine pack-horses. He did not accomplish this feat however, until he had exhausted all the money which Braddock had furnished him, had spent over a thousand dollars of his own money, and had given bonds for the safe return of horses and wagons, whose money value was estimated at one hundred thousand dollars.

Braddock was lavish in his compliments. Franklin dined with him daily. The idea seemed never to have entered Braddock's mind that British Regulars, under his command, could ever be seriously annoyed by bands of French and Indians. He said one day,

"After taking Fort Duquesne, I shall go to Niagara. Having taken that, if the season will permit, I shall proceed to Fort Frontenac. Fort Duquesne can hardly detain me more than three or four days."

KARTINDO PUBLISHING HOUSE (Kartindo.Com)

Franklin, who was well aware that Braddock was entering upon a far more formidable campaign than he anticipated, ventured very modestly to suggest,

"To be sure, sir, if you arrive well before Duquesne with the fine troops so well provided with artillery, the fort, though completely fortified, and assisted with a very strong garrison, can probably make but a short resistance. The only danger I apprehend of obstruction to your march, is of ambuscades of the Indians, who, by constant practice, are dexterous in laying and executing them. And the slender line, near four miles long, which your army must make, may expose it to be attacked by surprise in its flanks, and to be cut like a thread into several pieces, which, from their distance, cannot come up in time to support each other."

Braddock smiled derisively, at this ignorance of a benighted American. "These savages may indeed," he said, "be a formidable enemy to your raw American militia. But upon the king's regular and disciplined troops, it is impossible that they should make any impression."

Colonel Washington regarded the wagons, and the long array of pack-horses, as so many nuisances, arresting the rapidity of their march, and inviting attacks which it would be impossible to repel. At length the army was in motion. The progress was very slow. Franklin was continually forwarding supplies; and even advanced between six and seven thousand dollars, from his own purse, to expedite purchases. A part of this he never received back.

The attack upon Braddock's army, and its terrible defeat soon came. A minute account of the conflict is given in the Life of George Washington, one of the volumes of this series. The teamsters cut the traces of their horses, mounted the swiftest, and, in the frenzy of their panic, rushed for home. The other horses and the wagons, with their abounding supplies, were left to magnify the triumph of the exultant Indians. Disastrous as was the campaign, Franklin obtained much credit for the efficient services he had rendered.

War, with all its horrors, had now penetrated the beautiful region of Pennsylvania, which had enjoyed eighty years of peace, through the Christian philanthropy of William Penn. Nearly all of the Indians, beyond the mountains, were allies of the French. The news of Braddock's defeat reached Philadelphia about the middle of July, 1755. Immediately a violent conflict arose between the royalist governor Morris, and the Colonial Assembly. The Legislative body voted liberal taxes for the public defence. But very justly it was enacted that

KARTINDO PUBLISHING HOUSE (Kartindo.Com)

these taxes should be assessed impartially upon all estates alike, upon those of the wealthy Proprietaries, as well as upon the few hundred acres which were owned by the humble farmers. The Proprietaries, consisting of two of the sons of William Penn, revolted against this. The Governor, appointed by them, as their agent of course, united with them in opposition. For many weeks the conflict between the Assembly and the Governor as agent of the Proprietaries, raged fiercely. Under these circumstances no military supplies could be voted, and the peril of the community was very great.

Franklin warmly espoused and eloquently advocated the claim of the Assembly. During the months of July and August, the Indians, satiated with the vast plunder of Braddock's camp, made no attempt to cross the Alleghanies, in predatory excursions against the more settled portions of Pennsylvania. But September and October ushered in scenes of horror and carnage, too awful to be depicted. Villages were laid in ashes, cottages were burned, families tomahawked and scalped, women and children carried into captivity, and many poor creatures perished at the stake, in the endurance of all the tortures which savage ingenuity could devise.

And still the Quakers, adhering to their principle of non-resistance, refused to contribute any money, or in any way to unite in any military organization for self-defence. But in candor it must be admitted, that had the principles of the Quakers been adopted by the British court, this whole disastrous war might have been avoided. It was a war of invasion commenced by the English. They were determined, by force of arms, to drive the French out of the magnificent valleys beyond the mountains. In the conflict which ensued, both parties enlisted all the savages they could, as allies. Will not England at the judgment be held responsible for this war and its woes?

To rouse the Quakers to a sense of shame, the bodies of a whole murdered family, mutilated and gory, were brought to Philadelphia and paraded through all its streets, in an open wagon. In November, as the Indians, often led by French officers, were sweeping the frontier in all directions, killing, burning, destroying, the antagonistic parties in the Assembly, for a time laid aside their quarrels, and with the exception of the Quakers, adopted vigorous military measures. The Quakers were generally the most opulent people in the State. It is not strange that the common people should be reluctant to volunteer to defend the property of the Quakers, since they refused either to shoulder a musket, or to contribute a dollar.

The pen of Franklin rendered wonderful service in this crisis. With his accustomed toleration, he could make allowance for the frailties of conscience-bound men. He wrote a very witty pamphlet which was very widely read, and produced a powerful impression. Its character may be inferred from the following brief quotation:

"'For my part,' says A., 'I am no coward; but hang me if I fight to save the Quakers.'

"'That is to say,' B. replied, 'you will not pump the sinking ship, because it will save the rats as well as yourselves.'"

The dialogue ends with the following admirable words:

"O! my friends, the glory of serving and saving others is superior to the advantage of being served and secured. Let us resolutely and generously unite in our country's cause, in which to die is the sweetest of all deaths; and may the God of armies bless our honest endeavors."

The colonists of Pennsylvania now generally rushed to arms. There were, on the frontiers, several flourishing Moravian villages. They were occupied by a peculiarly industrious and religious people. The traveller through their quiet streets heard, morning and evening, the voice of prayer ascending from many firesides, and the melody of Christian hymns. Guadenhutton, perhaps the most flourishing of them, was attacked by the Indians, burned, and the inhabitants all massacred or carried into captivity. Terrible was the panic in the other villages. They were liable at any day, to experience the same fate.

Under these circumstances the Governor raised five hundred and forty volunteers, and placed them under the command of Franklin, with the title of General. He was to lead them, as rapidly as possible, to Northampton county, for the protection of these people. His son, William, was his aid-de-camp. He proved an efficient and valiant soldier.

It was the middle of December when this heroic little band commenced its march. Snow whitened the hills. Wintry gales swept the bleak plains, and moaned through the forests. The roads were almost impassable. Fierce storms often entirely arrested their march. The wilderness was very thinly inhabited. It required the toil of a month, for Franklin to force his way through these many obstructions to the base of his operations, though it was distant not more than ninety miles.

KARTINDO PUBLISHING HOUSE (Kartindo.Com)

The troops moved very cautiously to guard against ambush. The philosopher, Franklin, though he had never received a military education, and was quite inexperienced in military affairs, was the last man to be drawn into such a net as that in which the army of Braddock was destroyed.

Franklin, as a philosopher, could appreciate the powerful influence of religious motives upon the mind. Rev. Mr. Beatty was his chaplain, whose worth of character Franklin appreciated. Before commencing their march, all the troops were assembled for a religious service. After an earnest exhortation to fidelity and duty, a fervent prayer was offered.

The march was conducted with great regularity. First, scouts advanced in a semi-circular line, ranging the woods. Then came the advanced guard, at a few hundred paces behind. The centre followed, with all the wagons and baggage. Then came the rear guard, with scouts on each flank, and spies on every hill.

Upon reaching Guadenhutton, an awful scene of desolation and carnage met the eye. The once happy village presented now but a revolting expanse of blackened ruins. The mangled bodies of the dead strewed the ground, mutilated alike by the savages and the howling wolves. Franklin ordered huts immediately to be reared to protect his troops from the inclemency of the weather. No man knew better than he, how to make them comfortable and cheerful with the least expense.

A fort was promptly constructed, which he called Fort Allen, and which could easily repel any attack the Indians might make, unless they approached with formidable French artillery. There were many indications that the Indians, in large numbers, were hovering around, watching all their movements. But the sagacity of Franklin baffled them. They kept concealed without any attack. The savages were very cautious men; they would seldom engage in a battle, unless they were sure of victory.

A trifling incident occurred at this time, worthy of record as illustrative of the shrewdness of General Franklin.

The chaplain complained that the men were remiss in attending prayers. Franklin suggested that though it might not be exactly consistent with the dignity of the chaplain to become himself the steward of the rum, still, if he would order it to be distributed immediately after prayers, he would probably have all the men gathering around him.

KARTINDO PUBLISHING HOUSE (Kartindo.Com)

"He liked the thought," Franklin wrote, "under took the task, and with the help of a few hands to measure out the liquor, executed it to satisfaction. Never were prayers more generally and more punctually attended. So that I think this method preferable to the punishment inflicted by some military laws for non-attendance on divine worship."

Bitter quarrels were renewed in the Assembly. The presence of Franklin was indispensable to allay the strife. Governor Morris wrote entreating him immediately to return to Philadelphia. It so happened at this time, that Col. Clapham, a New England soldier of experience and high repute, visited the camp at Guadenhutton. Franklin placed him in command, and warmly commending him to the confidence of the troops, hurried home. He reached Philadelphia on the 10th of February, 1756, after two months' service in the field. Universal applause greeted him. Several military companies, in Philadelphia, united in a regiment of about twelve hundred men. Franklin was promptly elected their colonel, which office he accepted.

In tracing the disasters of war, it is interesting to observe how many of those disasters are owing to unpardonable folly. Some months after Franklin's departure, on a cold, bleak day in November, a large part of the garrison, unmindful of danger, were skating, like school-boys on the Lehigh river. The vigilant Indians saw their opportunity. Like howling wolves they made a rush upon the fort, entered its open gates, and killed or captured all its inmates. The skaters fled into the woods. They were pursued. Some were killed or captured. Some perished miserably of cold and starvation. Probably a few escaped. The triumphant savages, having plundered the fort and the dwellings of all their contents, applied the torch, and again Guadenhutton was reduced to a pile of ashes.

The controversy which arose between the Governor and the Assembly became acrimonious in the extreme. The principles there contended for, involved the very existence of anything like American liberty. For fifteen years the pen and voice of Franklin were influential in this controversy. He probably did more than any other man to prepare the colonists to resist the despotism of the British court, and to proclaim their independence.

On the 5th of January, 1681, King Charles the Second had conferred upon William Penn twenty-six million acres of the "best land in the universe." This land was in the New World, and received the name of Pennsylvania. In return for this grant, Penn agreed to pay annually, at Windsor Castle, two beaver skins, and one-fifth of the gold and silver which the province might yield. He

KARTINDO PUBLISHING HOUSE (Kartindo.Com)

also promised to govern the province in conformity with the laws of England.

He could treat with the savages, appoint ordinary magistrates, and pardon petty crimes. But he could lay no tax, and impose no law without consent of the freemen of the province, represented in the Assembly.

Of this whole wide realm, Penn was the absolute proprietor. He refused to sell a single acre, absolutely, but in all the sales reserved for himself what may be called a ground-rent. Immense tracts were sold at forty shillings, about ten dollars, for one hundred acres, reserving a rent of one shilling for each hundred acres. He also reserved, entirely to himself, various portions of the territory which promised to become the site of important cities and villages. All these rights descended to the heirs of William Penn.

Seventy-four years passed away, when the estate thus founded, was estimated to be worth ten millions sterling, and popular belief affirmed that it produced a revenue of one hundred thousand pounds.

Penn, when he died, bequeathed the province to his three sons, John, Thomas, and Richard. To John he gave a double part, or one-half of Pennsylvania. John died and left his half to Thomas, who thus became proprietor of three-fourths of the province, while Richard held one-fourth. Thus there were but two proprietors, Thomas and Richard Penn. They were both weak men; resided in England, were thoroughly imbued with Tory principles, and, in the consciousness of their vast estates, assumed to be lords and princes.

They ruled their province by a deputy-governor. His position was indeed no sinecure. The two proprietaries, who appointed him, could at any time deprive him of office. The Assembly could refuse to vote his salary, and if he displeased the king of England, he might lose, not only his office, but his head.

The controversy which had arisen, in consequence of these involvements between the proprietaries and the people, engrossed universal attention. During the four years between 1754 and 1758, the ravaged colony of Pennsylvania had raised the sum of two hundred and eighteen thousand pounds sterling, (over a million of dollars,) for defending its borders. And still the two lordly proprietaries demanded that their vast possessions should be entirely exempt from taxation.

To an earnest remonstrance of the Assembly, they returned an insulting answer, in which they said,

"We are no more bound to pay taxes than any other chief governor of the King's colonies. Your agitation of this matter is a new trick to secure your re-election. We advise you to show us the respect due to the rank which the crown has been pleased to bestow upon us. The people of Pennsylvania, in ordinary times, are so lightly taxed, that they hardly know that they are taxed. What fools you are to be agitating this dangerous topic of American taxation. It is beneath the dignity of the Assembly to make trouble about such small sums of money. We do not deny that you have been at some expense in pacifying the Indians, but that is no affair of ours. We already give the province a larger sum per annum, than our share of the taxes would amount to. One of us, for example, sent over four hundred pounds' worth of cannon, for the defence of our city of Philadelphia."

Such was their answer. It was conveyed in sixteen sentences which were numbered and which were very similar to the ones we have given. The communication excited great displeasure. It was considered alike false and insolent. Even the tranquil mind of Franklin was fired with indignation. He replied to the document with a power of eloquence and logic which carried the convictions of nearly all the colonists.

KARTINDO PUBLISHING HOUSE (Kartindo.Com)

CHAPTER IX

Franklin's Mission to England

New marks of respect--Lord Loudoun--Gov. Denny and Franklin--Visit the Indians--Franklin commissioner to England--His constant good nature--Loudoun's delays--Wise action of an English captain--The voyagers land at Falmouth--Journey to London--Franklin's style of living in London--His electrical experiments--He teaches the Cambridge professor--Complimentary action of St. Andrews--Gov. Denny displaced, and dark clouds arising--Franklin's successful diplomacy--His son appointed Governor of New Jersey--Great opposition--The homeward voyage--Savage horrors--Retaliating cruelties--Franklin's efforts in behalf of the Moravian Indians.

The general impression, produced throughout the colonies, by the controversy with the proprietaries, was that they were very weak men. Indeed it does not appear that they were much regarded even in London. A gentleman, writing from that city, said, "They are hardly to be found in the herd of gentry; not in court, not in office, not in parliament."

In March, Franklin left his home for a post-office tour. Some forty of the officers of his regiment, well mounted, and in rich uniform, without Franklin's knowledge, came to his door, to escort him out of the village. Franklin says,

"I had not previously been made acquainted with their project, or I should have prevented it, being naturally averse to the assuming of state on any occasion."

The proprietaries in London heard an account of this affair. They were very much displeased, saying they had never been thus honored, and that princes of the blood alone were entitled to such distinction. The war was still raging. Large bodies of troops were crossing the ocean to be united with the colonial forces.

Lord Loudoun was appointed by the court commander-in-chief for America. He was an exceedingly weak and inefficient man; scarcely a soldier in the ranks could be found more incompetent for the situation. Governor Morris, of Pennsylvania, worn out with his unavailing conflicts with the Assembly, was withdrawn, and the proprietaries sent out Captain William Denny as their

KARTINDO PUBLISHING HOUSE (Kartindo.Com)

obsequious servant in his stead. The Philadelphians, hoping to conciliate him, received him cordially, and with a public entertainment. William Franklin wrote:

"Change of devils, according to the Scotch proverb, is blithesome."

At the close of the feast, when most of the party were making themselves merry over their wine, Governor Denny took Franklin aside into an adjoining room, and endeavored, by the most abounding flattery, and by the bribe of rich promises, to induce him to espouse the cause of the proprietaries. But he soon learned that Franklin could not be influenced by any of his bribes.

There was but a brief lull in the storm. Governor Denny had no power of his own. He could only obey the peremptory instructions he had received. These instructions were irreconcilably hostile to the resolves of the Assembly. Franklin was the all-powerful leader of the popular party. There was something in his imperturbable good nature which it is difficult to explain. No scenes of woe seemed to depress his cheerful spirits. No atrocities of oppression could excite his indignation. He could thrust his keen dagger points into the vitals of his antagonist, with a smile upon his face and jokes upon his lips which would convulse both friend and foe with laughter. He was the most unrelenting antagonist of Governor Denny in the Assembly, and yet he was the only man who remained on good terms with the governor, visiting him, and dining with him.

Governor Denny was a gentleman, and well educated, and few men could appear to better advantage in the saloons of fashion. But he was trammeled beyond all independent action, by the instructions he had received from the proprietaries. He was right in heart, was in sympathy with Franklin, and with reluctance endeavored to enforce the arbitrary measures with which he was entrusted.

Franklin was one of the most companionable of men. His wonderful powers of conversation, his sweetness of temper, and his entire ignoring of all aristocratic assumption, made him one of the most fascinating of guests in every circle. He charmed alike the rich and the poor, the learned and the ignorant.

In November, 1756, he accompanied Governor Denny to the frontier to confer with the chiefs of several Indian tribes. The savages, to say the least, were as punctilious in the observance of the laws of honor, in securing the safety of the ambassadors on such an occasion, as were the English.

The governor and the philosopher rode side by side on horseback, accompanied by only a few body servants. The governor, familiar with the clubs and the wits of England, entertained Franklin, in the highest degree, with the literary gossip of London, and probably excited in his mind an intense desire to visit those scenes, which he himself was so calculated to enjoy and to embellish. On the journey he wrote the following comic letter to his wife. He had been disappointed in not receiving a line from her by a certain messenger.

"I had a good mind not to write to you by this opportunity, but I never can be ill-natured enough even when there is most occasion. I think I won't tell you that we are well, and that we expect to return about the middle of the week, nor will I send you a word of news; that's poz. My duty to mother, love to the children, and to Miss Betsy and Gracie. I am your *loving* husband.

"P. S. I have *scratched out the loving words*, being writ in haste by mistake, when I forgot I was angry."

Gov. Denny, unable to accomplish his purposes with the Assembly, resolved to make a final appeal to the king. The House promptly decided to imitate his example. Its Speaker, Mr. Norris, and Benjamin Franklin, were appointed commissioners. The Speaker declined the office, and Franklin was left as sole commissioner. He probably was not at all reluctant to be introduced to the statesmen, the philosophers, and the fashionable circles of the Old World. To defray his expenses the Assembly voted a sum of nearly eight thousand dollars. He had also wealth of his own. By correspondence, he was quite intimately acquainted with very many of the scientific men of England and France. It was very certain that he would have the *entrée* to any circle which he might wish to honor with his presence.

It was at that time a very serious affair to cross the Atlantic. The ocean swarmed with pirates, privateers, and men-of-war. On the fourth of April, 1757, Franklin, with his son William, set out from Philadelphia. His cheerfulness of spirits did not forsake him as he left a home where he had been remarkably happy for twenty-six years. The family he left behind him consisted of his wife, his wife's aged mother, his daughter Sarah, a beautiful child of twelve years, one or two nieces, and an old nurse of the family.

Franklin had written to the governor to ascertain the precise time when the packet would sail. The reply he received from him was,

"I have given out that the ship is to sail on Saturday next. But I may let you know *entre nous* that if you are there by Monday morning you will be in time; but do not delay any longer."

Franklin was accompanied by a number of his friends as far as Trenton, where they spent a very joyful evening together. At one of the ferries on this road, they were delayed by obstructions so that they could not reach the Hudson River until noon of Monday. Franklin feared that the ship might sail without him; but upon reaching the river he was relieved by seeing the vessel still in the stream.

Eleven weeks passed before Lord Loudoun would issue his permission for the ship to sail. Every day this most dilatory and incompetent of men announced that the packet would sail to-morrow. And thus the weeks rolled on while Franklin was waiting, but we do not hear a single word of impatience or remonstrance from his lips. His philosophy taught him to be happy under all circumstances. With a smiling face he called upon Lord Loudoun and dined with him. He endeavored, but in vain, to obtain a settlement of his claims for supplies furnished to Braddock's army.

He found much in the society of New York to entertain him. And more than all, and above all, he was doing everything that could be done for the accomplishment of his mission. Why, then, should he worry?

"New York," he records, "was growing immensely rich by money brought into it from all quarters for the pay and subsistence of the troops."

Franklin was remarkably gallant in his intercourse with ladies. He kept up quite a brisk correspondence with several of the most brilliant ladies of the day. No man could more prettily pay a compliment. To his lively and beautiful friend Miss Ray he wrote upon his departure,

"Present my best compliments to all that love me; I should have said all that love you, but that would be giving you too much trouble."

At length Lord Loudoun granted permission for the packet to drop down to the Lower Bay, where a large fleet of ninety vessels was assembled, fitted out for

KARTINDO PUBLISHING HOUSE (Kartindo.Com)

an attack upon the French at Louisburg. Franklin and his friends went on board, as it was announced that the vessel would certainly sail "to-morrow." For six weeks longer the packet rode there at anchor. Franklin and his companions had for the third time consumed all the provisions they had laid in store for the voyage. Still we hear not a murmur from our imperturbable philosopher.

At length the signal for sailing was given. The whole squadron put to sea, and the London packet, with all the rest, was swept forward toward Louisburg. After a voyage of five days, a letter was placed in the hands of the captain, authorizing him to quit the fleet and steer for England.

The days and nights of a long voyage came and went, when the packet at midnight in a gale of wind, and enveloped in fogs, was approaching Falmouth. A light-house, upon some rocks, had not been visible. Suddenly the lifting of the fog revealed the light-house and the craggy shore, over which the surf was fearfully breaking, at the distance of but a few rods. A captain of the Royal Navy, who chanced to be near the helmsman, sprang to the helm, called upon the sailors instantly to wear ship, and thus, at the risk of snapping every mast, saved the vessel and the crew from otherwise immediate and certain destruction.

There was not, at that time, a single light-house on the North American coast. The event impressed the mind of Franklin deeply, and he resolved that upon his return, light-houses should be constructed.

About nine o'clock the next morning the fog was slowly dispersed, and Falmouth, with its extended tower, its battlemented castles, and the forests of masts, was opened before the weary voyagers. It was Sunday morning and the bells were ringing for church. The vessel glided into the harbor, and joyfully the passengers landed. Franklin writes,

"The bell ringing for church, we went thither immediately, and with hearts full of gratitude returned sincere thanks to God far the mercies we had received."

We know not whether this devout act was suggested by Franklin, or whether he courteously fell in with the arrangement proposed, perhaps, by some religious companion. It is, however, certain that the sentence which next followed, in his letter, came gushing from his own mind.

"Were I a Roman Catholic, perhaps I should, on this occasion, vow to build a

KARTINDO PUBLISHING HOUSE (Kartindo.Com)

chapel to some saint. But as I am not, if I were to vow at all it should be to build a *light-house*."

It required a journey of two hundred and fifty miles to reach London. Franklin and his son *posted* to London, which was the most rapid mode of traveling in those days. They seem to have enjoyed the journey in the highest degree, through blooming, beautiful, highly cultivated England. Almost every thing in the charming landscape, appeared different from the rude settlements which were springing up amid the primeval forests of the New World.

They visited the Cathedral at Salisbury, Stonehenge, Wilton Hall, the palatial mansion of the Earl of Pembroke. England was in her loveliest attire. Perhaps there could not then be found, upon this globe, a more lovely drive, than that through luxuriant Devonshire, and over the Hampshire Downs.

Peter Collinson, a gentleman of great wealth, first received the travelers to his own hospitable mansion. Here Franklin was the object of marked attentions from the most distinguished scientists of England. Other gentlemen of high distinction honored themselves by honoring him. Franklin visited the old printing house, where he had worked forty years before, and treated the workmen with that beer, which he had formerly so efficiently denounced in that same place.

Soon he took lodgings with a very agreeable landlady, Mrs. Stevenson, No. 7, Craven street, Strand. He adopted, not an ostentatious, but a very genteel style of living. Both he and his son had brought with them each a body servant from America. He set up a modest carriage, that he might worthily present himself at the doors of cabinet ministers and members of parliament.

The Proprietaries received him very coldly, almost insolently. They were haughty, reserved and totally uninfluenced by his arguments. He presented to them a brief memorandum, which very lucidly explained the views of the Assembly. It was as follows,

1. "The Royal Charter gives the Assembly the power to make laws; the proprietary instructions deprive it of that power. 2. The Royal Charter confers on the Assembly the right to grant or withhold supplies; the instructions neutralize that right. 3. The exemption of the proprietary estate from taxation is unjust. 4. The proprietaries are besought to consider these grievances seriously and redress them, that harmony may be restored."

KARTINDO PUBLISHING HOUSE (Kartindo.Com)

The Penn brothers denounced this brief document, as vague, and disrespectful. It was evident that Franklin had nothing to hope from them. He therefore directed all his energies to win to his side the Lords of Trade, and the members of the King's Council, to whom the final decision must be referred. Twelve months elapsed, during which nothing was accomplished. But we hear not a murmur from his lips. He was not only contented but jovial. For two whole years he remained in England, apparently accomplishing nothing. These hours of leisure he devoted to the enjoyment of fashionable, intellectual and scientific society. No man could be a more welcome guest, in such elevated circles, for no man could enjoy more richly the charms of such society, or could contribute more liberally to its fascination. Electricity was still a very popular branch of natural science. The brilliant experiments Franklin performed, lured many to his apartments. His machine was the largest which had been made, and would emit a spark nine inches in length. He had invented, or greatly improved, a new musical machine of glass goblets, called the Armonica.

It was listened to with much admiration, as it gave forth the sweetest tones. He played upon this instrument with great effect.

The theatre was to Franklin an inexhaustible source of enjoyment. Garrick was then in the meridian of his fame. He loved a good dinner, and could, without inconvenience, empty the second bottle of claret. He wrote to a friend,

"I find that I love company, chat, a laugh, a glass, and even a song as well as ever."

At one time he took quite an extensive tour through England, visiting the University at Cambridge. He was received with the most flattering attentions from the chancellor and others of the prominent members of the faculty. Indeed every summer, during his stay in England, Franklin and his son spent a few weeks visiting the most attractive scenes of the beautiful island. Wherever he went, he left an impression behind him, which greatly increased his reputation.

At Cambridge he visited the chemical laboratory, with the distinguished Professor of Chemistry, Dr. Hadley. Franklin suggested that temperature could be astonishingly reduced by evaporation. It was entirely a new idea to the Professor. They both with others repaired to Franklin's room. He had ether there, and a thermometer. To the astonishment of the Professor of Chemistry in Cambridge University, the printer from Philadelphia showed him that by dipping the ball into the ether, and then blowing upon it with bellows to

KARTINDO PUBLISHING HOUSE (Kartindo.Com)

increase the evaporation, the mercury rapidly sunk twenty-five degrees below the freezing point. Ice was formed a quarter of an inch thick, all around the ball. Thus, surrounded by the professors of one of the most distinguished universities of Europe, Benjamin Franklin was the teacher of the teachers.

The father and the son visited the villages where their ancestors had lived. They sought out poor relations, and examined the tombstones. In the spring of 1769, they spent six weeks in Scotland. The University of St. Andrews conferred upon Franklin the honorary title of doctor, by which he has since been generally known. Other universities received him with great distinction. The corporation of Edinburgh voted him the freedom of the city. All the saloons of fashion were not only open to receive him, but his presence, at every brilliant entertainment, was eagerly sought. The most distinguished men of letters crowded around him. Hume, Robertson and Lord Kames became his intimate friends.

These were honors sufficient to turn the head of almost any man. But Franklin, who allowed no adversity to annoy him, could not be unduly elated by any prosperity or flattery.

"On the whole," writes Franklin, "I must say, that the time we spent there (Scotland) was six weeks of the *densest* happiness I have met with in any part of my life."

Still it is evident that occasionally he felt some slight yearnings for the joys of that home, over which his highly esteemed wife presided with such economy and skill. He wrote to her,

"The regard and friendship I meet with from persons of worth, and the conversation of ingenuous men give me no small pleasure. But at this time of life, domestic comforts afford the most solid satisfaction;[20] and my uneasiness at being absent from my family and longing desire to be with them, make me often sigh, in the midst of cheerful company."

[Footnote 20: Franklin was then 53 years of age.]

An English gentleman, Mr. Strahan, wrote to Mrs. Franklin, urging her to come over to England and join her husband. In this letter he said,

KARTINDO PUBLISHING HOUSE (Kartindo.Com)

"I never saw a man who was, in every respect, so perfectly agreeable to me. Some are amiable in one view, some in another; he in all."

Three years thus passed away. It must not be supposed that the patriotic and faithful Franklin lost any opportunity whatever, to urge the all important cause with which he was entrusted. His philosophy taught him that when he absolutely could not do any thing but *wait*, it was best to wait in the most agreeable and profitable manner.

It was one of his strong desires, which he was compelled to abandon, to convert the proprietary province of Pennsylvania into a royal province. After Franklin left Philadelphia, the strife between the Assembly, and Governor Denny, as the representative of the proprietaries, became more violent than ever. The governor, worn out by the ceaseless struggle, yielded in some points. This offended the proprietaries. Indignantly they dismissed him and appointed, in his place, Mr. James Hamilton, a more obsequious servant.

By the royal charter it was provided that all laws, passed by the Assembly and signed by the governor, should be sent to the king, for his approval. One of the bills which the governor, compelled as it were by the peril of public affairs, had signed, allowed the Assembly to raise a sum of about five hundred thousand dollars, to be raised by a *tax on all estates*. This was a dangerous precedent. The aristocratic court of England repealed it, as an encroachment upon the rights of the privileged classes. It was a severe blow to the Assembly. The speaker wrote to Franklin:

"We are among rocks and sands, in a stormy season. It depends upon you to do every thing in your power in the present crisis. It is too late for us to give you any assistance."

When Franklin received the crushing report against the Assembly he was just setting off for a pleasant June excursion in Ireland. Immediately he unpacked his saddle-bags, and consecrated all his energies to avert the impending evils. He enlisted the sympathies of Lord Mansfield, and accomplished the astonishing feat in diplomacy, of inducing the British Lords of Commission to reverse their decision, and to vote that the act of the Assembly should stand unrepealed.

His business detained Franklin in London all summer. In the autumn he took a tour into the west of England and Wales. The gales of winter were now sweeping the Atlantic. No man in his senses would expose himself to a winter passage across the ocean, unless it was absolutely necessary. Indeed it would appear that Franklin was so happy in England, that he was not very impatient to see his home again. Though he had been absent three years from his wife and child, still two years more elapsed before he embarked for his native land.

On the 25th of October George II. died. His grandson, a stupid, stubborn fanatically conscientious young man ascended the throne, with the title of George III. It would be difficult to compute the multitudes in Europe, Asia and America, whom his arrogance and ambition caused to perish on the battle field. During these two years there was nothing of very special moment which occurred in the life of Franklin. Able as he was as a statesman, science was the favorite object of his pursuit. He wrote several very strong pamphlets upon the political agitations of those tumultuous days, when all nations seem to have been roused to cutting each other's throats. He continued to occupy a prominent position wherever he was, and devoted much time in collecting his thoughts upon a treatise to be designated "The Art of Virtue." The treatise, however, was never written.

His influential and wealthy friend, Mr. Strahan, was anxious to unite their two families by the marriage of his worthy and prosperous son to Mr. Franklin's beautiful daughter, Sarah. But the plan failed. Franklin also made an effort to marry his only son William, who, it will be remembered, was not born in wedlock, to a very lovely English lady, Miss Stephenson. But this young man, who, renouncing revealed religion, was a law unto himself, had already become a father without being a husband. Miss Stephenson had probably learned this fact and, greatly to the disappointment of Franklin, declined the alliance. The unhappy boy, the dishonored son of a dishonored father, was born about the year 1760. Nothing is known of what became of the discarded mother. He received the name of William Temple Franklin.

Benjamin Franklin, as in duty bound, recognized him as his grandson, and received him warmly to his house and his heart. The reader will hereafter become better acquainted with the character and career of this young man. In the spring of 1762, Franklin commenced preparations for his return home. He did not reach Philadelphia until late in the autumn. Upon his departure from England, the University of Oxford conferred upon him the distinction of an honorary degree.

William Franklin, though devoid of moral principle, was a man of highly respectable abilities, of pleasing manners, and was an entertaining companion.

KARTINDO PUBLISHING HOUSE (Kartindo.Com)

Lord Bute, who was in power, was the warm friend of Dr. Franklin. He therefore caused his son William to be appointed governor of New Jersey. It is positively asserted that Franklin did not solicit the favor. Indeed it was not a very desirable office. Its emoluments amounted to but about three thousand dollars a year. The governorship of the colonies was generally conferred upon the needy sons of the British aristocracy. So many of them had developed characters weak and unworthy, that they were not regarded with much esteem.

William Franklin was married on the 2d of September, 1762, to Miss Elizabeth Downes. The announcement of the marriage in London, and of his appointment to the governorship of New Jersey, created some sensation. Mr. John Penn, son of one of the proprietaries, and who was soon to become governor of Pennsylvania, affected great indignation in view of the fact that William Franklin was to be a brother governor. He wrote to Lord Stirling,

"It is no less amazing than true, that Mr. William Franklin, son of Benjamin Franklin of Philadelphia, is appointed to be governor of the province of New Jersey. I make no doubt that the people of New Jersey will make some remonstrances at this indignity put upon them. You are full as well acquainted with the character and principles of this person as myself, and are as able to judge of the impropriety of such an appointment. What a dishonor and a disgrace it must be to a country to have such a man at the head of it, and to sit down contented. I should hope that some effort will be made before our Jersey friends would put up with such an insult. If any *gentleman* had been appointed, it would have been a different case. But I cannot look upon the person in question in that light by any means. I may perhaps be too strong in my expressions, but I am so extremely astonished and enraged at it, that I am hardly able to contain myself at the thought of it."

Franklin sailed from Portsmouth the latter part of August. Quite a fleet of American merchantmen sailed together. The weather during a voyage of nine weeks, was most of the time delightful. Often the vessels glided along so gently over a waveless sea, that the passengers could visit, and exchange invitations for dinner parties.

On the first of November, Franklin reached his home. He had been absent nearly six years. All were well. His daughter, whom he had left a child of twelve, was now a remarkably beautiful and accomplished maiden of eighteen. Franklin was received not only with affection, but with enthusiasm. The Assembly voted him fifteen thousand dollars for his services in England.

KARTINDO PUBLISHING HOUSE (Kartindo.Com)

His son William, with his bride, did not arrive until the next February. Franklin accompanied him to New Jersey. The people there gave the governor a very kind greeting. He took up his residence in Burlington, within fifteen miles of the home of his father.

Franklin had attained the age of fifty-seven. He was in perfect health, had an ample fortune, and excelled most men in his dignified bearing and his attractive features. Probably there never was a more happy man. He had leisure to devote himself to his beloved sciences. It was his dream, his castle in the air, to withdraw from political life, and devote the remainder of his days to philosophical research.

In the year 1763 terminated the seven years' war. There was peace in Europe, peace on the ocean, but not peace along the blood crimsoned frontiers of the wilderness of America. England and France had been hurling savage warriors by tens of thousands against each other, and against the helpless emigrants in their defenceless villages and their lonely cabins. The belligerent powers of Europe, in their ambitious struggles, cared very little for the savages of North America. Like the hungry wolf they had lapped blood. Plunder had become as attractive to them as to the privateersman and the pirate. During the summer of 1763, the western regions of Pennsylvania were fearfully ravaged by these fierce bands. Thousands of settlers were driven from their homes, their buildings laid in ashes, and their farms utterly desolated.

In all the churches contributions were raised, in behalf of the victims of this insane and utterly needless war. Christ Church alone raised between three and four thousand dollars; and sent a missionary to expend the sum among these starving, woe-stricken families. The missionary reported seven hundred and fifty farms in Pennsylvania alone, utterly abandoned. Two hundred and fifty women and children, destitute and despairing, had fled to Fort Pitt for protection.

In the midst of these awful scenes, Governor Hamilton resigned, and the weak, haughty John Penn arriving, took his place. The Assembly, as usual, gave him a courteous reception, wishing, if possible, to avert a quarrel. There were many fanatics in those days. Some of these assumed that God was displeased, because the heathen Indians had not been entirely exterminated. The savages had perpetrated such horrors, that by them no distinction was made between those friendly to the English, and those hostile. The very name of Indian was loathed.

KARTINDO PUBLISHING HOUSE (Kartindo.Com)

In the vicinity of Lancaster, there was the feeble remnant of a once powerful tribe. The philanthropy of William Penn had won them to love the English. No one of them had ever been known to lift his hand against a white man. There were but twenty remaining, seven men, five women and eight children. They were an industrious, peaceful, harmless people, having adopted English names, English customs and the Christian religion.

A vagabond party of Scotch-Irish, from Paxton, set out, in the morning of the 14th of December, for their destruction. They were well mounted and well armed. It so happened that there were but six Indians at home. They made no defence. Parents and children knelt, as in prayer, and silently received the death blow. Every head was cleft by the hatchet. These poor creatures were very affectionate, and had greatly endeared themselves to their neighbors. This deed of infamous assassination roused the indignation of many of the most worthy people in the province. But there were thousands of the baser sort, who deemed it no crime to kill an Indian, any more than a wolf or a bear.

Franklin wrote, to the people of Pennsylvania, a noble letter of indignant remonstrance, denouncing the deed as atrocious murder. Vividly he pictured the scene of the assassination, and gave the names, ages and characters of the victims. A hundred and forty Moravian Indians, the firm and unsuspected friends of the English, terrified by this massacre, fled to Philadelphia for protection. The letter of Franklin had excited much sympathy in their behalf. The people rallied for their protection. The Paxton murderers, several hundred in number, pursued the fugitives, avowing their determination to put every one to death. The imbecile governor was at his wits' end. Franklin was summoned.

He, at once, proclaimed his house headquarters; rallied a regiment of a thousand men, and made efficient arrangements to give the murderers a warm reception. The Paxton band reached Germantown. Franklin, anxious to avoid bloodshed, rode out with three aids, to confer with the leaders. He writes,

"The fighting face we had put on, and the reasonings we used with the insurgents, having turned them back, and restored quiet to the city, I became a less man than ever; for I had, by this transaction, made myself many enemies among the populace."

KARTINDO PUBLISHING HOUSE (Kartindo.Com)

CHAPTER X

Franklin's Second Mission to England

Fiendish conduct of John Penn--Petition to the crown--Debt of England--Two causes of conflict--Franklin sent to England--His embarkation--Wise counsel to his daughter--The stamp act--American resolves--Edmund Burke--Examination of Franklin--Words of Lord Chatham--Dangers to English operatives--Repeal of the stamp act--Joy in America--Ross Mackay--New taxes levied--Character of George III--Accumulation of honors to Franklin--Warlike preparations--Human conscientiousness--Unpopularity of William Franklin--Marriage of Sarah Franklin--Franklin's varied investigations--Efforts to civilize the Sandwich Islands.

It is scarcely too severe to say that Governor John Penn was both knave and fool. To ingratiate himself with the vile Paxton men and their partisans, he issued a proclamation, offering for every captive male Indian, of any hostile tribe, one hundred and fifty dollars, for every female, one hundred and thirty-eight dollars. For the scalp of a male, the bounty was one hundred and thirty-eight dollars; for the scalp of a female fifty dollars. Of course it would be impossible, when the scalps were brought in to decide whether they were stripped from friendly or hostile heads.

Curiously two political parties were thus organized. The governor, intensely inimical to Franklin, led all the loose fellows who approved of the massacre of the friendly Indians. Franklin was supported by the humane portion of the community, who regarded that massacre with horror.

There was much bitterness engendered. Franklin was assailed and calumniated as one of the worst of men. He, as usual, wrote a pamphlet, which was read far and wide. Earnestly he urged that the crown, as it had a right to do, should, by purchase, take possession of the province and convert its government into that of a royal colony. It should be remembered that this was several years before the troubles of the revolution arose. The people were in heart true Englishmen. Fond of their nationality, sincere patriotism glowed in all bosoms. They ever spoke of England as "home." When the Assembly met again three thousand citizens, influenced mainly by Franklin's pamphlet, sent in a petition that the province might revert to the crown. The Penns succeeded in presenting a counter petition signed by three hundred.

KARTINDO PUBLISHING HOUSE (Kartindo.Com)

The British cabinet, in its insatiable thirst for universal conquest, or impelled by necessity to repel the encroachments of other nations, equally wicked and equally grasping, had been by fleet and army, fighting all over the world. After spending every dollar which the most cruel taxation could extort from the laboring and impoverished masses, the government had incurred the enormous debt of seventy-three millions sterling. This amounted to over three hundred and sixty-five millions of our money.

The government decided to tax the Americans to help pay the interest on this vast sum. But the colonies were already taxed almost beyond endurance, to carry on the terrible war against the French and Indians. This war was not one of their own choosing. It had been forced upon them by the British Cabinet, in its resolve to drive the French off the continent of North America. The Americans were allowed no representation in Parliament. They were to be taxed according to the caprice of the government. Franklin, with patriotic foresight, vehemently, and with resistless force of logic, resisted the outrage.

It will be perceived that there were now two quite distinct sources of controversy. First came the conflict with the proprietaries, and then rose the still more important strife with the cabinet of Great Britain, to repel the principle of taxation without representation. This principle once admitted, the crown could tax the Americans to any amount whatever it pleased. Many unreflecting people could not appreciate these disastrous results.

Thus all the partisans of the Penns, and all the office holders of the crown and their friends, and there were many such, became not only opposed to Franklin, but implacable in their hostility. The majority of the Assembly was with him. He was chosen Speaker, and then was elected to go again to England, to carry with him to the British Court the remonstrances of the people against "taxation without representation," and their earnest petition to be delivered from the tyranny of the Penns. More unwelcome messages to the British Court and aristocracy, he could not well convey. It was certain that the Penns and their powerful coadjutors, would set many influences in array against him. Mr. Dickinson, in the Assembly, remonstrating against this appointment, declared that there was no man in Pennsylvania who was more the object of popular dislike than Benjamin Franklin.

But two years had elapsed since Franklin's return to America, after an absence from his home of six years. He still remembered fondly the "dense happiness" which he had enjoyed in the brilliant circles abroad. This, added to an intensity of patriotism, which rendered him second to none but Washington, among the heroes of the Revolution, induced him promptly to accept the all important mission. He allowed but twelve days to prepare for his embarkation. The treasury was empty, and money for his expenses had to be raised by a loan. A packet ship, bound for London was riding at Chester, fifteen miles below the city. Three hundred of the citizens of Philadelphia, on horseback, escorted Franklin to the ship.

He seldom attended church, though he always encouraged his wife and daughter to do so. It was genteel; it was politic. A family could scarcely command the respect of the community, which, in the midst of a religious people, should be living without any apparent object of worship. The preacher of Christ Church, which the family attended, was a partisan of the Penns. Sometimes he "meddled with politics." Franklin in his parting letter, from on shipboard, wrote to his daughter:

"Go constantly to church, whoever preaches. The active devotion in the common prayer-book, is your principal business there, and if properly attended to, will do more towards amending the heart, than sermons generally can do. For they were composed by men of much greater piety and wisdom, than our common composers of sermons can pretend to be. Therefore I wish that you would never miss the prayer days. Yet I do not mean you should despise sermons, even of the preachers you dislike; for the discourse is often much better than the man, as sweet and clear waters come through very dirty earth."

The voyage was stormy; it lasted thirty days. On the evening of the tenth of December, 1764, he again took up his residence in the house of Mrs. Stephenson and her daughter, where he was received with delight. He found several other agents of the colonies in London, who had also been sent to remonstrate against the despotic measures which the British Cabinet threatened, of taxing the Americans at its pleasure, without allowing them to have any voice in deciding upon the sums which they should pay.

Grenville was prime minister. He was about to introduce the Stamp Act, as an initiatory measure. It imposed but a trivial tax, in itself of but little importance, but was intended as an experiment, to ascertain whether the Americans would submit to the principle. This fact being once established, the government could then proceed to demand money at its pleasure. Franklin opposed the tax with all his energies. He declared it, in his own forceful language, to be the "mother of mischiefs." With four other colonial agents, he held an interview with Lord Grenville. The usual arguments were employed on both sides. Lord Grenville was courteous, but very decided. The Americans he declared must help

England pay the interest on her debt, and the parliament of Great Britain alone could decide how large an amount of money the Americans should pay. The bill was introduced to parliament, and passed by a large majority. The king signed it in a scrawling hand, which some think indicated the insanity he was beginning to develop.

The trivial sum expected to be raised by the Stamp Act amounted to scarcely one hundred thousand pounds a year. It was thought that the Americans would not venture upon any decisive opposition to England for such a trifle. Franklin wrote to a friend:

"I took every step in my power, to prevent the passing of the Stamp Act. But the tide was too strong against us. The nation was provoked by American claims of legislative independence; and all parties joined in resolving, by this act, to settle the point."

Thus Franklin entirely failed in arresting the passing of the Stamp Act. He was also equally unsuccessful in his endeavor to promote a change of government, from the proprietary to the royal. And still his mission proved a success. By conversations, pamphlets and articles in the newspapers, he raised throughout the country such an opposition to the measure that parliament was compelled to repeal it. The tidings of the passage of the Stamp Act was received in intelligent America, with universal expressions of displeasure, and with resolves to oppose its operation in every possible way.

It is remarked of a celebrated theological professor, that he once said to his pupils,

"When you go to the city to preach, take your best coat; when to the country, take your best sermon."

The lords and gentry of England were astonished at the intelligence displayed in the opposition, by the rural population of America. They fancied the colonists to be an ignorant, ragged people, living in log cabins, scattered through the wilderness, and, in social position, two or three degrees below European and Irish peasantry. Great was their surprise to hear from all the colonies, and from the remotest districts in each colony, the voice of intelligent and dignified rebuke.

The Act was to go into execution on the first of November, 1765. Before that

KARTINDO PUBLISHING HOUSE (Kartindo.Com)

time, Franklin had spread, through all the mechanical, mercantile and commercial classes, the conviction that they would suffer ten-fold more, by the interruptions of trade which the Stamp Act would introduce, than government could hope to gain by the measure. He spread abroad the intelligence which came by every fresh arrival, that the Americans were resolving, with wonderful unanimity, that they would consume no more English manufactures, that they would purchase no more British goods, and that, as far as possible, in food, clothing, and household furniture, they would depend upon their own productions. They had even passed resolves to eat no more lamb, that their flocks might so increase that they should have wool enough to manufacture their own clothing.

England had thus far furnished nearly all the supplies for the rapidly increasing colonies, already numbering a population of between two and three millions. The sudden cessation of this trade was felt in nearly every warehouse of industry. No more orders came. Goods accumulated without purchasers. Violent opposition arose, and vast meetings were held in the manufacturing districts, to remonstrate against the measures of the government. Edmund Burke, a host in himself, headed the opposition in parliament.

Burke and Franklin were intimate friends, and the renowned orator obtained from the renowned philosopher, many of those arguments and captivating illustrations, which, uttered on the floor of parliament, astonished England, and reaching our shores, electrified America. The state of affairs became alarming. In some places the stamps were destroyed, in others, no one could be found who would venture upon the obnoxious task of offering to sell them. The parliament resolved itself into a committee of the whole house, and spent six weeks in hearing testimony respecting the operation of the act in America. The hall was crowded with eager listeners. The industrial prosperity of the nation seemed at stake. Franklin was the principal witness. His testimony overshadowed all the rest. The record of it was read with admiration. Seldom has a man been placed in a more embarrassing situation, and never has one, under such circumstances, acquitted himself more triumphantly.

He was examined and cross-examined, before this vast and imposing assemblage, by the shrewdest lawyers of the crown. Every attempt was made to throw him into embarrassment, to trip him in his speech. But never for a moment did Franklin lose his self-possession. Never for an instant, did he hesitate in his reply. In the judgment of all his friends, not a mistake did he make. His mind seemed to be omnisciently furnished, with all the needful statistics for as rigorous an examination as any mortal was ever exposed to.

Burke wrote to a friend, "that Franklin, as he stood before the bar of parliament, presented such an aspect of dignity and intellectual superiority, as to remind him of a schoolmaster questioned by school boys." Rev. George Whitefield wrote,

"Our worthy friend, Dr. Franklin, has gained immortal honor, by his behavior at the bar of the house. The answer was always found equal, if not superior to the questioner. He stood unappalled, gave pleasure to his friends, and did honor to his country."

After great agitation and many and stormy debates, the haughty government was compelled to yield to the demands of the industrial classes. Indeed, with those in England, who cried most loudly for the repeal of the stamp act, there were comparatively few who were influenced by any sympathy for the Americans, or by any appreciation of the justice of their cause. The loss of the American trade was impoverishing them. Selfish considerations alone,--their own personal interests--moved them to action.

There were individuals, in and out of Parliament, who recognized the rights of Englishmen, and regarding the Americans as Englishmen, and America as a portion of the British empire, were in heart and with all their energies, in sympathy with the Americans in their struggle for their rights. When the despotism of the British court led that court to the infamous measure of sending fleets and armies, to compel the Americans to submission, and the feeble colonists, less than three millions in number, performing the boldest and most heroic deeds ever yet recorded in history, grasped their arms in self-defence, thus to wage war against the most powerful naval and military empire upon this globe, Lord Chatham, with moral courage rarely surpassed, boldly exclaimed in the House of Lords, "Were I an American, as I am an Englishman, I would never lay down my arms, never, *never*, NEVER."

In all England, there was no man more determined in his resolve to bring the Americans to servile obedience, than the stubborn king, George III. The repeal gave him intense offence. The equally unprincipled, but more intelligent, ministers were compelled to the measure, as they saw clearly that England was menaced with civil war, which would array the industrial classes generally against the aristocracy. In such a conflict it was far from improbable that the aristocracy would be brought to grief. Horace Walpole wrote,

"It was the clamor of trade, of merchants, and of manufacturing towns, that had borne down all opposition. A general insurrection was apprehended, as the immediate consequence of upholding the bill. The revolt of America, and the destruction of trade, was the prospect in future."

Still the question of the repeal was carried in the House but by a majority of one hundred and eight votes. Of course Franklin now solicited permission to return home. The Assembly, instead of granting his request, elected him agent for another year. It does not appear that Franklin was disappointed.

The report of his splendid and triumphant examination, before the Commons, and the republication of many of his pamphlets, had raised him to the highest position of popularity. The Americans, throughout all the provinces, received tidings of the Repeal with unbounded delight. Bells were rung, bon-fires blazed, cannon were fired.

"I never heard so much noise in my life," wrote Sally to her "honored papa." "The very children seemed distracted."

The Tory party in England developed no little malignity in their anger, in view of the discomfiture of their plans. The bigoted Tory, Dr. Johnson, wrote to Bishop White of Pennsylvania, that if he had been Prime Minister, instead of repealing the act, he would have sent a man-of-war, and laid one or more of our largest cities in ashes.[21]

[Footnote 21: Wilson's Life of Bishop White, p. 89.]

The king felt personally aggrieved. His denunciations of those who favored the Repeal were so indecent, that some of his most influential friends ventured to intimate to him that it was highly impolitic. Indeed, as the previous narrative has shown, many who were in entire sympathy with the king, and who were bitterly opposed to any concession to the Americans, felt compelled to vote for the Repeal.

To propitiate the unrelenting and half-crazed monarch, with his obdurate court, a Declaratory Act, as it was called, was passed, which affirmed the *absolute supremacy* of Parliament over the colonies.

We hear very much of the corruption of our own Congress. It is said that votes are sometimes bought and sold. Sir Nathaniel Wraxall, who was a member of

Parliament during all this period, declares, in his intensely interesting and undoubtedly honest Memoir, that under the ministry of Lord Bute, Ross Mackay was employed by him as "corrupter-general" whose mission it was to carry important measures of government by bribery. Wraxall writes that Ross Mackay said to him, at a dinner party given by Lord Besborough, as the illustrious guests were sipping their wine,

"The peace of 1763 was carried through and approved by a pecuniary dispensation. Nothing else could have surmounted the difficulty. I was myself the channel through which the money passed. With my own hand I secured above one hundred and twenty votes on that most important question to ministers. Eighty thousand pounds were set apart for the purpose. Forty members of the House of Commons received from me a thousand pounds each. To eighty others I paid five hundred pounds a-piece."

The unrelenting king was still determined that the Americans, unrepresented in Parliament, should still pay into his treasury whatever sums of money he might exact. Calling to his aid courtiers more shrewd than himself, they devised a very cunning act, to attain that object in a way which would hardly be likely to excite opposition. They laid a tax, insignificant really in its amount, upon paper, paint, glass, and tea. This tax was to be collected at the custom-houses in the few ports of entry in the colonies. The whole amount thus raised would not exceed forty thousand pounds. It was thought that the Americans would never make opposition to so trivial a payment.

But it established a principle that England could tax the colonies without allowing those colonies any representation in Parliament. If the Court had a right thus to demand forty thousand pounds, they had a right to demand so many millions, should it seem expedient to king and cabinet so to do.

The great blunder which the court committed, was in not appreciating the wide-spread intelligence of the American people. In New England particularly, and throughout the colonies generally, there was scarcely a farmer who did not perceive the trick, and despise it. They deemed it an insult to their intelligence.

Instantly there arose, throughout all the provinces, the most determined opposition to the measure. It was in fact merely a renewal of the Stamp Act, under slightly modified forms. If they admitted the justice of this act, it was only declaring that they had acted with unpardonable folly, in opposing the tax under the previous form.

KARTINDO PUBLISHING HOUSE (Kartindo.Com)

Dr. Franklin, with honest shrewdness, not with trickery or with cunning, but with a sincere and penetrating mind, eagerly scrutinized all the measures of the Court. George III. was a gentleman. He was irreproachable in all his domestic relations. He was, in a sense, conscientious; for certainly he was not disposed to do anything which he thought to be wrong. Conscientious men have burned their fellow-Christians at the stake. It is said that George the Third was a Christian. He certainly was a full believer in the religion of Jesus Christ; and earnestly advocated the support and extension of that religion. God makes great allowance for the frailties of his fallen children. It requires the wisdom of omniscience to decide how much wickedness there may be in the heart, consistently with piety. No man is perfect.

During the reign of George III., terrible wars were waged throughout all the world, mainly incited by the British Court. Millions perished. The moans of widows and orphans ascended from every hand. This wicked Christian king sent his navy and his army to burn down our cities and villages, and to shoot husbands, fathers, and sons, until he could compel America to submit to his despotism. The population of England being exhausted by those wide spread wars, he hired, of the petty princes of Europe, innocent peasantry, to abandon their homes in Germany, to burn and destroy the homes of Americans. Finding that not sufficient, he sent his agents through the wilderness to rouse, by bribes, savage men, who knew no better, to ravage our frontiers, to burn the cabins of lonely farmers, to tomahawk and scalp their wives and children.

Such a man may be a good Christian. God, who can read the secrets of the heart, and who is infinite in his love and charity, alone can decide. But if we imagine that man, George Guelph, at the bar of judgment, and thronging up as witnesses against him, the millions whose earthly homes he converted into abodes of misery and despair, it is difficult to imagine in our frail natures, how our Heavenly Father, who loves all his children alike, and who, as revealed in the person of Jesus, could weep over the woes of humanity, could look with a loving smile upon him and say, "Well done, good and faithful servant, enter thou into the joy of thy Lord."

Franklin of course continued in as determined an opposition to the new tax as to the old one. He wrote,

"I have some little property in America. I will freely spend nineteen shillings in the pound to defend my right of giving or refusing the other shilling. And after all, if I cannot defend that right, I can retire cheerfully with my little family into the boundless woods of America, which are sure to afford freedom and

KARTINDO PUBLISHING HOUSE (Kartindo.Com)

subsistence to any man who can bait a hook or pull a trigger."

The ability which Franklin had displayed as the agent of Pennsylvania before the court of St. James, gave him, as we have said, a high reputation in all the colonies. In the spring of 1768 he was highly gratified by the intelligence that he was appointed, by the young colony of Georgia, its London agent. The next year New Jersey conferred the same honor upon him, and the year after, he was appointed agent of his native province of Massachusetts. These several appointments detained him ten years in England.

During all this time he did not visit home. The equanimity of his joyful spirit seems never to have been disturbed. His pen describes only pleasant scenes. No murmurs are recorded, no yearnings of home-sickness.

But month after month the animosity of the British Court towards the Americans was increasing. The king grew more and more fixed in his purpose, to compel the liberty-loving Americans to submission. Hostile movements were multiplied to indicate that if the opposition to his measures was continued, English fleets and armies would soon commence operations.

Several thousand troops were landed in Boston. Fourteen men-of-war were anchored before the town, with the cannon of their broad-sides loaded and primed, ready, at the slightest provocation to lay the whole town in ashes. Protected by this terrible menace, two British regiments paraded the streets, with their muskets charged, with gleaming sabres and bayonets, with formidable artillery prepared to vomit forth the most horrible discharges of grape shot, with haughty English officers well mounted, and soldiers and officers alike in imposing uniforms. This invincible band of highly disciplined soldiers, as a peace measure, took possession of the Common, the State House, the Court House and Faneuil Hall.

Even now, after the lapse of more than a hundred years, it makes the blood of an American boil to contemplate this insult. Who can imagine the feelings of exasperation that must have glowed in the bosoms of our patriotic fathers!

Franklin, in England, was treated with ever increasing disrespect. Lord Hillsborough, then in charge of American affairs, told him peremptorily, even insolently, that America could expect no favors while he himself was in power, and that he was determined to persevere with firmness in the policy which the king was pursuing. The king was so shielded by his ministers that Franklin

KARTINDO PUBLISHING HOUSE (Kartindo.Com)

knew but little about him. Even at this time he wrote,

"I can scarcely conceive a king of better dispositions, of more exemplary virtues, or more truly desirous of promoting the welfare of his subjects."

Franklin never had occasion to speak differently of his domestic virtues. Nay, it is more than probable that the king daily, in prayer, looked to God for guidance, and that he thought that he was doing that which was promotive of the interests of England. Alas for man! He can perpetrate the most atrocious crimes, honestly believing that he is doing God's will. He can burn aged women under the charge of their being witches. He can torture, in the infliction of unutterable anguish, his brother man--mothers and daughters, under the charge of heresy. He can hurl hundreds of thousands of men against each other in most horrible and woe-inflicting wars, while falling upon his knees and praying to God to bless his murderous armies.

Franklin had with him his grandson, William Temple Franklin, the dishonored son of William Franklin, then Governor of New Jersey. He was a bright and promising boy, and developed an estimable character, under the guidance of his grandfather, who loved him.

William Franklin in New Jersey was, however, becoming increasingly the scourge of his father. It would seem that Providence was thus, in some measure, punishing Franklin for his sin. The governor, appointed by the Court of England to his office, which he highly prized, and which he feared to lose, was siding with the Court. He perceived that the storm of political agitation was increasing in severity. He felt that the power of the colonies was as nothing compared with the power of the British government. Gradually he became one of the most violent of the Tories.

The moderation of Franklin, and his extraordinarily charitable disposition, led him to refrain from all denunciations of his ungrateful son, or even reproaches, until his conduct became absolutely infamous. In 1773, he wrote, in reference to the course which the governor was pursuing,

"I only wish you to act uprightly and steadily, avoiding that duplicity which, in Hutchinson, adds contempt to indignation. If you can promote the prosperity of your people, and leave them happier than you found them, whatever your political principles are, your memory will be honored."

KARTINDO PUBLISHING HOUSE (Kartindo.Com)

While Franklin was absent, a young merchant of Philadelphia, Richard Bache, offered his hand to Franklin's only daughter, from whom the father had been absent nearly all of her life. Sarah was then twenty-three years of age, so beautiful as to become quite a celebrity, and she was highly accomplished. Mr. Bache was not successful in business, and the young couple resided under the roof of Mrs. Franklin for eight years. The husband, with an increasing family, appealed to his illustrious father-in-law, to obtain for him a governmental appointment. Franklin wrote to his daughter,

"I am of opinion, that almost any profession a man has been educated in, is preferable to an office held at pleasure, as rendering him more independent, more a free man, and less subject to the caprices of his superiors. I think that in keeping a store, if it be where you dwell, you can be serviceable to him, as your mother was to me; for you are not deficient in capacity, and I hope you are not too proud. You might easily learn accounts; and you can copy letters, or write them very well on occasion. By industry and frugality you may get forward in the world, being both of you very young. And then what we may leave you at our death, will be a pretty addition, though of itself far from sufficient to maintain and bring up a family."

Franklin gave his son-in-law about a thousand dollars to assist him in the purchase of a stock of merchandise. The children, born to this happy couple, were intelligent and beautiful, and they greatly contributed to the happiness of their grandmother, who cherished them with a grandmother's most tender love. In the year 1862, there were one hundred and ten surviving descendants of Richard Bache and Sarah Franklin. Ten of these were serving in the Union army perilling their lives to maintain that national fabric, which their illustrious ancestor had done so much to establish. Franklin was by no means a man of one idea. His comprehensive mind seemed to grasp all questions of statesmanship, of philanthropy, of philosophy.

During the ten years of his residence in England he visited the hospitals, carefully examined their management, and transmitted to his home the result of his observations. This was probably the origin of the celebrity which the medical schools of Philadelphia have attained. He visited the silk manufactories, and urged the adoption of that branch of industry, as peculiarly adapted to our climate and people. Ere long he had the pleasure of presenting to the queen a piece of American silk, which she accepted and wore as a dress. As silk was an article not produced in England, the government was not offended by the introduction of that branch of industry. For Hartford college he procured a telescope, which cost about five hundred dollars. This was, in those days, an important event.

The renowned Captain Cook returned from his first voyage around the world. The narrative of his adventures, in the discovery of new islands, and new races of men, excited almost every mind in England and America. Franklin was prominent in the movement, to raise seventy-five thousand dollars, to fit out an expedition to send to those benighted islanders the fowls, the quadrupeds and the seeds of Europe. He wrote, in an admirable strain,

"Many voyages have been undertaken with views of profit or of plunder, or to gratify resentment. But a voyage is now proposed to visit a distant people on the other side of the globe, not to cheat them, not to rob them: not to seize their lands or to enslave their persons, but merely to do them good, and make them, as far as in our power lies, to live as comfortable as ourselves."

There can be no national prosperity without virtue. There can not be a happy people who do not "do justly, love mercy, and walk humbly with God." It was a noble enterprise to send to those naked savages corn and hoes, with horses, pigs and poultry. But the Christian conscience awoke to the conviction that something more than this was necessary. They sent, to the dreary huts of the Pacific, ambassadors of the religion of Jesus, to gather the children in schools, to establish the sanctity of the family relation, and to proclaim to all, the glad tidings of that divine Saviour, who has come to earth "to seek and to save the lost."

KARTINDO PUBLISHING HOUSE (Kartindo.Com)

CHAPTER XI

The Intolerance of King and Court

Parties in England--Franklin the favorite of the opposition--Plans of the Tories--Christian III--Letter of Franklin--Dr. Priestley--Parisian courtesy--Louis XV--Visit to Ireland--Attempted alteration of the Prayer Book--Letter to his son--Astounding letters from America--Words of John Adams--Petition of the Assembly--Violent conspiracy against Franklin--His bearing in the court-room--Wedderburn's infamous charges--Letter of Franklin--Bitter words of Dr. Johnson--Morals of English lords--Commercial value of the Colonies--Dangers threatening Franklin.

Wherever there is a government there must be an opposition. Those who are out of office wish to eject those in office, that they may take their places. There was a pretty strong party in what was called the Opposition. But it was composed of persons animated by very different motives. The first consisted of those intelligent, high minded, virtuous statesmen, who were indignant in view of the wrong which the haughty, unprincipled Tory government was inflicting upon the American people. The second gathered those who were in trade. They cared nothing for the Americans. They cared nothing for government right or wrong. They wished to sell their hats, their cutlery, and their cotton and woolen goods to the Americans. This they could not do while government was despotically enforcing the Stamp Act or the Revenue Bill. Then came a third class, who had no goods to sell, and no conscience to guide to action. They were merely ambitious politicians. They wished to thrust the Tories out of office simply that they might rush into the occupancy of all the places of honor, emolument or power.

Franklin was in high favor with the opposition. He furnished their orators in Parliament with arguments, with illustrations, with accurate statistical information. Many of the most telling passages in parliamentary speeches, were placed on the lips of the speakers by Benjamin Franklin. He wrote pamphlets of marvellous popular power, which were read in all the workshops, and greatly increased the number and the intelligence of the foes of the government measures. Thus Franklin became the favorite of the popular party. They lavished all honors upon him. In the same measure he became obnoxious to the haughty, aristocratic Tory government. Its ranks were filled with the lords, the governmental officials, and all their dependents. This made a party very powerful in numbers, and still more powerful in wealth and influence. They were watching for opportunities to traduce Franklin, to ruin his reputation, and if possible, to bring him into contempt.

This will explain the honors which were conferred upon him by one party, and the indignities to which he was subjected from the other. At times, the Tories would make efforts by flattery, by offers of position, of emolument, by various occult forms of bribery, to draw Franklin to their side. He might very easily have attained almost any amount of wealth and high official dignity.

The king of Denmark, Christian VII., was brother-in-law of George III. He visited England; a mere boy in years, and still more a weak boy in insipidity of character. A large dinner-party was given in his honor at the Royal Palace. Franklin was one of the guests. In some way unexplained, he impressed the boy-king with a sense of his inherent and peculiar greatness. Christian invited a select circle of but sixteen men to dine with him. Among those thus carefully selected, Franklin was honored with an invitation. Though sixty-seven years of age he still enjoyed in the highest degree, convivial scenes. He could tell stories, and sing songs which gave delight to all. It was his boast that he could empty his two bottles of wine, and still retain entire sobriety. He wrote to Hugh Roberts,

"I wish you would continue to meet the Junto. It wants but about two years of forty since it was established. We loved, and still love one another; we have grown grey together, and yet it is too early to part. Let us sit till the evening of life is spent; the last hours are always the most joyous. When we can stay no longer, it is time enough to bid each other good night, separate, and go quietly to bed."

Franklin was the last person to find any enjoyment in the society of vulgar and dissolute men. In those days, it was scarcely a reproach for a young lord to be carried home from a festivity in deadly intoxication. Witticisms were admitted into such circles which respectable men would not tolerate now. Franklin's most intimate friends in London were found among Unitarian clergymen, and those philosophers who were in sympathy with him in his rejection of the Christian religion. Dr. Richard Price, and Dr. Joseph Priestly, men both eminent for intellectual ability and virtues, were his bosom friends.

Dr. Priestly, who had many conversations with Franklin upon religious topics, deeply deplored the looseness of his views. Though Dr. Priestly rejected the

KARTINDO PUBLISHING HOUSE (Kartindo.Com)

divinity of Christ, he still firmly adhered to the belief that Christianity was of divine origin. In his autobiography, Dr. Priestly writes:

"It is much to be lamented that a man of Dr. Franklin's generally good character and great influence, should have been an unbeliever in Christianity, and also have done so much as he did to make others unbelievers. To me, however, he acknowledged that he had not given so much attention as he ought to have done to the evidences of Christianity; and he desired me to recommend him a few treatises on the subject, such as I thought most deserving his notice."

Priestly did so; but Franklin, all absorbed in his social festivities, his scientific researches, and his intense patriotic labors, could find no time to devote to that subject--the immortal destiny of man,--which is infinitely more important to each individual than all others combined.[22] It was indeed a sad circle of unbelievers, into whose intimacy Franklin was thrown. Dr. Priestly writes,

"In Paris, in 1774, all the philosophical persons to whom I was introduced, were unbelievers in Christianity, and even professed atheists. I was told by some of them, that I was the only person they had ever met, of whose understanding they had any opinion, who professed to believe in Christianity. But I soon found they did not really know what Christianity was."

[Footnote 22: Mr. Parton, in his excellent Life of Franklin, one of the best biographies which was ever written, objects to this withholding of the Christian name from Dr. Franklin. He writes,

"I do not understand what Dr. Priestly meant, by saying that Franklin was an unbeliever in Christianity, since he himself was open to the same charge from nine-tenths of the inhabitants of christendom. Perhaps, if the two men were now alive, we might express the theological difference between them by saying that Priestly was a Unitarian of the Channing school, and Franklin of that of Theodore Parker." Again he writes, "I have ventured to call Franklin the consummate Christian of his time. Indeed I know not who, of any time, has exhibited more of the Spirit of Christ."--*Parton's Franklin Vol. 1. p. 546. Vol. 2. p. 646.*]

It was Franklin's practice to spend a part of every summer in traveling. In 1767, accompanied by Sir John Pringle, he visited Paris. With Franklin, one of the first of earthly virtues was courtesy. He was charmed with the politeness of the French people. Even the most humble of the working classes, were gentlemanly; and from the highest to the lowest, he, simply as a stranger, was treated with consideration which surprised him. He writes,

"The civilities we everywhere receive, give us the strongest impressions of the French politeness. It seems to be a point settled here universally, that strangers are to be treated with respect; and one has just the same deference shown one here, by being a stranger, as in England, by being a lady."

Two dozen bottles of port-wine were given them at Bordeaux. These, as the law required, were seized by the custom-house officers, as they entered Paris by the Porte St. Denis; but as soon as it was ascertained that they were strangers, the wine was remitted.

There was a magnificent illumination of the Church of Notre Dame, in honor of the deceased Dauphiness. Thousands could not obtain admission. An officer, learning merely that they were strangers, took them in charge, conducted them through the vast edifice, and showed them every thing.

Franklin and his companion had the honor of a presentation to the king, Louis XV., at Versailles. This monarch was as vile a man as ever occupied a throne. But he had the virtue of courtesy, which Franklin placed at the head of religious principle. The philosopher simply records,

"The king spoke to both of us very graciously and very cheerfully. He is a handsome man, has a very lively look, and appears younger than he is."

In 1772, Franklin visited Ireland. He was treated there with great honor; but the poverty of the Irish peasantry overwhelmed his benevolent heart with astonishment and dismay. He writes,

"I thought often of the happiness of New England, where every man is a free-holder, has a vote in public affairs, lives in a tidy, warm house, has plenty of good food and fuel, with whole clothes from head to foot, the manufacture perhaps of his own family. Long may they continue in this situation."

In the year 1773, Franklin spent several weeks in the beautiful mansion of his friend, Lord Despencer. We read with astonishment, that Franklin, who openly renounced all belief in the divine origin of Christianity, should have undertaken, with Lord Despencer, an abbreviation of the prayer-book of the

Church of England. It is surprising, that he could have thought it possible, that the eminent Christians, clergy and laity of that church, would accept at the hands of a deist, their form of worship. But Franklin was faithful in the abbreviation, not to make the slightest change in the evangelical character of that admirable work, which through ages has guided the devotion of millions. The abbreviated service, cut down one-half, attracted no attention, and scarcely a copy was sold.

At this time, Franklin's reputation was in its meridian altitude. There was scarcely a man in Europe or America, more prominent. Every learned body in Europe, of any importance, had elected him a member. Splendid editions of his works were published in London; and three editions were issued from the press in Paris.

In France, Franklin met with no insults, with no opposition. All alike smiled upon him, and the voices of commendation alone fell upon his ear.

Returning to England, his reputation there, as a man of high moral worth, and of almost the highest intellectual attainments, and a man honored in the most remarkable degree with all the highest offices which his countrymen could confer upon him, swept contumely from his path, and even his enemies were ashamed to manifest their hostility. From London he wrote to his son,

"As to my situation here, nothing can be more agreeable. Learned and ingenious foreigners that come to England, almost all make a point of visiting me; for my reputation is still higher abroad, than here. Several of the foreign ambassadors have assiduously cultivated my acquaintance, treating me as one of their corps, partly, I believe, from the desire they have from time to time, of hearing something of American affairs; an object become of importance in foreign courts, who begin to hope Britain's alarming power will be diminished by the defection of her colonies."[23]

[Footnote 23: "For dinner parties Franklin was in such demand that, during the London season, he sometimes dined out six days in the week for several weeks together. He also confesses that occasionally he drank more wine than became a philosopher. It would indeed have been extremely difficult to avoid it, in that soaking age, when a man's force was reckoned by the number of bottles he could empty."--*Parton's Life of Franklin*, Vol. i, p. 540.

As an illustration of the state of the times, I give the following verse from one of the songs which Franklin wrote, and which he was accustomed to sing with great applause. At the meetings of the Junto, all the club joined in the chorus,

"Fair Venus calls; her voice obey In beauty's arms spend night and day. The joys of love all joys excel, And loving's certainly doing well.

Chorus.

Oh! no! Not so! For honest souls still know Friends and the bottle still bear the bell."

"It is well," Mr. Parton writes, "for us, in these days, to consider the spectacle of this large, robust soul, sporting in this simple, homely way. This superb Franklin of ours, who spent some evenings in mere jollity, passed nearly all his days in labor most fruitful of benefit to his country."--*Life of Franklin*, Vol. i, p. 262.]

In the latter part of the year 1772, Franklin, in his ever courteous, but decisive language, was conversing with an influential member of Parliament, respecting the violent proceedings of the ministry, in quartering troops upon the citizens of Boston. The member, in reply, said,

"You are deceived in supposing these measures to originate with the ministry. The sending out of the troops, and all the hostile measures, of which you complain, have not only been suggested, but solicited, by prominent men of your own country. They have urged that troops should be sent, and that fleets should enter your harbors, declaring that in no other way, than by this menace of power, can the turbulent Americans be brought to see their guilt and danger, and return to obedience."

Franklin expressed his doubts of this statement. "I will bring you proof," the gentleman replied. A few days after, he visited Franklin, and brought with him a packet of letters, written by persons of high official station in the colonies, and native born Americans. The signatures of these letters were effaced; but the letters themselves were presented, and Franklin was confidentially informed of their writers. They were addressed to Mr. William Whately, an influential member of Parliament, who had recently died.

Franklin read them with astonishment and indignation. He found the representation of the gentleman entirely true. Six of the letters were written by Thomas Hutchinson, Governor of Massachusetts. He was a native of the colony he governed, a graduate of Harvard, and in his religious position a Puritan. Four were written by Andrew Oliver, Lieutenant-governor, and also a native of Massachusetts.

The rest were written by custom-house officers and other servants of the Crown. The openly avowed design of these letters was, that they should be exhibited to the Ministry, to excite them to prompt, vigorous and hostile measures. They teemed with misrepresentations, and often with downright falsehoods. The perusal of these infamous productions elicited from Franklin first a burst of indignation. The second effect was greatly to mitigate his resentment against the British government. The ministry, it seemed, were acting in accordance with solicitations received from Americans, native born, and occupying the highest posts of honor and influence.

The gentleman who obtained these letters and showed them to Franklin, was very unwilling to have his agency in the affair made public. After much solicitation, he consented to have Franklin send the letters to America, though he would not give permission to have any copies taken. It was his hope, that the letters would calm the rising animosity in America, by showing that the British ministry was pursuing a course of menace, which many of the most distinguished Americans declared to be essential, to save the country from anarchy and ruin. Franklin's object was to cause these traitorous office-holders to be ejected from their positions of influence, that others, more patriotic, might occupy the stations which they disgraced.

On the 2d of December, 1772, Franklin inclosed the letters in an official package, directed to Thomas Cushing. He wrote,

"I am not at liberty to make the letters public. I can only allow them to be seen by yourself, by the other gentlemen of the Committee of Correspondence, by Messrs. Bowdoin and Pitts of the Council, and Drs. Chauncy, Cooper, and Winthrop, and a few such other gentlemen as you may think fit to show them to. After being some months in your possession, you are requested to return them to me."

The reading of the letters created intense anger and disgust. John Adams, after perusing them, recorded in his diary, alluding to Hutchinson, "Cool, thinking deliberate villain, malicious and vindictive." He carried the documents around to read to all his male and female friends, and was not sparing in his vehement comments.

Again he wrote, "Bone of our bone; born and educated among us! Mr. Hancock is deeply affected; is determined, in conjunction with Major Hawley, to watch the vile serpent, and his deputy, Brattle. The subtlety of this serpent is equal to that of the old one."

For two months the letters were privately yet extensively circulated. Hutchinson himself soon found out the storm which was gathering against him. The hand-writing of all the writers was known. In June, the Massachusetts Assembly met. In secret session the letters were read. Soon some copies were printed. It was said that some one had obtained, from England, copies of the letters from which the printed impressions were taken. But the mystery of their publication was never solved.

The Assembly sent a petition to the king of England, imploring that Thomas Hutchinson and Andrew Oliver, should be removed from their posts, and that such good men as the king might select, should be placed in their stead. The petition, eminently respectful, but drawn up in very forcible language, expressive of the ruinous consequences caused by the measures which these officials had recommended, was transmitted to Franklin, the latter part of the summer of 1773. He immediately forwarded it to Lord Dartmouth. With it he sent a very polite and conciliatory letter, in which he declared, that the Americans were very desirous of being on good terms with the mother country, that their resentment against the government was greatly abated, by finding that Americans had urged the obnoxious measures which had been adopted; and that the present was a very favorable time to introduce cordial, friendly relations between the king and the colonists.

Lord Dartmouth returned a very polite reply, laid the all-important petition aside, and for five months never alluded to it, by word or letter. In the meantime, some of the printed copies reached London. The Tories thought that perhaps the long sought opportunity had come when they might pounce upon Franklin, and at least greatly impair his influence. Franklin had nothing to conceal. He had received the letters from a friend, who authorized him to send them to America, that their contents might be made known there.

In all this he had done absolutely nothing, which any one could pronounce to be wrong. But the Court, being determined to stir up strife, began to demand

KARTINDO PUBLISHING HOUSE (Kartindo.Com)

who it was that had obtained and delivered up the letters. Franklin was absent from London. He soon heard tidings of the great commotion that was excited, and that two gentlemen, who had nothing to do with the matter, were each accused of having dishonorably obtained the letters. This led to a duel. Franklin immediately wrote,

"I think it incumbent for me to declare that I alone am the person who obtained and transmitted to Boston, the letters in question."

The Court decided to summon Franklin to meet the "Committee for Plantation Affairs," to explain the reasons for the petition against Hutchinson and Oliver. To the surprise of Franklin, it appeared that they were organizing quite a formidable trial; and very able counsel was appointed to defend the culprits.

Thus Franklin, who simply presented the petition of the Assembly, was forced into the obnoxious position of a prosecutor. The array against him was so strong, that it became necessary for him also to have counsel. It was manifest to all the friends of Franklin, that the British Court was rousing all its energies to crush him.

The meeting was held on the 11th of January, 1773. Four of the Cabinet ministers were present, and several Lords of the Privy Council. They addressed Franklin as a culprit, who had brought slanderous charges against his majesty's faithful officers in the colonies. He was treated not only with disrespect but with absolute insolence. But nothing could disturb his equanimity. Not for one moment did he lose serenity of mind.

There was an adjournment, to meet on the 29th of the month. In the meantime one of the court party, who had received many favors from Franklin, commenced a chancery suit against him, accusing him of stealing the letters, and being by trade a printer, of having secretly published them, and sold immense numbers, the profits of which he had placed in his own pocket. All this Franklin denied on oath. The charge was so absurd, and so manifestly malignant, that his foes withdrew the suit. Franklin was however assured that the Court was clamoring for his punishment and disgrace.

All London was agitated by the commotion which these extraordinary events created. At the appointed day, the Council again met. The assembly was held in a large apartment in the drawing-room style. At one end was the entrance door; at the other the fire-place, with recesses on each side of the chimney. A broad

KARTINDO PUBLISHING HOUSE (Kartindo.Com)

table extended from the fire-place to the door. The Privy Council, thirty-five in number, sat at this table. They were inveterate Tories, resolved to bring the Americans down upon their knees, and, as a preliminary step, to inflict indelible disgrace upon Franklin. Lord North, the implacable Prime Minister was there. The Archbishop of Canterbury was present. As Franklin cast his eye along the line of these haughty nobles, he could not see the face of a friend.

The remainder of the room was crowded with spectators. From them many a sympathizing glance fell upon him. Priestly and Burke gave him their silent but cordial sympathy. There were also quite a number of Americans and prominent members of the opposition, whose presence was a support to Franklin, during the ordeal through which he was to pass. He stood at the edge of the recess formed by the chimney, with one elbow resting upon the mantel, and his cheek upon his hand. He was motionless as a statue, and had composed his features into such calm and serene rigidity, that not the movement of a muscle could be detected. As usual, he was dressed simply, but with great elegance. A large flowing wig, with abundant curls, such as were used by elderly gentlemen at that day, covered his head. His costume, which was admirably fitted to a form as perfect as Grecian sculptor ever chiseled, was of rich figured silk velvet. In all that room, there was not an individual, who in physical beauty, was the peer of Franklin. In all that room there was not another, who in intellectual greatness could have met the trial so grandly.

It will be remembered that the Assembly of Massachusetts had petitioned for the removal of an obnoxious governor and lieutenant governor. Franklin, as the agent in London of that colony, had presented the petition to the crown. He was now summoned to appear before the privy council, to bring forward and substantiate charges against these officers. The council had appointed a lawyer to defend Hutchinson and Oliver. His name was Wedderburn. He had already obtained celebrity for the savage skill with which he could browbeat a witness, and for his wonderful command of the vocabulary of vituperation and abuse. Before commencing the examination, he addressed the assembly in a long speech. After eulogizing Governor Hutchinson, as one of the best and most loyal of the officers of the crown, who merited the gratitude of king and court, he turned upon Franklin, and assailed him with a storm of vituperative epithets, such as never before, and never since, has fallen upon the head of a man. The council were in sympathy with the speaker. Often his malignant thrusts would elicit from those lords a general shout of derisive laughter.

Such was the treatment which one of the most illustrious and honored of American citizens received from the privy council of king George III., when he

KARTINDO PUBLISHING HOUSE (Kartindo.Com)

appeared before that council as a friendly ambassador from his native land, seeking only conciliation and peace.

Wedderburn accused Franklin of stealing private letters, of misrepresenting their contents, that he might excite hostility against the loyal officers of the king. He accused him of doing this that he might eject them from office, so as to obtain the positions for himself and his friends. Still more, he accused him of having in an unexampled spirit of meanness, availed himself of his skill as a printer, to publish these letters, and that he sold them far and wide, that he might enrich himself. Charges better calculated to ruin a man, in the view of these proud lords, can scarcely be conceived. It is doubtful whether there were another man in the world, who could have received them so calmly, and in the end could have so magnificently triumphed over them.

During all this really terrific assailment, Franklin stood with his head resting on his left hand, apparently unmoved. At the close, he declined answering any questions. The committee of the council reported on that same day, "the lords of the committee, do agree humbly to report as their opinion to your majesty, that the said petition is founded upon resolution's, formed upon false and erroneous allegations, and that the same is false, vexatious and scandalous; and calculated only for the seditious purposes of keeping up a spirit of clamor and discontent in said province." The king accepted the report, and acted accordingly. Franklin went home alone. We know not why his friends thus apparently deserted him.

The next morning, which was Sunday, Priestly breakfasted at Franklin's table. He represents him as saying that he could not have borne the insults heaped upon him by the privy council, but for the consciousness, that he had done only that which was right. On Monday morning Franklin received a laconic letter from the Postmaster General, informing him that the king had found it necessary to dismiss him from the office of deputy Postmaster General in America.

This outrage, inflicted by the privy council of Great Britain, upon a friendly ambassador from her colonies, who had visited her court with the desire to promote union and harmony, was one of the most atrocious acts ever perpetrated by men above the rank of vagabonds in their drunken carousals. Franklin, in transmitting an account to Massachusetts, writes in a noble strain:

"What I feel on my own account, is half lost in what I feel for the public. When

I see that all petitions and complaints of grievances, are so odious to government, that even the mere pipe which conveys them, becomes obnoxious, I am at a loss to know how peace and union are to be maintained, and restored between the different parts of the empire. Grievances cannot be redressed, unless they are known. And they cannot be known, but through complaints and petitions. If these are deemed affronts, and the messengers punished as offenders, who will henceforth send petitions? and who will deliver them?"

The speech of Wedderburn gave great delight to all the Tory party. It was derisively said, "that the lords of the council, went to their chamber, as to a bull-baiting, and hounded on the Solicitor General with loud applause and laughter." Mr. Fox, writing of the assault said, "All men tossed up their hats and clapped their hands, in boundless delight."

When the tidings of the affair reached America, it added intensity to the animosity, then rapidly increasing, against the British government. The dismissal of Franklin from the post-office, was deemed equivalent to the seizure, by the crown, of that important branch of the government. None but the creatures of the Ministry were to be postmasters. Consequently patriotic Americans could no longer entrust their letters to the mail. Private arrangements were immediately made for the conveyance of letters; and with so much efficiency, that the general office, which had heretofore contributed fifteen thousand dollars annually to the public treasury, never after paid into it one farthing.[24]

[Footnote 24: It may be worthy of record, that Wedderburn became the hero of the clubs and the favorite of the Tory party. Wealth and honors were lavished upon him. He rose to the dignity of an earl and lord chancellor, and yet we do not find, in any of the annals of those days, that he is spoken of otherwise than as a shallow, unprincipled man. When his death, after a few hours' illness, was announced to the king, he scornfully said, "He has not left a worse man behind him."]

The spirit of the Tories may be inferred from that of one of the most applauded and influential of their leaders. Dr. Samuel Johnson, who wrote the notorious "Taxation no Tyranny," said,

"The Americans are a race of convicts. They ought to be thankful for any thing we can give them. I am willing to love all mankind except an American." Boswell in quoting one of his insane tirades writes, "His inflammable corruption, bursting into horrid fire, he breathed out threatenings and slaughter, calling them rascals, robbers, pirates, and exclaiming that he would burn and destroy them."

It was a day of vicious indulgence, of dissipation in every form, when it was fashionable to be godless, and to sneer at all the restraints of the Christian religion. Volumes might be filled with accounts of the atrocities perpetrated by drunken lords at the gaming table and in midnight revel through the streets. Such men of influence and rank as Fox, Lord Derby, the Duke of Ancaster, inflamed with wine, could set the police at defiance. They were constantly engaged in orgies which would disgrace the most degraded wretches, in the vilest haunts of infamy in our cities. Instead of gambling for copper, they gambled for gold. Horace Walpole testifies that at one of the most fashionable clubs, at Almack's, they played only for rouleaux of two hundred and fifty dollars each. There were often fifty thousand dollars in specie on the gaming tables, around which these bloated inebriates were gathered. It is said that Lord Holland paid the gambling debts of his two sons to the amount of one hundred thousand dollars.

The trade of the colonies had become of immense value to the mother country. It amounted to six and a half millions sterling a year. Philadelphia numbered forty thousand inhabitants. Charleston, South Carolina, had become one of the most beautiful and healthy cities in America. The harbor was crowded with shipping, the streets were lined with mansions of great architectural beauty. Gorgeous equipages were seen, almost rivaling the display in French and English capitals. But there were many Tories in Charleston, as malignant in their opposition to the popular cause in America, as any of the aristocrats to be found in London.

The unpardonable insult which Franklin had received, closed his official labors in London. His personal friends and the Opposition rallied more affectionately than ever around him. But he ceased to appear at court and was seldom present at the dinner-parties of the ministers. Still he was constantly and efficiently employed in behalf of his country. The leaders of the opposition were in constant conference with him. He wrote many pamphlets and published articles in the journals, which exerted an extended and powerful influence. He wrote to his friends at home, in October, 1774,

"My situation here is thought, by many, to be a little hazardous; for if by some accident the troops and people of New England should come to blows, I should probably be taken up; the ministerial people, affecting everywhere to represent me as the cause of all the misunderstanding. And I have been frequently cautioned to secure all my papers, and by some advised to withdraw. But I venture to stay, in compliance with the wish of others, till the result of the Congress arrives, since they suppose my being here might, on that occasion, be of use. And I confide in my innocence, that the worst that can happen to me will be an imprisonment upon suspicion; though that is a thing I should much desire to avoid, as it may be expensive and vexatious, as well as dangerous to my health."

KARTINDO PUBLISHING HOUSE (Kartindo.Com)

CHAPTER XII

The Bloodhounds of War Unleashed

The mission of Josiah Quincy--Love of England by the Americans--Petition to the king--Sickness and death of Mrs. Franklin--Lord Chatham--His speech in favor of the colonists--Lord Howe--His interview with Franklin--Firmness of Franklin--His indignation--His mirth--Franklin's fable--He embarks for Philadelphia--Feeble condition of the colonies--England's expressions of contempt--Franklin's reception at Philadelphia--His letter to Edmund Burke--Post-office arrangements--Defection and conduct of William Franklin--His arrest.

Young Josiah Quincy, of Boston, one of the noblest of patriots, who was dying of consumption, visited London, with instructions to confer with Franklin upon the posture of affairs. He wrote home, in the most commendatory terms, of the zeal and sagacity with which Franklin was devoting himself to the interests of his country. Tory spies were watching his every movement, and listening to catch every word which fell from his lips. Lord Hillsborough, in a debate in the House of Lords, said,

"There are two men, walking in the streets of London, who ought to be in Newgate or at Tyburn."

The duke of Richmond demanded their names, saying that if such were the fact the ministry were severely to be blamed. Hillsborough declined to give their names; but it was generally known that he referred to Dr. Franklin and Josiah Quincy.

The policy of Franklin was clearly defined, and unchanging. He said virtually, to his countrymen, "Perform no political act against the government, utter no menace, and do no act of violence whatever. But firmly and perseveringly unite in consuming no English goods. There is nothing in this which any one will pronounce to be, in the slightest degree, illegal. The sudden and total loss of the trade with America, will, in one year, create such a clamor, from the capitalists and industrial classes of England, Ireland and Scotland, that the despotic government will be compelled to retrace its steps."

KARTINDO PUBLISHING HOUSE (Kartindo.Com)

Even at this time the Americans had no desire to break loose from the government of Great Britain. England was emphatically their home. Englishmen were their brothers. In England their fathers were gathered to the grave. The Americans did not assume a new name. They still called themselves Englishmen. They were proud to be members of the majestic kingdom, which then stood at the head of the world.

Congress met. Its members, perhaps without exception, were yearning for reconciliation with the mother-country, and for sincere and cordial friendship. It was resolved to make another solemn appeal to the king, whom they had ever been accustomed to revere, and, in a fraternal spirit, to address their brethren, the people of England, whom they wished to regard with all the respect due to elder brothers.

The intelligence of Christendom has applauded the dignity and the pathos of these documents. The appeal fell upon the profane, gambling, wine-bloated aristocrats of the court, as if it had been addressed to the marble statuary in the British Museum. Nay worse. Those statues would have listened in respectful silence. No contemptuous laughter, and no oaths of menace, would have burst from their marble lips. The following brief extract will show the spirit which pervaded these noble documents. It is one of the closing sentences of the address to the king:

"Permit us then, most gracious sovereign, in the name of all your faithful people in America, with the utmost humility to implore you, for the honor of Almighty God, whose pure religion our enemies are undermining; for the glory which can be advanced only by rendering your subjects happy and keeping them united; for the interests of your family, depending on an adherence to the principle that enthroned it; for the safety and welfare of your kingdom and dominions, threatened with unavoidable dangers, and distresses; that your majesty, as the loving father of your whole people, connected by the same bands of law, loyalty, faith and blood, though dwelling in various countries, will not suffer the transcendent relation, formed by these ties, to be further violated, in uncertain expectation of effects which, if attained, never can compensate for the calamities through which they must be gained."

This petition was sent to Franklin, and the other colony agents, to be presented by them to the king. They were instructed also to publish both the Petition and the Address, in the newspapers, and to give them as wide a circulation as possible.

KARTINDO PUBLISHING HOUSE (Kartindo.Com)

Dr. Franklin, with two other agents, Arthur Lee and Mr. Bollan, presented to Lord Dartmouth the petition to be handed by him to the king. They were soon informed that the king received it graciously, and would submit the consideration of it to Parliament. It was thought not respectful to the king to publish it before he had presented it to that body. But as usual, the infatuation of both king and court was such, that everything that came from the Americans was treated with neglect, if not with contempt. The all-important petition was buried in a pile of documents upon all conceivable subjects, and not one word was said to commend it to the consideration of either house. For three days it remained unnoticed. Dr. Franklin, then, with his two companions, solicited permission to be heard at the bar of the house. Their request was refused. This brought the question into debate.

The House of Commons was at that time but a reflected image of the House of Lords. It was composed almost exclusively, of the younger sons of the nobles, and such other obsequious servants of the aristocracy, as they, with their vast wealth and patronage, saw fit to have elected. There was an immense Tory majority in the House. They assailed the petition with vulgarity of abuse, which could scarcely be exceeded; and then dismissed it from further consideration. Noble lords made themselves merry in depicting the alacrity with which a whole army of Americans would disperse at the very sound of a British cannon.

While these disastrous events were taking place in England--events, sure to usher in a cruel and bloody war, bearing on its wings terror and conflagration, tears and blood, a domestic tragedy was taking place in the far distant home of Franklin on the banks of the Delaware. Mrs. Franklin had been separated from her husband for nearly ten years. She was a cheerful, motherly woman, ever blessing her home with smiles and with kindly words; and in the society of her daughter and her grandchildren, she found a constant joy. The lapse of three-score years and ten, had not brought their usual infirmities. Though yearning intensely for the return of her husband, she did not allow the separation seriously to mar her happiness. Every spring she was confident that he would return the next autumn, and then bore her disappointment bravely in the assurance that she should see him the coming spring.

In December, 1774, she was suddenly stricken down by a paralytic stroke. Five days of unconscious slumber passed away, when she fell into that deep and dreamless sleep, which has no earthly waking. Her funeral was attended by a large concourse of citizens, with every testimonial of respect. Some of Franklin's oldest friends bore the coffin to the churchyard, where the remains of the affectionate wife and mother who had so nobly fulfilled life's duties, were

KARTINDO PUBLISHING HOUSE (Kartindo.Com)

placed by the side of her father, her mother, and her infant son.

Feelingly does Mr. Parton write, "It is mournful to think that for so many years, she should have been deprived of her husband's society. The very qualities which made her so good a wife, rendered it possible for him to remain absent from his affairs."

Franklin, all unconscious of the calamity which had darkened his home, and weary of the conflict with the British court, was eagerly making preparations to return to Philadelphia.

The aged, illustrious, eloquent Earl of Chatham, one of the noblest of England's all grasping and ambitious sons, sought an interview with Franklin. He utterly condemned the policy of the British cabinet. His sympathies were, not only from principles of policy, but from convictions of justice, cordially with the Americans. He felt sure that unless the court should retrace its steps, war would ensue, and American Independence would follow, and that England, with the loss of her colonies, would find mercantile impoverishment and political weakness. In the course of conversation, he implied that America might be even then, contemplating independence. Franklin, in his account of the interview writes,

"I assured him that having more than once traveled almost from one end of the continent to the other, and kept a great variety of company, eating, drinking and conversing with them freely, I had never heard in any conversation from any person, drunk or sober, the least expression of a wish for a separation, or a hint that such a thing would be advantageous to America."

In a subsequent interview, the Earl of Chatham, alluding to the conduct of Congress, in drawing up the petition and address, said,

"They have acted with so much temper, moderation and wisdom, that I think it the most honorable assembly of statesmen since those of the Greeks and Romans, of the most virtuous times."

In a subsequent interview, Dr. Franklin expressed, to the earl, his apprehension that the continuance of the British army in Boston, which was the source of constant irritation to the people, might eventually lead to a quarrel, perhaps between a drunken porter and a soldier, and that thus tumult and bloodshed might be introduced, leading to consequences which no one could foresee.

KARTINDO PUBLISHING HOUSE (Kartindo.Com)

Lord Chatham felt the force of these remarks, which soon received their striking illustration, in what was called the Boston Massacre. He therefore declared his intention of repairing to the House of Lords, to introduce a resolve for the immediate withdrawal of the troops from Boston. The tidings were soon noised abroad that the eloquent earl, then probably the most illustrious man in England, was to make a speech in favor of America. The eventful day arrived. The hall was crowded. Dr. Franklin had a special invitation from the earl to be present. The friends of America were there, few in numbers, and the enemies in all their strength.

Lord Chatham made a speech, which in logical power and glowing eloquence, has perhaps never been surpassed. Franklin had impressed him with the conviction that the determination of the Americans to defend their rights was such, that if, with fleet and army, the government were to ravage all the coast and burn all the cities, the Americans would retreat back into the forests, in the maintenance of their liberty. Full of this idea, Lord Chatham exclaimed, with prophetic power,

"We shall be forced ultimately to retract. Let us retract while we can, not when we must. I say we must necessarily undo these violent oppressive acts. You will repeal them. I pledge myself for it. I stake my reputation on it. I will consent to be taken for an idiot, if they are not finally repealed."

Franklin writes, "All availed no more than the whistling of the wind. The motion was rejected. Sixteen Scotch peers and twenty-four bishops, with all the lords in possession or expectation of places, when they vote together unanimously for ministerial measures, as they generally do, make a dead majority, that renders all debate ridiculous in itself, since it can answer no end."

Though the speech produced no impression upon the obdurate House of Lords, it had a very powerful effect upon the public mind. It was read in America, in collegiate halls, in the work-shop and at the farmer's fireside, with delight which cannot be described. A few days after the speech, Dr. Franklin, writing to Lord Stanhope, said,

"Dr. Franklin is filled with admiration of that truly great man. He has seen, in the course of life, sometimes eloquence without wisdom, and often wisdom without eloquence; in the present instance he sees both united, and both he thinks in the highest degree possible."

KARTINDO PUBLISHING HOUSE (Kartindo.Com)

Slowly the ministry were awaking to the conviction that American affairs, if not settled, might yet cause them much trouble. In various underhand ways, they approached Franklin. It was generally understood that every man had his price; that the influence of one man could be bought for a few hundred pounds; that another would require a lucrative and honorable office. Though the reputation of Franklin was such, that it was a delicate matter to approach him with bribes, still some of them now commenced a course of flattery, endeavoring to secure his coöperation. It was thought that his influence with his countrymen was so great, that they would accede to any terms he should recommend.

Lord Howe called upon Franklin, and, in the name of Lord North and Lord Dartmouth, the two most influential members of the ministry, informed him that they sincerely sought reconciliation, and that they were prepared to listen favorably, to any reasonable propositions he might offer. Lord Howe was the friend of Franklin and of America. These unexpected and joyful tidings affected Franklin so deeply, that he could not conceal the tears which rolled down his cheeks.

Lord Howe then added that he was instructed to say, that the service he would thus render both England and America, would be of priceless value, and that though the ministers could not think of influencing him by any selfish motives, he might expect, in return, *any reward which it was in the power of government to bestow.* "This," said Franklin, "was what the French vulgarly called *spitting in the soup.*"

But again there was a meeting of Parliament. Again it became evident that the ministry would accede to no terms, which did not secure the entire subjugation of America. Lord Chatham made a renewed attempt to conciliate. His propositions were rejected with scorn. In the meantime Dr. Franklin had presented some Hints, drawn up in the most liberal spirit of compromise, but which still maintained the American principle, that the colonists could not be taxed at the pleasure of the court, without having any voice themselves in the amount which they were to pay.

Soon after this, Mr. Barclay called upon Franklin in the name of the government, and after a long, and to Franklin, disgusting diplomatic harangue, ventured to say to him, that if he would only comply with the wishes of the ministry, he might expect almost any reward he could wish for. Even the imperturbable spirit of Franklin was roused. He replied,

"The ministry, I am sure, would rather give me a place in a cart to Tyburn, than any other place whatever. I sincerely wish to be serviceable; and I need no other inducement that I might be so."

In another interview, which soon followed, it appeared that the government refused to concede a single point which the Americans deemed essential. They refused to withdraw the troops; refused to allow the colonial governors to appoint the collectors of the customs; persisted in building fortresses to hold the people in subjection; and adhered to the claim of Parliament to legislate for the colonies. Franklin said,

"While Parliament claims the power of altering our constitution at pleasure, there can be no agreement. We are rendered unsafe in every privilege, and are secure in nothing."

Mr. Barclay insolently replied, "It would be well for the Americans to come to an agreement with the court of Great Britain. They ought not to forget how easy a thing it will be for the British men-of-war to lay all their seaport towns in ashes."

"I grew warm," writes Franklin; "said that the chief part of my little property consisted of houses in those towns; that they might make bon-fires of them whenever they pleased; that the fear of losing them would never alter my resolution to resist to the last, such claims of Parliament; and that it behoved this country to take care what mischief it did us; for that sooner or later it would certainly be obliged to make good all damages, with interest."

Still again these corrupt men, who are selling themselves and buying others, approached Franklin with attempts to bribe him. "They could not comprehend that any man could be above the reach of such influences. It was contemplated sending Lord Howe to America as a Commissioner. He applied to Franklin to go with him as friend, assistant or secretary.

Lord Howe said to Franklin, that he could not think of undertaking the mission without him; that if he effected any thing valuable, it must be owing to the advice Franklin would afford him; and that he should make no scruple of giving him the full honor of it. He assured him that the ministry did not expect his assistance without a proper consideration; that they wished to make generous and ample appointments for those who aided them, and also would give them the promise of subsequent more ample rewards.

KARTINDO PUBLISHING HOUSE (Kartindo.Com)

"And," said he, with marked emphasis, "that the ministry may have an opportunity of showing their good disposition toward yourself, will you give me leave, Mr. Franklin, to procure for you, previously, some mark of it; suppose the payment here, of the arrears of your salary as agent for New England, which, I understand, they have stopped for some time past."

It will be remembered that Lord Howe was sincerely the friend of America, and that he anxiously desired to see friendly relations restored. Franklin therefore restrained his displeasure, and courteously replied,

"My Lord, I shall deem it a great honor to be, in any shape, joined with your lordship in so good a work. But if you hope service from any influence I may be supposed to have, drop all thoughts of procuring me any previous favors from ministers. My accepting them would destroy the very influence you propose to make use of. They would be considered as so many bribes to betray the interests of my country. Only let me see the propositions and I shall not hesitate for a moment."

Repeated interviews ensued, between Franklin and both the friends and the enemies of the Americans. There were interminable conferences. But the court was implacable in its resolve, to maintain a supreme and exclusive control over the colonies. Every hour of Franklin's time was engrossed. Merchants and manufacturers, Tories and the opposition, lords temporal, and lords spiritual, all called upon him with their several plans. There were many Americans in London, including a large number of Quakers. These crowded the apartment of Franklin. The negotiations were terminated by a debate in the House of Lords, in which the Americans were assailed in the vilest language of insult and abuse which can be coined. Franklin was present. He writes,

"We were treated with the utmost contempt, as the lowest of mankind, and almost of a different species from the English of Britain. Particularly American honesty was abused by some of the lords, who asserted that we were all knaves, and wanted only, by this dispute, to avoid paying our debts."

Franklin returned to his home, with feelings of indignation, which his calm spirit had rarely before experienced. He resolved no longer to have any thing to do with the hostile governing powers of England. He had loved the British empire. He felt proud of its renown, and that America was but part and parcel of its greatness. But there was no longer hope, that there could be any escape from the awful appeal to arms. Though that measure would be fraught with

KARTINDO PUBLISHING HOUSE (Kartindo.Com)

inconceivable woes for his countrymen, he was assured that they would never submit. They would now march to independence though the path led through scenes of conflagration, blood and unutterable woe. His experience placed him in advance of all his countrymen.

Franklin immediately commenced packing his trunks. Astonishing, almost incredible as it may appear, the evidence seems conclusive that through all these trying scenes, Franklin was a cheerful, it is hardly too strong a word to use, a *jovial* man. It has been well said, that to be angry is to punish one's self for the sins of another. Our philosopher had no idea of making himself unhappy, because British lords behaved like knaves. He continued to be one of the most entertaining of companions. A cloudless sun seemed to shine wherever he moved. He made witty speeches. He wrote the most amusing articles for the journals, and the invariable gayety of his mind caused his society to be eagerly sought for.

One evening he attended quite a brilliant party at a nobleman's house, who was a friend to America. The conversation chanced to turn upon Esop's fables. It was said that that mine of illustration was exhausted. Franklin, after a moment's thought, remarked, that many new fables could be invented, as instructive as any of those of Esop, Gay, or La Fontaine. Can you think of one now, asked a lord. "I think so," said Franklin, "if you will furnish me with pencil and paper." He immediately sat down, surrounded by the gay assembly, and wrote, as rapidly as his pencil could move,

"THE EAGLE AND THE CAT."

"Once upon a time an eagle, scaling round a farmer's barn, and espying a hare, darted down upon him like a sunbeam, seized him in his claws, and remounted with him into the air. He soon found that he had a creature of more courage and strength than the hare; for which he had mistaken a cat. The snarling and scrambling of his prey were very inconvenient. And what was worse, she had disengaged herself from his talons, grasped his body with her four limbs, so as to stop his breath, and seized fast hold of his throat, with her teeth.

"'Pray,' said the eagle, 'let go your hold, and I will release you.'

"'Very fine,' said the cat. 'But I have no fancy to fall from this height, and to be crushed to death. You have taken me up, and you shall stoop and let me down.'

KARTINDO PUBLISHING HOUSE (Kartindo.Com)

"The eagle thought it necessary to stoop accordingly."

This admirable fable was read to the company; and, as all were in sympathy with America, it was received with great applause. Little, however, did any of them then imagine, how invincible was the animal the British government was about to clutch in its talons, supposing it to be a defenseless hare.

Franklin spent his last day in London with Dr. Priestly. The Doctor bears glowing testimony to his admirable character. Many thought Dr. Franklin heartless, since, in view of all the horrors of a civil war, his hilarity was never interrupted. Priestly, alluding to this charge against Franklin, says, that they spent the day looking over the American papers, and extracting from them passages to be published in England. "In reading them," he writes, "Franklin was frequently not able to proceed for the tears literally running down his cheeks." Upon his departure, he surrendered his agency to Arthur Lee. It was the 21st of March, 1775, when Franklin embarked at Portsmouth, in a Pennsylvania packet.

Franklin was apprehensive until the last moment, that he would not be permitted to depart; that the court, which had repeatedly denounced him as a traitor, would arrest him on some frivolous charge. On the voyage he wrote a minute narrative of his diplomatic career, occupying two hundred and fifty pages of foolscap. This important document was given to his son William Franklin, who was daily becoming a more inveterate Tory, endeavoring to ingratiate himself into favor with the court, from which he had received the appointment of governor.

Franklin also sent a copy to Mr. Jefferson, perhaps apprehensive that his son might not deal fairly with a document which so terribly condemned the British government. The Governor subsequently published the narrative. But there is reason to suppose that he suppressed those passages, which revealed most clearly the atrocious conduct of the British cabinet. Jefferson wrote some years later, alluding to this document:

"I remember that Lord North's answers were dry, unyielding, in the spirit of unconditional submission, and betrayed an absolute indifference to the occurrence of a rupture. And he said to the mediators distinctly, at last, that *a rebellion was not to be deprecated on the part of Great Britain; that the confiscations it would produce, would provide for many of their friends.*"

KARTINDO PUBLISHING HOUSE (Kartindo.Com)

The idea that the feeble Americans, scattered along a coast more than a thousand miles in extent, without a fortress, a vessel of war, or a regiment of regular troops, could withstand the fleets and armies of Great Britain, was never entertained for a moment. Indeed, as we now contemplate the fearful odds, it causes one's heart to throb, and we cannot but be amazed at the courage which our patriotic fathers displayed.

It was a common boast in England, that one regiment of British regulars could march from Boston to Charleston, and sweep all opposition before them. A band of ten wolves can put a flock of ten thousand sheep to flight. It was quite a pleasant thought, to the haughty court, that one or two ships of war, and two or three regiments could be sent across the Atlantic, seize and hang Washington, Franklin, Adams, Jefferson, and others of our leading patriots, and confiscate the property of hundreds of others, for the enrichment of the favorites of the crown.

[Illustration]

"There will be no fighting;" these deluded men said, "it will be a mere holiday excursion. The turbulent and foolhardy Americans will be brought to their senses, and, like whipped spaniels, will fawn upon the hand which has chastised them."

The voyage across the Atlantic occupied six weeks. In the evening twilight of the 5th of May, the ship dropped anchor in the Delaware, opposite Philadelphia. Franklin landed, and walked alone through the darkened streets towards his home. It is difficult to imagine the emotions with which his heart must have been agitated in that hour. Ten years had elapsed since he left his home. In the meantime his wife had reared another dwelling, in Market street, and there she had died. He had left his daughter Sarah, a child of twelve years. He was to find her a matron surrounded by her babes.

Cordially Franklin was welcomed home. The whole country resounded with the praises he so richly merited. The morning after his arrival he was unanimously chosen by the Assembly, then in session, as a member of the Continental Congress, which was to meet on the 10th of the month, in that city. Sixteen days before Franklin's arrival the memorable conflicts of Lexington and Concord had taken place. Probably never were men more astounded, than were the members of the British cabinet, in learning that the British regulars had been defeated, routed and put to precipitate flight by American farmers with their fowling-pieces. In this heroic conflict, whose echoes reverberated around the world, the Americans lost in killed and wounded eighty-three. The British lost two hundred and seventy-three. Franklin wrote to his friend Edmund Burke,

"Gen. Gage's troops made a most vigorous retreat--twenty miles in three hours--scarce to be paralleled in history. The feeble Americans, who pelted them all the way, could scarce keep up with them."

On the 10th of May Congress met. There were still two parties, one in favor of renewed attempts at conciliation, before drawing the sword and throwing away the scabbard; the other felt that the powers of conciliation were exhausted, and that nothing now remained, but the arbitrament of war.

George Washington was chosen, by the Assembly, Commander-in-Chief of the American forces. On the 17th of June the battle of Bunker Hill was fought. Mr. John Dickinson trembled in view of his great wealth. His wife entreated him to withdraw from the conflict. Piteously she urged the considerations, that he would be hung, his wife left a widow, and his children beggared and rendered infamous. He succeeded in passing a resolution in favor of a second petition to the king, which he drew up, and which the Tory Governor Richard Penn was to present. John Adams, who was weary of having his country continue in the attitude of a suppliant kneeling at the foot of the throne, opposed this petition, as a "measure of imbecility."

One of the first acts of Congress was to organize a system for the safe conveyance of letters, which could no longer be trusted in the hands of the agents of the British Court. Franklin was appointed Postmaster General. He had attained the age of sixty nine years. Notwithstanding his gravity of character and his great wisdom, he had unfortunately become an inveterate joker. He could not refrain from inserting, even in his most serious and earnest documents, some witticism, which men of the intensity of soul of John Adams and Thomas Jefferson, felt to be out of place. Still the wisdom of his counsels invariably commanded respect. Upon learning of the burning of Charleston, he wrote to Dr. Priestly,[25]

"England has begun to burn our seaport towns, secure, I suppose, that we shall never be able to return the outrage in kind. She may, doubtless, destroy them all. But if she wishes to recover our commerce, are these the probable means? She must certainly be distracted; for no tradesman, out of Bedlam, ever thought of increasing the number of his customers by knocking them in the head; or of enabling them to pay their debts by burning their houses."

[Footnote 25: "And here perhaps we have one of the reasons why Dr. Franklin, who was universally confessed to be the ablest pen in America, was not always asked to write the great documents of the Revolution. He would have put a joke into the Declaration of Independence, if it had fallen to him to write it. At this time he was a humorist of fifty years standing, and had become fixed in the habit of illustrating great truths by grotesque and familiar similes. His jokes, the circulating medium of Congress, were as helpful to the cause, as Jay's conscience or Adams' fire; they restored good humor, and relieved the tedium of delay, but were out of place in formal, exact and authoritative papers."-- *Parton's Franklin*, Vol. 2. p. 85.]

One of Franklin's jokes, in Congress, is very characteristic of the man. It was urged that the Episcopal clergy should be directed to refrain from praying for the king. Franklin quenched the injudicious movement with a witticism.

"The measure is quite unnecessary," said he. "The Episcopal clergy, to my certain knowledge, have been constantly praying, these twenty years, that 'God would give to the king and council wisdom.' And we all know that not the least notice has been taken of that prayer. So it's plain that those gentlemen have no interest in the court of Heaven."

If we sow the wind we must reap the whirlwind. Terrible was the mortification and mental suffering which Franklin endured from the governor of New Jersey. He had lived down the prejudices connected with his birth and had become an influential and popular man. He, with increasing tenacity adhered to the British Government, and became even the malignant opponent of the Americans. He pronounced the idea of their successfully resisting the power of Great Britain, as utterly absurd. His measures became so atrocious, as to excite the indignation of the people of New Jersey. The Assembly finally arrested him and sent him, under guard, to Burlington. As he continued contumacious and menacing, Congress ordered him to be removed to Connecticut. The Constitutional Gazette of July 13th, 1776, contains the following allusion to this affair:

"Day before yesterday Governor Franklin, of New Jersey, passed through Hartford, on his way to Governor Trumbull. Mr. Franklin is a noted Tory and ministerial tool, and has been exceedingly busy in perplexing the cause of liberty, and in serving the designs of the British king and his ministers.

"He is son to Dr. Benjamin Franklin, the genius of the day, and the great patron of American liberty. If his excellency escapes the vengeance of the people, due to the enormity of his crimes, his redemption will flow, not from his personal merit, but from the high esteem and veneration which the country entertains for his honored father."

His family was left in deep affliction. Franklin sent them both sympathy and money. The captive governor resided at Middletown on parole. Here the infatuated man gathered around him a band of Tories, many of whom were rich, and held convivial meetings exceedingly exasperating, when British armies were threatening the people with conflagration and carnage.

Inflamed with wine, these bacchanals sang treasonable songs, the whole company joining in chorus, with uproar which drew large groups around the house. The Tories professed utterly to despise the patriots, and doubted not that their leaders would all soon be hung. One midnight the governor, with his boon companions, having indulged in the wildest of their orgies, sallied into the streets, with such uproar as to make night hideous. The watch found it needful to interfere. The drunken governor called one of them a damned villain and threatened to flog him. A report of these proceedings was sent to Congress.

Soon after it was ascertained that he was an active agent for the British ministry. He was then confined in Litchfield jail, and deprived of pen, ink and paper. For two years he suffered this well-merited imprisonment. Mrs. governor Franklin never saw her husband again. Grief-stricken, she fell sick, and died in New York in July, 1778.

After an imprisonment of two years and four months, William Franklin was exchanged, and he took refuge within the British lines at New York. He received a pension from the British government, lived hilariously, and devoted his energies to a vigorous prosecution of the war against his countrymen. Franklin felt deeply this defection of his son. After the lapse of nine years he wrote,

"Nothing has ever affected me with such keen sensations, as to find myself deserted in my old age by my only son; and not only deserted but to find him taking up arms in a cause wherein my good fame, fortune and life were at stake."[26]

KARTINDO PUBLISHING HOUSE (Kartindo.Com)

[Footnote 26: Upon the overthrow of the royalist cause, Governor Franklin with other Tories went to England. Government gave him outright eighteen hundred pounds, and settled upon him a pension of eight hundred pounds a year. After the lapse of ten years he sought reconciliation with his father. He lived to the age of eighty-two and died in London, in 1813.]

KARTINDO PUBLISHING HOUSE (Kartindo.Com)

CHAPTER XIII

Progress of the War, both of Diplomacy and the Sword

Letter of Henry Laurens--Franklin visits the army before Boston--Letter of Mrs. Adams--Burning of Falmouth--Franklin's journey to Montreal--The Declaration of Independence--Anecdote of the Hatter--Framing the Constitution--Lord Howe's Declaration--Franklin's reply--The Conference--Encouraging letter from France--Franklin's embassy to France--The two parties in France--The voyage--The reception in France.

The spirit which, almost to that hour, had animated the people of America,--the most illustrious statesmen and common people, was attachment to Old England. Their intense desire to maintain friendly relations with the mother country, their "home," their revered and beloved home, may be inferred from the following extract from a letter, which one of the noblest of South Carolinians, Hon. Henry Laurens, wrote to his son John. It bears the date of 1776. He writes, alluding to the separation from England, then beginning to be contemplated:

"I can not rejoice in the downfall of an old friend, of a parent from whose nurturing breasts I have drawn my support and strength. Every evil which befalls old England grieves me. Would to God she had listened, in time, to the cries of her children. If my own interests, if my own rights alone had been concerned, I would most freely have given the whole to the demands and disposal of her ministers, in preference to a separation. But the rights of posterity were involved in the question. I happened to stand as one of their representatives, and dared not betray their trust."

Washington, Adams, Jay, would have made almost any conceivable sacrifice of their personal interest, if they could have averted the calamity of a separation from the home of their ancestors. But the conduct of the British Cabinet was not only despotic, in the highest degree, but it was insolent and contemptuous beyond all endurance. It seemed to be generally assumed that a man, if born on the majestic continent of North America, instead of being born on their little island, must be an inferior being. They regarded Americans as slave-holders were accustomed to regard the negro. Almost every interview resolved itself into an insult. Courteous intercourse was impossible. Affection gave place to detestation.

On the 13th of September, 1775, Congress assembled in Philadelphia. Lexington, Bunker Hill, and other hostile acts of our implacable foes, had thrown the whole country into the most intense agitation. Military companies were every where being organized. Musket manufactories and powder mills were reared. Ladies were busy scraping lint, and preparing bandages. And what was the cause of all this commotion, which converted America, for seven years, into an Aceldama of blood and woe?

It was that haughty, insolent men in England, claimed the right to impose taxes, to whatever amount they pleased, upon their brother men in America. They did not blush to say, "It is the prerogative of us Englishmen to demand of you Americans such sums of money as we want. Unless, like obsequious slaves, you pay the money, without murmuring, we will burn your cities and deluge your whole land in blood."

Washington was assembling quite an army of American troops around Boston, holding the foe in close siege there. Franklin was sent, by Congress, as one of a committee of three, to confer with Washington upon raising and supplying the American army. Amidst all these terrific excitements and perils this wonderful man could not refrain from giving expression to his sense of the ludicrous. The day before leaving Philadelphia, he wrote to Dr. Priestly the following humorous summary of the result of the British operations thus far.

"Britain at the expense of three millions, has killed one hundred and fifty Yankees this campaign, which is twenty thousand pounds a head. And, at Bunker Hill, she gained a mile of ground, half of which she lost again by our taking post on Ploughed Hill. During the same time sixty thousand children have been born in America. From these data, Dr. Price's mathematical head will easily calculate the time and expense necessary to kill us all, and conquer our whole territory."

It required a journey of thirteen days, for the Commissioners to pass from Philadelphia to Cambridge. On the 4th of October they reached the camp. Mrs. John Adams, who was equal to her husband in patriotism, in intellectual ability and in self-denial, writes,

"I had the pleasure of dining with Dr. Franklin, and of admiring him whose character, from infancy, I had been taught to venerate. I found him social, but not talkative; and when he spoke, something useful dropped from his tongue. He was grave, yet pleasant and affable. You know I make some pretensions to physiognomy, and I thought that I could read in his countenance, the virtues of his heart; and with that is blended every virtue of a Christian."

The conference lasted four days, and resulted in the adoption of very important measures. While in the camp, news came of the burning of Portland, then Falmouth. It was a deed which would have disgraced American savages. The town was entirely defenceless. It held out no menace whatever to the foe. The cold blasts of a Maine winter were at hand. A British man-of-war entered the harbor, and giving but a few hours notice, that the sick and the dying might be removed, and that the women and children might escape from shot and shell, to the frozen fields, one hundred and thirty humble, peaceful homes were laid in ashes. The cruel flames consumed nearly all their household furniture, their clothing and the frugal food they had laid in store for their long and dreary winter. A few houses escaped the shells. Marines were landed to apply the torch to them, that the destruction might be complete.

There were several vessels in the harbor. The freezing, starving, homeless wives and daughters who had not strength to toil through the wilderness to seek distant cabins of refuge, might perhaps escape in them. To prevent this they were burned to the water's edge. It was an infernal deed. It struck to the very heart of America. Even now, after a lapse of one hundred years, no American can read an account of this outrage without the flushed cheek and the moistened eye which indignation creates. Mrs. Adams wrote,

"I could not join to-day in the petitions of our worthy pastor for a reconciliation between our no longer parent, but tyrant state, and these colonies. Let us separate. They are no longer worthy to be our brethren. Let us renounce them, and instead of supplications, as formerly for their prosperity and happiness, let us beseech the Almighty to blast their councils and bring to naught all their devices."

Though Franklin was the sweetest tempered of men, he returned to Philadelphia with his spirit greatly embittered against the demoniac foes of his country. For some time no jokes escaped his lips or pen. In December, Arnold, then a patriot and a brave soldier, had made an unsuccessful attack upon Quebec. He had retired to Montreal. Franklin was again appointed one of these commissioners, to visit Arnold and advise respecting Canadian affairs.

KARTINDO PUBLISHING HOUSE (Kartindo.Com)

Most of the Canadians were Catholics. One of the commissioners was Charles Carroll of Carollton. He had a brother John, a Catholic priest, a man of high culture, of irreproachable character and a sincere patriot. He was perfectly familiar with the French language. By the solicitation of Congress he was induced to accompany his brother on this mission. It was hoped that he would be able to exert a powerful influence over the Canadian clergy. Franklin and John Carroll became intimate and loving friends. It speaks well for both, that the free-thinking philosopher, and the Catholic priest could so recognize each other's virtues, as to forget their speculative differences in mutual regard.

There was before the commissioners, a very laborious journey of five hundred miles, much of it leading through an almost unexplored wilderness. It shows great zeal in Franklin, that at the age of seventy, he was willing to encounter such exposure.

Late in March, the commissioners left Philadelphia. In two days they reached New York. They found the place deserted of its inhabitants. It was held but by a few soldiers, as it was hourly expected that the British, from their fleet and batteries, would open upon it a terrific bombardment. How little can we imagine the sufferings which must ensue, when thousands of families are driven, in terror, from their homes, from all their means of support, to go they know not where, and to live they know not how.

A few sad days were passed in the ruined town, and on the 2d of April the party embarked, at five in the afternoon, in a packet for Albany. At seven o'clock in the morning of the 4th day, after an eventful voyage, in which they narrowly escaped shipwreck from a gale in the Highlands, they landed at Albany, where they were hospitably entertained by General Schuyler.

After a brief rest, on the 9th, they set out for Saratoga, which was distant about thirty-two miles. They were conveyed over an exceedingly rough road of rocks, and corduroy and mire, in a large, heavy, country wagon. From this place, Franklin wrote,

"I begin to apprehend that I have undertaken a fatigue which, at my time of life, may prove too much for me."

After a short tarry at the country seat of General Sullivan at Saratoga, the party moved on toward Lake George. In those northern latitudes the ground was still covered with snow, and the lake was filled with floating ice. Two days of very exhausting travel brought them to the southern shore of the beautiful but then dreary lake. Here they took a large boat, thirty-six feet long, and eight broad. It was what was called a bateau, which was flat-bottomed, and was but one foot in depth. There was one mast, and a blanket sail, which was available when the wind was directly aft. There was no cabin. A mere awning sheltered partially from wind and rain.

Thus they crept across the lake, through masses of ice, a distance of thirty-six miles, in thirty-six hours. There was a neck of land, four miles in breadth, which separated Lake George from Lake Champlain. The heavy boat, placed on wheels, was dragged across by six yoke of oxen. A delay of five days was thus caused, before they were ready to embark on the latter lake. The navigation of this small sheet of water, surrounded by the primeval forest, and with scarcely the cabin of a white man to be seen, must have been romantic indeed.

They sailed when the wind favored, and rowed when it was adverse. At night they ran ashore, built their camp fire, which illumined lake and forest, boiled their coffee, cooked their viands, and, some under the awning, and some under the shelter of a hastily constructed camp, slept sweetly. The ice greatly impeded their progress. In three and a half days, they reached St. John's, near the upper end of the lake. The toilsome journey of another day, brought them to Montreal. None of the commissioners were accustomed to thus roughing it. All were greatly exhausted.

A council of war was convened. Canada was clearly lost to the Americans. It was at once decided that nothing remained but to withdraw the troops. Early in June, Franklin reached Philadelphia, from his toilsome journey. He had been absent about ten weeks. The doom of the proprietary government over Pennsylvania, was now sealed. Congress had voted that all authority derived from the king of England, was extinct. A conference of delegates was appointed to organize a new government for the province. Franklin was, of course, one of these delegates. A committee had been appointed, by Congress, to draw up a Declaration of Independence. The committee consisted of Jefferson, Franklin, Adams, Livingston, and Sherman.

The immortal document, as all the world knows, came from the pen of Jefferson. It was offered to Congress for acceptance. Many frivolous objections were, of course, presented. One man thought this phrase a little too severe. Another thought that a little too lenient. Franklin sat by the side of Jefferson, as the admirable document was subjected to this assailment. Turning to him he

KARTINDO PUBLISHING HOUSE (Kartindo.Com)

said, in one of the most characteristic and popular of all his utterances,

"When I was a journeyman printer, one of my companions, an apprenticed hatter, was about to open a shop for himself. His first concern was to have a handsome sign-board, with a proper inscription. He composed it in these words,

"John Thompson, Hatter, makes and sells Hats for ready Money."

But he thought he would submit it to his friends for their amendments. The first he showed it to, thought the word *hatter* tautologous; because followed by the words *makes hats*, which showed that he was a hatter. It was struck out. The next observed that the word *makes*, might as well be omitted, because his customers would not care who made the hats; if good, and to their mind, they would buy, by whomsoever made. He struck it out. A third said he thought the words, for *ready money*, were useless; as it was not the custom of the place to sell on credit. Every one who purchased, expected to pay. They were parted with. The inscription now stood,

"John Thompson sells hats."

"*Sells* hats," says his next friend. "Why nobody will expect you to give them away. What then is the use of that word?" It was stricken out, and *hats* followed, the rather as there was one painted on the board. So his inscription was reduced ultimately to *John Thompson*, with the figure of a hat subjoined."

It will be remembered the readiness with which Dr. Franklin, on the spur of the moment, threw off the admirable fable of the Eagle and the Hare. It is altogether probable that, in the inexhaustible resources of his genius, he improvised this anecdote to meet the exigencies of the occasion.

When the Hessian troops, whom England had hired of a German prince, arrived, intelligent men in this country pitied rather than blamed those simple hearted peasants, who had no animosity whatever, against the Americans. They had been compelled, by their feudal lord, who was really their slave master, to leave their lowly homes on the Rhine, to unite with English regulars and painted savages, in burning the homes and butchering the people struggling for existence in the wilderness of the New World.

Again the all availing pen of Franklin was called into requisition. By direction of Congress he drew up a friendly address to these unfortunate men, offering every German, who would abandon the ignominious service to which his prince had sold him, a tract of rich land sufficient for an ample farm. The address was translated into German. Various were the devices adopted, to give the document circulation in the Hessian camp. It doubtless exerted a powerful influence, in disarming these highly disciplined troops of all animosity. The effect was perhaps seen in the spectacle witnessed a few weeks afterwards, when nine hundred of these soldiers were led through the streets of Philadelphia, prisoners of war. It is not improbable that many of them were more than willing to throw down their arms.

On the 20th of July, 1776, Franklin was chosen by the Convention, one of nine delegates to represent Pennsylvania in the national Congress. One of the great difficulties to be surmounted, in a union of the States, was to give the great States, like New York and Pennsylvania, their own preponderance in the confederacy, while the minor states, like New Jersey and Delaware, should not be shorn of their influence. The difficulty was finally obviated by the present admirable arrangement, by which each State, great or small, has two representatives in the Senate, while their representation in the House depends upon the number of the population.

Franklin excelled in the art of "putting things." He silenced the demand of the smaller States, to be, in all respects, on an equality with the larger, by saying,

"Let the smaller colonies give equal money and men, and then have an equal vote. But if they have an equal vote, without bearing equal burdens, a confederation, upon such iniquitous principles, will never last long."

The convention, to form a constitution for the State of Pennsylvania, met at Philadelphia on the 16th of July, 1776. Franklin was unanimously chosen President. No pen can describe the intensity of his labors. All appreciated his consummate wisdom, and yielded readily to his suggestions. Troops were hurrying to and fro. One hundred and twenty British war vessels were in New York harbor. No one knew upon what seaport the thunderbolts of this formidable armament would be hurled. The Americans had been defeated on Long Island in August, 1776, and had almost miraculously escaped with their field pieces and stores, across the East River to New York. This brilliant retreat was deemed, by the Americans, almost equivalent to a victory.

Lord Howe, the old friend of Franklin and a humane and respected Englishman,

KARTINDO PUBLISHING HOUSE (Kartindo.Com)

who was sincerely desirous of peace with the Colonies, was appointed Admiral of the king's naval forces. He accepted the appointment, with the hope that, by the aid of Franklin, reconciliation might be effected. Still he was an Englishman and could not conceive that Americans had any rights which the English government was bound to respect. The degree of his infatuation may be inferred from the fact that, as soon as he reached our shores, he published a Declaration, which he circulated far and wide, stating that if the Americans would only give up the conflict and return to implicit submission, the British Government would forgive their sins, pardon the guilty ones, with a few exceptions, and receive them again to favor. The weak man seemed really to think, that this was an extraordinary act of clemency on the part of the English Court.

The reply, which Franklin drew up, to the Declaration, was grand. And it was the more grand when we reflect that it was addressed to a man who was supported by an army, of we know not how many thousand British regulars, and by a fleet of one hundred and twenty war vessels, many of which were of gigantic armament. Admiral Howe had written a courteous private letter to Dr. Franklin, in which he enclosed the Declaration. Congress gave Franklin permission to reply. He wrote,

"My lord; the official despatches to which you refer me, contain nothing more than offers of pardon upon submission. Directing pardon to be offered to the colonies, who are the very parties injured, expresses indeed that opinion of our ignorance, baseness, and insensibility which your uninformed and proud nation has long been pleased to entertain of us. It is impossible that we should think of submission to a government that has, with the most wanton barbarity and cruelty, burnt our defenseless towns, in the midst of winter, excited the savages to massacre our farmers, and our slaves to murder their masters, and is, even now, bringing foreign mercenaries to deluge our settlements with blood."

I have not space to copy the remainder of this admirable letter. It was delivered to Lord Howe, on board his flag ship in New York harbor, ten days after its date. As he read it his countenance expressed surprise, and almost his only remark was, "My old friend has expressed himself very warmly."

A few weeks later this good natured but weak man paroled General Sullivan, who was a prisoner of war, and sent him to Philadelphia, with a message to Congress which Lord Howe cautiously declined to put upon paper. General Sullivan reduced the message to writing and presented it to Congress. It was in substance as follows:

"The government of England cannot admit that Congress is a legitimate body, to be recognized by any diplomatic relations whatever. It is but a tumultous assembly of men who have treasonably conspired against their lawful sovereign. Still the government is willing that Lord Howe should confer with some of the members of congress, as private gentlemen, to see if some terms of accommodation cannot be arranged."

After much and earnest discussion, in which a great diversity of opinion prevailed, it was voted that General Sullivan should inform Admiral Howe, that a committee of three would be sent to ascertain whether he "has any authority to treat with persons, *authorized by Congress* for that purpose."

Benjamin Franklin, John Adams and Edward Rutledge composed this committee. An antique house, nearly a hundred years old, formerly the abode of wealth and splendor, which stood in a green lawn, but a few rods from the beach on the western shore of Staten Island, was chosen as the place for the conference. A two days' journey conveyed the committee to Amboy, opposite the house. Adams traveled on horseback: Franklin and Rutledge in a two wheel chaise.

Admiral Howe sent a boat, under the protection of a flag of truce, with an officer, who stated that he was to be left behind as a hostage for their safe return. Promptly they declined manifesting any such distrust of the honor of Admiral Howe, and took the hostage back in the boat with them. The barge, propelled by lusty rowers, soon reached the Staten Island shore. A large apartment of the old stone house had been richly decorated with moss and branches in honor of the occasion.

A regiment of Hessians was posted at that spot. The colonel drew them up in two lines and through this lane of soldiers the commissioners advanced from the beach to the house. When Admiral Howe saw that the officer he had sent as a hostage had been returned, he said,

"Gentlemen, you pay me a high compliment."

Cordially the kind-hearted admiral received his guests, and invited them to an ample collation of cold ham, tongues, mutton and wine. Mr. Henry Strachey, secretary of Lord Howe, wrote a very full report of the interview, which accords entirely with the narrative which John Adams presented to Congress. In as sincere and friendly words as human lips could pronounce, the Admiral

KARTINDO PUBLISHING HOUSE (Kartindo.Com)

assured the American gentlemen of his earnest desire to promote reconciliation between the colonists and the mother country. He alluded to the fact that in England he had been regarded as the friend of America, and to the honor Massachusetts had conferred upon his family by rearing a monument to his brother, who had fallen at Ticonderoga. Franklin well knew that Howe was regarded as the friend of America.

"I assure you, gentlemen," said Lord Howe, "that I esteem that honor to my family, above all things in this world. Such is my gratitude and affection to this country, on that account, that I feel for America as for a brother. And if America should fall, I should feel and lament it like the loss of a brother." The reply of Franklin to these sincere words, seems a little discourteous. Assuming an air of great indifference and confidence, as though the fall of America was an idea not to be thought of, he bowed, and with one of his blandest smiles said, "I assure you, my lord, that we will do everything in our power to save your lordship from that mortification."

The admiral was feeling too deeply for jokes. He was wounded by the rebuke apparently contained in the reply of his old friend. But it must not be forgotten that Franklin, the sweetest tempered of men, had not yet recovered from the indignation caused by the barbarities inflicted by the British government upon the families of Falmouth. Every day was bringing tidings of the atrocities which England, through its savage allies, was perpetrating on the frontiers, burning the cabins of lonely farmers, and tomahawking and scalping women and children. And he was constrained to look upon Lord Howe as the agent of that government, commissioned to bear to the patriots of America only the insulting messages, that the king and his ministers would graciously pardon them the crime of attempting to resist their despotism, if they would ask forgiveness, and in future submit uncomplainingly to the requirements of the crown.

Thus, while the kind-hearted admiral, with a bosom glowing with brotherly sympathy, was acting upon the assumption that the Americans should cherish undying emotions of gratitude to the king, that he was so ready to forgive their disobedience to his commands, Franklin and his companions, found it difficult to restrain their emotions of indignation, in view of the truly diabolical course pursued by the British government. The court, in their judgment, merited the execrations not only of Americans but of all humanity.

Lord Howe very emphatically wished the commissioners to understand that he met them merely as private individuals, and that he could not, in the slightest degree, recognize any authority in Congress. Franklin coldly replied,

"Your lordship may consider us in any view you may think proper. We, on our part, are at liberty to consider ourselves in our real character."

John Adams replied with warmth, characteristic of his impetuous nature, "Your lordship may consider *me* in what light you please. Indeed I should be willing to consider myself, for a few moments, in any character which would be agreeable to your lordship, *except that of a British subject.*"

As the conversation was continued, Franklin said, "We have been deputed, by Congress, simply to inquire of your lordship what proposition you have to offer *for the consideration of Congress.* British troops have ravaged our country and burnt our towns. We cannot again be happy under the government of Great Britain. All former attachments are obliterated. America can never return to the domination of Great Britain."

Mr. Adams added, "My lord, it is not in our power to treat otherwise than as *independent states.* For my part, I avow my determination never to depart from the idea of *independency.*"

Mr Rutledge gave emphasis to these decisive words by saying, "With regard to the people consenting to come again under the English government, *it is impossible.* I can answer for South Carolina. The royal government there was very oppressive. At last we took the government into our own hands. The people are now settled, and happy, under that government. They would not now return to the king's government even if Congress should desire it."

Here the conference ended, by Lord Howe's stating, that, as they insisted upon *independence,* no accommodation was possible. Lord Howe courteously accompanied the American gentlemen to the barge, and they were rowed over to the New Jersey shore. In the report they made to Congress they stated, that the commission of Lord Howe only conferred upon him authority to grant pardon to the Americans, with a few exceptions, upon their entire submission to the king.

It required, in those days, a long time to cross the Atlantic. Seldom could an answer be obtained to a letter in less than four or five months. To the usual delays and perils attached to the navigation of that stormy sea, there was now to be added the danger of capture from the swarm of British cruisers. Congress

KARTINDO PUBLISHING HOUSE (Kartindo.Com)

had several agents on the continent. But months passed away, during which no letters were received from them. This painful suspense was relieved, in September, 1776, by a long letter to Dr. Franklin, from a French gentleman, Dr. Dubourg. He was one of the prominent philosophers of Paris, and, by the request of Count du Buffon, had translated into French, Franklin's treatise upon electricity.

This letter was very cautiously written. It covered many sheets of paper. The all important substance of the letter was almost concealed from view by the mass of verbiage in which it was enveloped. But a careful reading indicated that the French ministry and the nation were in sympathy with the Americans; that while the ministry wished to avoid war with England they would gladly, if it could be done secretly, send the Americans money and powder, cannon and muskets, and that many French generals of note were eager to join the American army, and confer upon it the benefit of their experience.

This news sent a thrill of joy through hearts which recent reverses had rendered somewhat desponding. It was decided immediately to send an embassy of highest character to France. Three were to be chosen by ballot. On the first ballot Dr. Franklin was unanimously elected. He was seventy years old. And yet probably there was not another man in America so well qualified to fill that difficult, delicate and responsible post. Franklin, in the saloons of diplomacy, was fully the peer of Washington on the field of war. When the result of the ballot was announced Franklin turned to Dr. Rush, who was at his side, and said,

"I am old and good for nothing. But as the store-keepers say of their remnants of cloth, 'I am but a fag end, and you may have me for what you please.'"

Thomas Jefferson, then thirty-three years of age, and as pure a patriot as ever lived, was next chosen. He was already renowned in France as the writer of the Declaration of Independence. Silas Deane, a native of Connecticut, and a graduate of Yale, then one of the agents in Europe, was the third.

It required no little courage to cross the ocean, swept by the fleets of Great Britain. Had Franklin or Jefferson fallen into the hands of the British government, it is certain that they would have suffered severe imprisonment; it is by no means improbable that they would have been promptly hung as traitors. It was a noble sacrifice for country which led Franklin, having numbered his three-score years and ten, to incur these perils.[27]

[Footnote 27: In the year 1780, Mr. Henry Laurens, formerly President of Congress, was sent as ambassador to Holland. The ship was captured off Newfoundland, after a chase of five hours. The unfortunate man was thrown into the Tower, where he was imprisoned fifteen months, "where" he wrote to Mr. Burke, "I suffered under a degree of rigor, almost if not altogether unexampled in modern British history."]

Jefferson was compelled to decline the mission, as his wife, whom he loved with devotion rarely equalled, and perhaps never surpassed, was sick and dying. Arthur Lee, then in Europe, was elected in his stead. He was a querulous, ill-natured man, ever in a broil. A more unsuitable man for the office could scarcely have been found.

There were two parties in France who favored the Americans. One consisted of enthusiastic young men, who were enamored with the idea of republican liberty. They were weary of Bourbon despotism. The character of Louis XV., as vile a king as ever sat upon a throne, was loathsome to them. They had read Jefferson's "Declaration," with delight; and had engraven its immortal principles upon their hearts. The Marquis de Lafayette was perhaps the most prominent member of this party.

France hated England. That haughty government had long been the most unpopular on the globe. England had made great conquests from France, and was rich, intelligent and powerful beyond any other nation. Prosperity had given her arrogance, and she had placed her heel upon her humiliated neighbors. There was not a court in Europe which would not have rejoiced to see England humbled. The despotic court of France, and the most haughty nobles, were ready to encounter any perils which held out a reasonable hope that England might be weakened. Thus the sympathies of all France were united in favor of America.

And now the hour had come. By aiding the Americans, who had boldly declared their independence, they might not only deprive England of those colonies whose trade was already invaluable to England, and which were rapidly increasing in population, wealth and power, but also they might awaken such gratitude in the bosoms of Americans, that the trade of the new nation would be mainly transferred to France.

Thus the court and the nobles, intent upon this object, did not hesitate to aid in the establishment of those principles of liberty, fraternity and equality in

KARTINDO PUBLISHING HOUSE (Kartindo.Com)

America, which eventually whelmed in ruin the palaces and the castles of France.

It was deemed important to conceal, as long as possible, from the British government the sympathy and aid which France was about to manifest for the Americans. Arthur Lee reported that an agent of the French government had promised to send from Holland, two thousand pounds worth of military stores. They were to be forwarded to one of the French West India islands, ostensibly for the service of those islands. The governor was, however, instructed to surrender them to a secret agent of the American Congress. The plan failed. I have not space to record all the various stratagems which were devised to aid the Americans, while the movement was carefully concealed from the vigilant eyes of the English.

Franklin, with nobility of soul which should command the love of every American, as one of his last deeds before he left his country perhaps never to return, collected all the money he could command, about twelve thousand dollars, and loaned it to the government, whose treasury was utterly impoverished. In those dark days, even that small sum was of essential aid. In one of the last of Franklin's letters, before he sailed, he wrote,

"As to our public affairs, I hope our people will keep up their courage. I have no doubt of their finally succeeding by the blessing of God; nor have I any doubt that so good a cause will fail of that blessing. It is computed that we have already taken a million sterling from the enemy. They must soon be sick of their piratical project."

Franklin embarked in the Reprisal, a rapid sailing sloop of war of sixteen guns. He took with him his grandson, William Temple Franklin, son of the Tory governor, then a very handsome boy of eighteen, and Benjamin Franklin Bache, eldest son of his daughter, a lad of seven years. William Temple Franklin adhered firmly to the political views of his grandfather. Dr. Franklin intended to place Benjamin in a school in Paris.

Tory spies were watching every movement of Congress. This mission to France was kept a profound secret. Had the British government known that Benjamin Franklin was about to cross the ocean, almost every ship in the British navy would have been sent in chase of him. On the 26th of October, 1776, he left Philadelphia, every precaution having been adopted to keep his departure a secret. The vessel was at anchor at Marcus Hook, in the Delaware, three miles beyond Chester.

Fierce gales drove them rapidly across the Atlantic. Captain Wickes had received instructions to avoid fighting, if possible. He was to devote all his energies to transporting his precious passenger as rapidly as possible, from shore to shore. They were often chased by cruisers. The vessel was small, and Franklin, in his old age, was sadly cramped by his narrow accommodations. He says that of all his eight voyages this was the most distressing. When near the coast of France they captured an English brig, with a cargo of lumber and wine. On the afternoon of the same day, they took another brig, loaded with brandy and flax seed. England was almost delirious with rage, in finding that the Americans were bearing away their prizes from the channel itself, thus bidding proud defiance to those frigates and fortresses of Great Britain which had overawed the world.

On the 29th of November the Reprisal cast anchor in Quiberon Bay. Franklin there obtained a post chaise to convey him to Nantes. He writes,

"The carriage was a miserable one, with tired horses, the evening dark, scarce a traveller but ourselves on the road. And to make it more *comfortable*, the driver stopped near a wood we were to pass through, to tell us that a gang of eighteen robbers infested that wood, who, but two weeks ago, had robbed and murdered some travellers on that very spot."

Though absolutely no one in Europe knew that Franklin was expected, his fame had preceded him. The scientists of France were eager to render him their homage. French statesmen had learned, at the Court of St. James, to respect his grandeur of character, and his diplomatic abilities. He was a very handsome man, with a genial smile, which won love at sight. The invariable remark of every one, who chanced to meet him for five minutes was, "What a delightful man." Franklin had none of the brusqueness which characterizes John Bull. He was always a gentleman, scrupulously attentive to his rich, elegant, yet simple dress. He manifested his knowledge of human nature, in carefully preserving his national garb,--the old continental costume.

Thus wherever he appeared he attracted attention. No man was ever more courteous. The French Court, at that time, was bound by the shackles of etiquette, to an almost inconceivable degree. But Franklin was never embarrassed. He needed no one to teach him etiquette. Instinct taught him what to do, so that, in the bearing of a well bred gentleman, he was a model man,

KARTINDO PUBLISHING HOUSE (Kartindo.Com)

even in the court where Louis XIV. and Louis XV. had reigned with omnipotent sway. The most beautiful duchess, radiant in her courtly costume, and glittering with jewels, felt proud of being seated on the sofa by the side of this true gentleman, whose dress, simple as it was, was in harmony with her own. The popular impression is entirely an erroneous one, that there was anything rustic, anything which reminded one of the work shop or the *blouse*, in the demeanor of Benjamin Franklin, as he moved, unembarrassed, in the highest circles of fashion then known in the world.

Franklin was received to the hospitalities of a French gentleman of wealth and distinction, by the name of Gruel. His elegant apartments were always crowded with visitors, eager to manifest their respect for the trans-Atlantic philosopher. Horace Walpole, a warm friend of the Americans, wrote,

"An account came that Dr. Franklin, at the age of 72, or 74, and, at the risk of his head, had bravely embarked, on board an American frigate, and, with two prizes taken on the way, had landed, at Nantes, in France, and was to be at Paris on the 14th, where the highest admiration and expectation of him were raised."

Upon his arrival Mr. Deane exultingly wrote, "Here is the hero and philosopher, and patriot, all united in this celebrated American, who, at the age of seventy four, risks all dangers for his country."

KARTINDO PUBLISHING HOUSE (Kartindo.Com)

CHAPTER XIV

The Struggles of Diplomacy

Anecdote of Gibbon--John Adams--Residence at Passy--Lafayette introduced--Cruise of the Reprisal--Paul Jones--Capture of Burgoyne--Alliance with France--Anecdote of the Cake--Excitement in England--Franklin's introduction to the king--Joy in America--Extraordinary letter of Count Wissenstein--The reply--Injustice to Paul Jones--French troops in America--Character of John Adams--Franklin's mature views of human nature--Anecdote of the Angel--Capture of Cornwallis--Its effect in England--Prejudices of Mr. Jay--Testimony of Dr. Sparks--Jealousy of Franklin--Shrewd diplomatic act--The treaty signed.

In the journey from Nantes to Paris, a curious incident occurred, which is well worth recording. It so admirably illustrates the character of two distinguished men, as to bear internal evidence of its truthfulness. At one of the inns, at which Franklin stopped, he was informed that Mr. Gibbon, the illustrious author of the "Decline and Fall of the Roman Empire," was also tarrying.

Mr. Gibbon was an Englishman. He was a deist, being in entire sympathy with Franklin in his views of Christianity. He was also a man of letters. Mr. Franklin addressed a very polite note to Mr. Gibbon, sending his compliments, and soliciting the pleasure of spending the evening with him. Mr. Gibbon, who was never renowned for amiability of character, replied, in substance, we have not his exact words,

"Notwithstanding my regard for Dr. Franklin, as a man and a philosopher, I cannot reconcile it with my duty to my king, to have any conversation with a revolted subject."

Franklin responded to this by writing, "Though Mr. Gibbon's principles have compelled him to withhold the pleasure of his conversation, Dr. Franklin has still such a respect for the character of Mr. Gibbon, as a gentleman and a historian, that when, in the course of his writing the history of the 'Decline and Fall of Empires,' the decline and fall of the British Empire shall come to be his subject, as will probably soon be the case, Dr. Franklin would be happy to furnish him with ample materials, which are in his possession."[28]

[Footnote 28: This anecdote has had a wide circulation in the newspapers. Mr. William Cobbett inserts it in his "Works," with the following comment, characteristic of the spirit of most of the higher class of Englishmen, in those days:

"Whether this anecdote record a truth or not I shall not pretend to say. But it must be confessed, that the expressions imputed to the two personages were strictly in character. In Gibbon, we see the faithful subject, and the man of candor and honor. In Franklin the treacherous and malicious old Zanga, of Boston."--*Works of William Cobbett. Vol. vii, p. 244.*]

Gibbon was a Tory. He supported Lord North in all his measures. The government rewarded him with a pension of eight hundred pounds a year. This was equivalent to considerable more than four thousand dollars at the present time. Franklin was received, in Paris, by the whole population, court and *canaille*, with enthusiasm which that excitable capital had rarely witnessed. The most humble of the population were familiar with the pithy sayings of Poor Richard. The *savants* admitted their obligations to him, for the solution of some of the most difficult problems of philosophy. The fashionable world were delighted with his urbanity; and in his society found rare and unequalled pleasure. The republicans regarded him as the personification of a free government; and even the nobles and the ministry were cheered by the hope that, with his aid, haughty England could be weakened and humbled, and that thus a new era of commercial prosperity was about to dawn upon France.

John Adams was not popular in Paris. He was a man of great abilities, of irreproachable character, and was animated by as pure principles of patriotism as ever glowed in a human bosom. But he was a genuine Puritan, inheriting the virtues and the foibles of the best of that class. Though not wanting in magnanimity, he could not fail from being disturbed, by the caresses with which Franklin was ever greeted, contrasted with the cold and respectful courtesy with which he was received. It was always the same, in the Court, in the saloons, and on the Boulevards. In Mr. Adams' diary, written some years later, we find the following insertion, which, in some degree, reveals his feelings. He is recording a conversation with the French minister.

"All religions," said Marbois, "are tolerated in America. The ambassadors have a right, in all the courts of Europe, to a chapel in their own way. But Mr. Franklin never had any."

KARTINDO PUBLISHING HOUSE (Kartindo.Com)

"No," said I laughing, "because Mr. Franklin has no----"

I was going to say what I did not say, and will not say here. I stopped short, and laughed.

"No," said M. Marbois. "Mr. Franklin adores only great Nature; which has interested a great many people of both sexes in his favor."

"Yes," said I laughing, "all the atheists, deists and libertines, as well as the philosophers and ladies are in his train."[29]

[Footnote 29: Works of John Adams, Vol. III, p. 220.]

The English lords were exasperated by the reception France had given Franklin. They fully comprehended its significance. France was in sympathy with the Americans, in their heroic endeavor to escape from the despotism of the British crown. Thus the traffic which had enriched England, would be transferred to France.

Even the Earl of Chatham said, in one of the most eloquent of his speeches,

"France, my lords, has insulted you. She has encouraged and sustained America. And whether America be wrong or right, the dignity of this country ought to spurn at the officiousness of the French interference. The ministers and ambassadors of those who are called rebels, are in Paris. In Paris they transact the reciprocal business of America and France. Can there be a more mortifying insult? Can even our ministers sustain a more humiliating disgrace? Do they dare to resent it?"

Franklin was assailed in England, in innumerable pamphlets of abuse. The sin of his youth still pursued him. Many an envenomed arrow pierced his heart.[30]

[Footnote 30: This is a delicate subject, but it must not be ignored. Mr. Parton writes,--"One penny-a-liner informed the public that Dr. Franklin had a son, who, though illegitimate, was a much more honest man than his father. As to the mother of that son, nothing was known of her, except that her seducer let her die in the streets."

There was no end to those attacks. They were attended by every exaggeration of malignity which hatred could engender. It is certain that Franklin would have been saved from these woes could he, as a young man, have embraced the *faith* of the religion of Jesus, and developed that *faith* in his *practice*.]

But it must not be forgotten that there were many of the noblest men in England, who were the warm friends of Franklin, and who cordially espoused the American cause. Among these were Fox, Burke, Rockingham, Shelburne, Chatham, Priestley and Price.

Many beautiful villages surrounded Paris. One of the most lovely, embowered in foliage, was Passy. It is now included within the city walls. It was then but two miles from the centre of the city. A munificent friend of America, M. de Chaumont, invited Franklin to the hospitality of one of his sumptuous mansions in that place. Franklin accepted the invitation, assuring him that at the close of the war, Congress would insist upon granting him a tract of land, in recognition of his kindness to America in the hour of need.

Early in the year 1777, Franklin took up his residence at Passy, and there he continued to reside while he remained in France. He lived liberally, had an ample retinue of servants, and entertained his guests with elegance. His annual expenditures were about thirteen thousand dollars. This sum would then purchase twice the amount of conveniences and luxuries which could be purchased by the same sum at the present day. He had his own servants, and commanded a handsome carriage with two horses.

Mrs. Adams writes, "With seven servants, and hiring a charwoman upon occasion of company, we may possibly keep house. With less we should be hooted at as ridiculous, and could not entertain any company."

Though Franklin took every thing by the smooth handle, he did not, on that account, intermit any intensity of labor to accomplish his purposes. There were then three American envoys in Paris, Franklin, Deane, and Lee. Five days after the arrival of Franklin, they, on the 28th of December, 1777, held their first interview with the French Minister, Count de Vergennes. They were received with all that cordiality and courtesy which are marked characteristics of the French people. But still the commissioners were embarrassed. The prospects of America were doubtful. General Burgoyne was on the eve of sailing for America with a formidable fleet, and an army of eight or ten thousand highly disciplined troops. In the course of the conversation, the minister said that

France was not yet ready to enter into open collision with England, and to declare war.

"But," said he, "if a *couple of millions* of francs, to be repaid without interest after the war, will be of use to you, they are at your service. Only do not say that you had it from *us*."

This was indeed, under the doubtful circumstances, a very generous offer. It was at this dark hour that the noble Lafayette decided to consecrate his fortune, and to peril his life, for the cause of American freedom. It was proclaimed that Burgoyne's expedition was fitted out to rouse the slaves to insurrection, and to lay the mansions of the planters in ashes. Arthur Lee was very much alarmed. These splendid estates were generally situated in romantic spots, upon the banks of the navigable rivers, where the dwellings, often quite magnificent, could easily be demolished by shot and shell thrown from any frigate.

The Reprisal, Captain Wickes, was the first American vessel of war which ventured into European waters. The channel swarmed with British vessels. The Reprisal took prize after prize, and conveyed them into Nantes. As France was not at war with England, Count de Vergennes was compelled to order the Reprisal, with her prizes, to leave the harbor. Captain Wickes took some of the Nantes merchants on board his vessel, and, just outside the port, sold the prizes to them. The French merchants then returned, with their property, into the harbor.

Captain Wickes soon united with him the Lexington of fourteen guns, and a cutter, the Dolphin, of ten guns. With this little fleet the hero sailed completely around Ireland, capturing or destroying sixteen prizes. The British were astounded at this audacity. Merchants and under-writers were quite terror-stricken. They had never dreamed that the despised Americans could strike *them* any blows. And when, soon after, Paul Jones, one of the noblest of all naval heroes, appeared in their waters, it is not too much to say that *consternation* pervaded the coasts of both England and Ireland.[31]

[Footnote 31: The wonderful achievements of this patriot are fully recorded in one of the volumes of this series.]

It requires many and aggravated wrongs to rouse a naturally amiable man to the highest pitch of indignation. But when thus roused, he is ready for any vigor of action. Franklin's blood was up. England was bribing slaves to murder their

KARTINDO PUBLISHING HOUSE (Kartindo.Com)

masters; was rousing the savages to massacre the families of poor, hard-working frontiersmen; was wantonly bombarding defenceless seaports, and with inhumanity, rarely known in civilized warfare, was laying villages in ashes, consigning women and children to beggary and starvation. In the prison hulks of New York, our most illustrious men were in the endurance, as prisoners of war, of woes unsurpassed by Algerine barbarism. Many of our common sailors, England was compelling, by the terrors of the lash, to man her ships, and to fight their own countrymen. Maddened by these atrocities, Mr. Franklin wrote to his English friend, David Hartley, a member of Parliament, a letter, which all the few friends of America in England, read with great satisfaction, and which must have produced a very powerful moral impression in France. It is too long to be inserted here. In conclusion he said to his friend,

"In reviewing what I have written, I found too much warmth in it, and was about to strike out some parts. Yet I let them go, as it will afford you this one reflection,

"'If a man naturally cool, and rendered still cooler by old age, is so warmed by our treatment of his country, how much must those people in general be exasperated against us. And why are we making inveterate enemies, by our barbarity, not only of the present inhabitants of a great country, but of their infinitely more numerous posterity; who will, in future ages, detest the name of Englishman, as much as the children in Holland now do those of Alva and Spaniard.'"

William Temple Franklin inherited the attractions of person, and the fascination of manners, so conspicuous in his grandfather. He was a great favorite in the social circles of the gay metropolis. Dark days came, with tidings of discomfiture. Franklin devoted twelve hours out of the twenty-four, to the arduous duties of his mission. Philadelphia fell.

"Well, Doctor," said an Englishman in Paris, with the customary courtesy of his nation, "Howe has taken Philadelphia."

"I beg your pardon," Franklin replied, "Philadelphia has taken Howe."

The result proved that Franklin's joke was almost a reality.

Burgoyne surrendered. His whole army was taken captive. Massachusetts immediately sent John Loring Austin to convey the rapturous tidings to

Franklin. This great success would doubtless encourage France to open action. No tongue can tell the emotions excited in the bosoms of Franklin, Lee and Deane, as Austin entered their presence at Passy, with the announcement, *"General Burgoyne and his whole army are prisoners of war."*

There were no shoutings, no rushing into each other's arms. But tears filled their eyes. They felt assured that France would come openly to their aid, and that the independence of their country was no longer doubtful. Silently they returned to Franklin's spacious apartment, where they spent the whole day in reading the enrapturing dispatches, and in preparing for immediate alliance with France. France made no attempt to conceal its joy. A treaty of alliance was soon formed. Nobly the Count de Vergennes said,

"We wish to take no advantage of your situation. We desire no terms which you may hereafter regret having made; but would enter into arrangements of mutual interest, which may last as long as human institutions endure."

England was now greatly alarmed from fear that the trade of the colonies might be transferred to France. Envoys were sent to Passy to offer the American ambassadors everything they had demanded at the commencement of the conflict. But it was too late. America now demanded *Independence*, and would accept nothing less.

A large cake was one day sent to the ambassador's apartment, at Passy, with the inscription "Le Digne Franklin," the worthy Franklin. Mr. Lee said, "Well, Doctor, we have to thank you for our accommodations, and to appropriate your present to our use."

"Not at all," said Franklin. "This cake is for all the Commissioners. The French, not being able to write good English, do not spell our names correctly. The meaning doubtless is Lee, Deane, Franklin."

The memorable treaty was signed on the 5th of February, 1778. It was stated that the object of the treaty was to establish the independence of the United States, and that neither party should conclude either truce or peace with England, without the consent of the other.

Tidings of the treaty, which for a short time was kept secret, had been whispered in England, causing intense excitement. On the 17th of February, 1778, the House of Parliament was crowded. Lord North, amid breathless silence, presented a "Conciliation Bill," granting everything which Franklin had demanded. Fox, who was in the Opposition, arose and announced the treaty. "The astonishment," writes Walpole, "was totally indescribable."

Soon the fact of the treaty of alliance, was formally announced in France. The American envoys were invited to an audience with the king. Franklin was richly dressed. His hair was carefully arranged by a French perruquier. He wore an admirably fitting suit of plain, black, silk velvet. Ruffles of elaborate embroidery and snowy whiteness adorned his wrists and bosom. White silk stockings aided in displaying the perfect proportions of his frame. Large silver buckles were on his shoes.

No one could accuse him of failing in due respect for the king, by appearing in his presence in slatternly dress. His costume was superb, and was such as was then worn, on important occasions, by American gentlemen of the highest rank. The audience took place at Versailles, on the morning of the 20th of March. Each of the American envoys rode in his own carriage, attended by the usual retinue of servants. On the way they were cheered with the utmost enthusiasm by the crowd. The king, Louis XVI., received them with extreme courtesy, and the queen, Marie Antoinette, was marked in her attentions to Franklin. The British ambassador, Lord Stormont, was so enraged, that, regardless of all the claims of courtesy, he immediately returned to England, without even taking leave of the king.

Who can describe the exultation, the rapture, the tears, with which these tidings were received by the patriots of America. On the 6th of May, George Washington drew up his little band at Valley Forge, to announce the great event, and to offer to God prayers and thanksgivings. The tone of the English was immediately changed. They abandoned threats and tried the effect of entreaties. Several emissaries, from the government, approached Dr. Franklin, all bearing in substance the same message. They said,

"We cannot endure the thought that our beloved colonists should enter into alliance with our hereditary natural enemy, France. Can you, who are Protestants, consent to unite with a nation of Roman Catholics? If you will remain firm in your adhesion to England, we will grant you all you ever wished for, and even more. But do not forsake your mother country to swell the pride and power of perfidious France."

But all these efforts were unavailing. The colonists began to despise England.

KARTINDO PUBLISHING HOUSE (Kartindo.Com)

They had no wish for war with their unnatural parent, and they knew that their independence was assured; and that no efforts which England could possibly make, could now prevent it. All alike felt disposed to spurn the bribes which England so lavishly offered.

A very extraordinary letter was sent to Dr. Franklin, which was signed, Charles de Wissenstein. Franklin, who was accustomed to sifting evidence, became satisfied that the message came from king George III. himself. The letter declared that the perfidious French would certainly deceive the Americans with false promises, and defraud them. After making the most liberal offers of popular rights, if the Americans would continue to remain colonists under the British crown, the document presented the following extraordinary promise to those American patriots whom England had denounced as traitors, and doomed to be hung. It was deemed a bribe which human virtue could not resist.

"As it is unreasonable that their (the American patriots) services to their country should deprive them of those advantages which their talents would otherwise have gained them, the following persons shall have offices or pensions for life, at their option, namely, Franklin, Washington, Adams, Hancock, etc. In case his Majesty, or his successors, should ever create American peers, then those persons, or their descendants, shall be among the first created if they choose it."

Franklin, after conference with his colleagues, replied to the letter. His soul was all on fire with the insults our country had received, and the wrongs she had endured. He wrote as if personally addressing the king. We can only give the concluding paragraph. After stating that the independence of America was secured, that all attempts of England to prevent it would be impotent, and that consequently it was quite a matter of indifference to the Americans whether England acknowledged it or not, he wrote,[32]

"This proposition, of delivering ourselves bound and gagged, ready for hanging, without even a right to complain, and without a friend to be found afterward among all mankind, you would have us embrace upon the faith of an Act of Parliament. Good God! an act of your Parliament. This demonstrates that you do not yet know us; and that you fancy that we do not know you. But it is not merely this flimsy faith that we are to act upon. You offer us hope, the hope of PLACES, PENSIONS and PEERAGES.

"These, judging from yourselves, you think are motives irresistible. This offer to corrupt us, sir, is with me, your credential; and convinces me that you are not a private volunteer in your application. It bears the stamp of British Court character. It is even the signature of your king. But think, for a moment, in what light it must be viewed in America.

"By PLACES, you mean places among us; for you take care, by a special article, to secure your own to yourselves. We must then pay the salaries in order to enrich ourselves with those places. But you will give us PENSIONS, probably to be paid too out of your expected American revenue, and which none of us can accept without deserving, and perhaps obtaining, *suspension.*

"PEERAGES! Alas! in our long observation of the vast servile majority of your peers, voting constantly for every measure proposed by a minister, however weak or wicked, leaves us small respect for that title. We consider it as a sort of tar-and-feather honor, or a mixture of foulness and folly, which every man among us, who should accept it from your king, would be obliged to renounce, or exchange for that confessed by the mobs of their own country, or wear it with everlasting infamy."[33]

[Footnote 32: In reference to the promises contained in the letter, Franklin referred to a book which it was said George III. had carefully studied, called *Arcana Imperii*. A prince, to appease a revolt, had promised indemnity to the revolters. The question was submitted to the keepers of the king's conscience, whether he were bound to keep his promises. The reply was,

"No! It was right to make the promises, because the revolt could not otherwise be suppressed. It would be wrong to keep them, because revolters ought to be punished."]

[Footnote 33: Sparks' Franklin, Vol. iii, p. 278.]

In the spring of 1778, Paul Jones entered upon his brilliant career, bidding defiance, with his infant fleet, to all the naval power of Great Britain, agitating entire England with the terror of his name. Franklin was his affectionate friend, and, in all his many trials, he leaned upon Franklin for sympathy. So tremendously was he maligned by the English press, that American historians, unconsciously thus influenced, have never done him justice. As a patriot, and a noble man, he deserves to take rank with his friends, Washington and Franklin.

In 1779, Lafayette, returning to France, from America, brought the news that

Franklin was appointed by Congress as sole plenipotentiary of the new nation of the United States, to the generous kingdom, which had acknowledged our independence, and whose fleets and armies were now united with ours. All France rejoiced. With great eclat the new ambassadors were presented to the king.

No man of force of character can escape having enemies. Franklin had many and bitter ones. A cabal plotted the removal of his excellent grandson, William Temple Franklin. It gives us an insight to the heart of this venerable septuagenarian to read from his pen,

"It is enough that I have lost my son. Would they add my *grandson*. An old man of seventy, I undertook a winter voyage, at the command of Congress, with no other attendant to take care of me. I am continued here, in a foreign country, where, if I am sick, his filial attention comforts me. And if I die, I have a child to close my eyes and take care of my remains. His dutiful behavior toward me, and his diligence and fidelity in business, are both pleasing and useful to me. His conduct, as my private secretary, has been unexceptionable; and I am confident the Congress will never think of separating us."

Franklin's great endeavor now was to obtain money. Without it we could have neither fleet nor army. The treasury of France was empty, almost to bankruptcy. Never did he struggle against greater obstacles than during the next three years. It has been truly said, that Franklin, without intending it, helped to bleed the French monarchy to death. In addition to the employment of both army and navy, the French government conferred upon Congress, in gifts or loans, the sum of twenty-six million francs.

The French troops were received in America with boundless enthusiasm. Their discipline was admirable. Their respect for the rights of property was such, that not a barn, orchard or hen-roost was robbed.

John Adams was sent to join Franklin, to aid him in framing terms of peace, whenever England should be disposed to make such advances. He was a man of great abilities, of irreproachable integrity, but he had inherited, from his English ancestry, not only repulsive brusqueness, but also a prejudice against the French, which nothing could remove. His want of courtesy; his unconcealed assumption that France was acting out of unmitigated selfishness, and that consequently the Americans owed the French no debt of gratitude, often caused Franklin much embarrassment. This blunt man, at one time wrote so

KARTINDO PUBLISHING HOUSE (Kartindo.Com)

uncourteous, not to say insulting a letter, to M. de Vergennes, that the French minister declined having any more correspondence with him. Both Franklin and Congress condemned the incivility of Mr. Adams. He only escaped a motion of censure from the full conviction of Congress of the purity of his patriotism, and of his intentions.[34]

[Footnote 34: Mr. Jefferson, after an intimacy of seven months with John Adams, in Paris, wrote of him: "He is vain, irritable, and a bad calculator of the force and probable effect of the motives which govern men. This is all the ill which can possibly be said of him. He is as disinterested as the Being who made him."]

Franklin had been requested to forward the correspondence to Congress. As in duty bound, he did so; accompanying it with a magnanimous letter. Mr. Adams was very angry. Every impartial reader will admit that, in this embarrassing affair, Franklin conducted with delicacy and discretion. The British troops in America were still conducting like savages. Congress requested Franklin to prepare a school-book, with thirty-five prints, each depicting one or more of the acts of English brutality. The object was to impress the minds of children with a deep sense of the insatiable and bloody malice with which the English had pursued the Americans. The plan was never executed.

In the year 1781, Franklin, then seventy-five years of age, and having been engaged in public service for fifty years, wrote to Congress, begging permission to retire from his responsible office. Congress could not spare his services. They gave him an additional appointment. He was commissioned to unite with Adams and Jay, in those negotiations for peace which, it was evident, must soon take place.

Franklin loved the French, he could smile at their foibles, in dressing their hair so that they could not wear a hat, but were compelled to carry it under their arms; also in filling their noses with tobacco. "These," said he, "are mere follies. There is nothing wanting, in the character of a Frenchman, that belongs to that of an agreeable and worthy man."

It may perhaps be mentioned, as a defect in the character of Franklin, that when in France he could see nothing but the beautiful. His eye was turned from every revolting spectacle. In the society of elegantly dressed, highly educated, refined French ladies,--at dinner parties, glittering with gold and silver plate,--in social intercourse with men whose philosophical attainments were of the highest order, and whose politeness of speech and bearing rendered them delightful companions, Franklin found his time and thoughts engrossed. In all his voluminous writings we find no allusion to those tremendous wrongs, which Louis XIV. and Louis XV. had entailed upon the people,--wrongs which soon convulsed society with the volcanic throes of the French revolution.

Jefferson, who succeeded Franklin, was cast in a different mould. He saw and fully comprehended the misery under which the millions of the French peasantry were groaning. And this led him to the conviction, that no people could be safe, unless the government were placed in their own hands.

Still Franklin, like his brother deists, Hume and Voltaire, seeing how impotent were all the motives they could urge to make man virtuous, became thoroughly disgusted with human nature. He even went beyond Paul in his description of the hopeless depravity of man. The idea of reclaiming him by his philosophy was abandoned entirely. And yet he was not prepared to embrace that gospel, which the experience of ages has proved to be the "wisdom of God and the power of God unto salvation."

"He enlarges," writes Mr. Parton, "upon this theme, in his most delightful manner, in another letter to Dr. Priestley." In this letter he says in his usual jocular strain, that the more he studies the moral part of nature the more he is disgusted; that he finds men very badly constructed; that they are more prone to do evil than to do good; that they take great pleasure in killing one another, and that he doubts whether the species is worth preserving. He intimates that every attempt to save their souls is "an idle amusement."

"As you grow older," he writes, "you may perhaps repent of having murdered, in mephitic air, so many honest, harmless mice, and wish that, to prevent mischief, you had used boys and girls instead of them."

In this singular letter he represents a young angel having been sent to this world, under the guidance of an old courier spirit. They arrive over the seas of Martinico, in the midst of the horrible fight between the fleets of Rodney and De Grasse.

"When," he writes, "through the clouds of smoke, he (the young angel) saw the fire of the guns, the decks covered with mangled limbs and bodies, dead or dying; the ships sinking, burning, or blown into the air; and the quantity of pain, misery and destruction the crews, yet alive, were with so much eagerness dealing round to one another, he turned angrily to his guide and said,

"'You blundering blockhead; you are ignorant of your business. You undertook to conduct me to the earth; and you have brought me into hell.'

"'No sir,' said the guide, 'I have made no such mistake. This is really the earth, and these are men. Devils never treat one another in this cruel manner. They have more sense, and more of what men (vainly) call humanity.'"

It was after the study of human nature, under the most favorable of possible circumstances, for more than three-quarters of a century, that this philosopher wrote these terrible comments upon our fallen race.

The latter part of October, 1781, Lord Cornwallis surrendered his whole army, of over seven thousand men, at Yorktown. The French fleet cut off his escape by sea. Seven thousand French soldiers, united with five thousand American troops, prevented any retreat by land. The Americans had thus captured two British armies. It was in vain for England to think of sending a third. The conflict was virtually decided.

"The Prime Minister," Lord North, it is said, "received the tidings as he would have taken a ball in his breast. He threw his arms apart. He paced wildly up and down the room, exclaiming, from time to time, 'Oh God! it is all over.'"

All England now was clamoring against the war. Thousands of persons had perished in the campaigns, and financial embarrassments had come to nearly all her institutions of industry. The English government made vigorous endeavors, offering great bribes, to induce the American envoys at Paris to abandon their French allies, and make a separate peace. Franklin wrote to Mr. Hartley, through whom he received these proposals,

"I believe there is not a man in America, a few *English Tories* excepted, that would not spurn the thought of deserting a noble and generous friend, for the sake of a truce with an unjust and cruel enemy."

British diplomacy tried all its arts of intrigue to separate America from France in the negotiations for peace, but all in vain. The British minister, Mr. Grenville, in an interview with Mr. Franklin, ridiculed the idea that America owed France any gratitude, urging that France sought only her own selfish

KARTINDO PUBLISHING HOUSE (Kartindo.Com)

interests.

"I told him," Franklin writes, "that I was so strongly impressed with the kind assistance afforded us by France, in our distress, and the generous and noble manner in which it was granted, without exacting or stipulating for a single privilege, or particular advantage to herself in our commerce or otherwise, that I could never suffer myself to think of such reasonings for lessening the obligation."

On the 28th of February, 1782, General Conway, one of the leaders of the Opposition, the same who had moved the repeal of the stamp act, seventeen years before, presented a resolution in the House of Commons that,

"THE REDUCTION OF THE COLONIES BY FORCE OF ARMS IS IMPRACTICABLE."

A violent, even fierce debate ensued, which was continued until one o'clock in the morning. Then the cry of *question* became general. The vote was carried by a majority of nineteen. This terminated the American war. The people of England had decided against it. "Acclamations," writes Wraxall, "pierced the roof, and might have been heard in Westminster Hall."

This great victory was followed by another resolve. It was an address to George III. soliciting him to "Stop the prosecution of any further hostilities against the revolted colonies, for the purpose of reducing them to obedience by force."

Notwithstanding the lateness of the hour, these votes were immediately communicated to the king, who was in a pitiable condition, aged, nearly blind, half crazed, and stubborn even to insanity, in his determination to subjugate the Americans. The poor old man, in his rage, threatened to abandon England, to renounce the crown, and to cloister himself in his estate of Hanover. He was however compelled to yield, to dismiss his Tory ministers and to accept a whig cabinet. Edmund Burke wrote a warm, congratulatory letter to Franklin.[35]

[Footnote 35: Edmund Burke wrote to Dr. Franklin that "The motion was the *declaration* of two hundred and thirty four members; but it was the *opinion*, he thought, of the whole house."]

And now the final struggle arose respecting the terms of peace. The three great questions discussed, as diplomatic arrangements, were gradually and very cautiously entered into, were: 1. What shall be the boundaries of the United States. 2. Shall the Americans be allowed to fish on the great banks. 3. What provision shall be made for the Tories in America, whose estates have been confiscated?

There were many preliminary meetings, private, semi-official, and official. There was a general impression that Franklin was the man whose opinion would entirely control that of his countrymen. He was approached in every way, and the utmost endeavors were made to induce the American Commissioners to enter into a private treaty, without consulting the French ministry.

A full account of the diplomatic conflict which ensued, would fill a volume. On one occasion the British minister, Mr. Grenville, said,

"In case England grants America Independence."

The French minister, M. de Vergennes, smiled and said, "America has already won her Independence. She does not ask it of you. There is Dr. Franklin; he will answer you on that point."

"To be sure," Franklin said, "we do not consider it necessary to bargain for that which is our own. We have bought our Independence at the expense of much blood and treasure, and are in full possession of it."

Many of these preliminary interviews took place in Paris. The amount of money and blood which the pugnacious government of England had expended in totally needless wars, can not be computed. The misery with which those wars had deluged this unhappy globe, God only can comprehend. Mr. Richard Oswald, a retired London merchant, of vast wealth, was sent, by Lord Shelburne, prime minister, as a confidential messenger, to sound Dr. Franklin. He was frank in the extreme.

"Peace," said he, "is absolutely necessary for England. The nation has been foolishly involved in four wars, and can no longer raise money to carry them on. If continued, it will be absolutely necessary to stop the payment of interest money on the public debt."

Mr. Adams and Mr. Jay were soon associated with Dr. Franklin in these negotiations. Mr. Jay was in entire sympathy with Mr. Adams in his antipathy to the French. They both assumed that France was meanly seeking only her own interests, making use of America simply as an instrument for the accomplishment of her selfish purposes.[36]

[Footnote 36: Mr. Adams wrote, in his diary, November, 1782, "Mr. Jay don't like any Frenchman. The Marquis de la Fayette is clever, but he is a Frenchman."]

Dr. Jared Sparks, after carefully examining, in the Office of Foreign Affairs in London, the correspondence of the French ministers with the American envoys, during the whole war, writes,

"After examining the subject, with all the care and accuracy which these means of information have enabled me to give to it, I am prepared to express my belief, most fully, that Mr. Jay was mistaken, both in regard to the aims of the French court and the plans pursued by them to gain their supposed ends."[37]

[Footnote 37: Diplomatic Correspondence of the American Revolution, V. viii, p. 209.]

Mr. Jay was so insanely suspicious of the French, that he was afraid that the French ministry would send spies, to pick the locks in his lodgings, and steal his important papers. He therefore always carried them about his person. He also believed that Count de Vergennes had actually proposed to the British minister, that they should unite their armies, seize the United States, and divide America between them.

Such were the colleagues united with Franklin, in the negotiations for peace. It required all his consummate wisdom to be able to guide affairs wisely under such difficult circumstances. It may be doubted whether there was another man in America, who could have surmounted the obstacles over which he triumphed. Both of Franklin's colleagues regarded him with suspicion. They believed that he had been won over to such sympathy with the French, that he would be willing to sacrifice the interests of his own country to please them. They wrote letters home severely denouncing him; and they seemed to stand more in fear of France than of England.

"Dr. Franklin," wrote Mr. Adams, "is very staunch against the Tories; more decided, a great deal, upon that point, than Mr. Jay or myself."

The British ministers insisted that the confiscated estates of the American Tories should be restored to them, and all their losses reimbursed. Franklin silenced the demand by drawing from his pocket the following articles, which he proposed should be added to the treaty,

"It is agreed that his Britannic Majesty will earnestly recommend it to his Parliament, to provide for and make a compensation to the merchants and shop-keepers of Boston, whose goods and merchandise were seized and taken out of their stores, ware-houses and shops, by order of General Gage, and others of his commanding officers there; and also to the inhabitants of Philadelphia for the goods taken away by his army there; and to make compensation also for the tobacco, rice, indigo and negroes seized and carried off by his armies, under Generals Arnold, Cornwallis and others, from the States of Virginia, North and South Carolina and Georgia, and for all the vessels and cargoes belonging to the inhabitants of the said United States, which were stopped, seized or taken, either in the ports or on the seas, by his governors or by his ships of war, before the declaration of war against the United States. And it is further agreed that his Britannic Majesty will also earnestly recommend it to his Parliament to make compensation for all the towns, villages and farms, burnt and destroyed by his troops, or adherents in these United States."

The three British commissioners were confounded by these counter demands, and said not another word about reimbursing the American Tories. On the 30th of November, 1782, the preliminaries were signed, subject to the assent of the French ministers, who were also to submit their preliminaries to the American envoys. By these articles: 1. The boundaries were established. 2. The Americans could fish on the banks of Newfoundland, and cure their fish on the unsettled shores of Nova Scotia and Labrador. 3. Congress was to recommend to the several States, to restore the confiscated property of real British subjects. 4. Private debts were to be paid. 5. There were to be no more confiscations or prosecutions, on either side, for acts during the war. 6. The British troops were to be withdrawn. 7. The navigation of the Mississippi was declared to be free. 8. And any place captured, after the signing of these articles, was to be restored.

On the 13th of January, Count de Vergennes, and the British minister Mr. Fitzherbert, signed their preliminaries in the presence of Dr. Franklin and Mr. Adams. Not till then did the English order hostilities to be suspended, and declare the senseless war to be at an end.

KARTINDO PUBLISHING HOUSE (Kartindo.Com)

There was universal satisfaction in America. With the exception of the king and a few of his ministers, there was general satisfaction in England. It is true that the national pride was sorely humiliated. But after all these woes which England had inflicted upon America, her own statesmen, with almost undivided voice, declared that the interests of both nations were alike promoted, by having a few feeble colonies elevated into the rich and flourishing republic of the United States. Thus the war of the American revolution must be pronounced to have been, on the part of England, which forced it, one of the most disastrous and senseless of those blunders which have ever accompanied the progress of our race.[38]

[Footnote 38: Contemplate the still greater blunder of our civil war. It was forced upon the nation by the slave traders, that they might *perpetuate slavery*. And now after the infliction of woes which no finite imagination can gauge, these very slave-holders declare with one voice, that nothing would induce them to *reinstate the execrable institution*. How much misery would have been averted, and what a comparative paradise would our southern country now have been, if before, instead of after the war, the oppressed had been allowed to go free!]

CHAPTER XV

Life's Closing Scenes

Advice to Thomas Paine--Scenes at Passy--Journey to the Coast--Return to America--Elected Governor of Pennsylvania--Attends the Constitutional Convention--Proposes prayers--Remarkable speech--Letter to Dr. Stiles--Christ on the Cross--Last sickness and death.

About this time some one, knowing Dr. Franklin's deistical views, presented, for his opinion, a treatise denouncing the idea, that there was any God, who manifested any interest in the affairs of men, that there was any *Particular Providence*. Though Franklin did not accept the idea, that Jesus Christ was a divine messenger, and that the Bible was a supernatural revelation of God's will, he certainly did not, in his latter years, deny that there was a God, who superintended the affairs of this world, and whom it was proper to worship. It is generally supposed that Thomas Paine was the author of this treatise, and that it was a portion of his Age of Reason. Franklin, in his memorable reply, wrote,

"I have read your manuscript with some attention. By the argument it contains against a particular Providence, though you allow a *general* Providence, you strike at the foundations of all religion. For without the belief of a providence that takes cognizance of, guards and guides and may favor particular persons, there is no motive to worship a deity, to fear his displeasure or to pray for his protection. I will not enter into any discussion of your principles, though you seem to desire it. At present I shall only give you my opinion that, though your reasonings are subtile, and may prevail with some readers, you will not succeed so as to change the general sentiments of mankind on that subject; and the consequence of printing this piece will be, a great deal of odium drawn upon yourself; mischief to you and no benefit to others. He that spits against the wind, spits in his own face.

"I would advise you, therefore, not to attempt unchaining the tiger, but to burn this piece before it is seen by any other person; whereby you will save yourself a great deal of mortification, by the enemies it may raise against you, and perhaps a good deal of regret and repentance. If men are so wicked *with religion*, what would they be if *without it*."

KARTINDO PUBLISHING HOUSE (Kartindo.Com)

Franklin testifies to the remarkable courtesy which characterized all the movements of the French minister, during these protracted and delicate negotiations. The definitive treaty was signed on the 3d of September, 1783. It was unanimously ratified by Congress on the 14th of January, 1784. The king of England gave it his signature on the 9th of April. Thus two years and three months passed between the beginning of negotiations and the conclusion of the treaty of peace.

At the termination of the war crowds of Englishmen flocked to Paris. Franklin was then recognized as incomparably the most illustrious man on the continent of Europe. His apartments were ever thronged with men of highest note from all the nations. He was then seventy-eight years of age, suffering severely from the gout and the gravel. He often received his guests in his bed chamber, sitting in his night gown, wrapped in flannels, and reclining on a pillow. Yet his mind retained all its brilliance. All who saw him were charmed. Mr. Baynes wrote,

"Of all the celebrated persons whom, in my life, I have chanced to see, Dr. Franklin, both from his appearance and his conversation, seemed to me the most remarkable. His venerable, patriarchal appearance, the simplicity of his manner and language, and the novelty of his observations impressed me as one of the most extraordinary men that ever existed."

At this time he wrote several essays, which are esteemed among the best of his writings. He was awaiting permission from Congress to return to America. His son, the governor, who was receiving a pension of eight hundred pounds from the British Government, came over from England to his illustrious father, soliciting reconciliation. This was after the separation of many years. Franklin responded kindly, though he said that nothing had ever wounded him so keenly as to find himself deserted in his old age, by his only son; and to see him taking up arms against a cause, upon which he had staked life, fortune and honor.

A year passed before Franklin was recalled. He was then so feeble that he could not walk, and could only ride in a litter. Mr. Jefferson succeeded him. Upon his arrival in Paris, the Count de Vergennes said,

"You replace Dr. Franklin, I understand."

"No!" Mr. Jefferson replied, "I *succeed* him. No man can *replace* him."

Franklin's infirmities were such that he could not call upon the king or the minister for an audience of leave. He, however, wrote to Count de Vergennes a very grateful and affectionate letter, in which he said,

"May I beg the favor of you, sir, to express respectfully for me, to his majesty, the deep sense I have of all the inestimable benefits his goodness has conferred on my country; a sentiment that it will be the business of the little remainder of the life now left me, to impress equally on the minds of all my countrymen. My sincere prayers are that God may shower down his blessings on the king, the queen, their children and all the royal family, to the latest generations."

The reply was equally cordial and affectionate. As a parting gift the king sent Franklin his portrait, decorated with four hundred and eight diamonds. Its estimated value was ten thousand dollars.

On the 12th of July, 1785, Franklin, accompanied by many admiring friends in carriages, commenced his slow journey in a litter, from Passy to Havre. It was four o'clock in the afternoon. The litter was borne by two mules. The first night they stopped at St. Germain. Thence the journey was continued at the rate of about eighteen miles a day. The motion of the litter did not seriously incommode him. The cardinal of Rochefoucald, archbishop of Rouen, insisted upon his accepting the hospitality of his mansion at Gaillon. It was a superb chateau, commanding a magnificent prospect, with galleries crowded with paintings and the most valuable works of art.

"The cardinal," writes Franklin, "is much respected, and beloved by the people of this country; bearing in all respects, a most excellent character."

Though entreated to prolong his visit, Franklin resumed his journey at an early hour the next morning. At Rouen he was again received with the most flattering attentions. The *elite* of the city gave a very brilliant supper in his honor. Thus journeying in a truly triumphant march, Franklin reached Havre on the 18th of July. After a delay of three days he crossed the channel to Southampton. His old friends came in crowds, and from great distances, to see him. Even the British government had the courtesy to send an order exempting his effects from custom-house duties.

It will be remembered that Franklin was a remarkable swimmer. There are some human bodies much more buoyant than others. He records the singular fact that, taking a warm, salt water bath here, he fell asleep floating on his back, and did not awake for an hour. "This," he writes, "is a thing which I never did before, and would hardly have thought possible."

On the 28th of July, 1785, the ship spread her sails. The voyage lasted seven weeks. This extraordinary man, then seventy-nine years of age, wrote, on the passage, three essays, which are estimated among the most useful and able of any which emanated from his pen.

On the 13th of September the ship entered Delaware Bay, and the next morning cast anchor opposite Philadelphia. He wrote,

"My son-in-law came with a boat for us. We landed at Market street wharf, where we were received by a crowd of people with huzzahs, and accompanied with acclamations, quite to my door. Found my family well. God be praised and thanked for all his mercies."

The Assembly was in session, and immediately voted him a congratulatory address. Washington also wrote to him a letter of cordial welcome. The long sea voyage proved very beneficial to his health. He was immediately elected to the Supreme Executive, and was chosen chairman of that body. It is evident that he was gratified by this token of popular regard. He wrote to a friend,

"I had not firmness enough to resist the unanimous desire of my country folk; and I find myself harnessed again in their service for another year. They engrossed the prime of my life. They have eaten my flesh and seem resolved now to pick my bones."

Soon after he was elected President, or as we should now say, Governor of Pennsylvania. The vote rested with the Executive Council and the Assembly, seventy-seven in all. He received seventy-six votes. Notwithstanding the ravages of war, peace came with her usual blessings in her hand. The Tory journals of England, were presenting deplorable views of the ruin of the country since deprived of the beneficial government of the British cabinet. Franklin wrote to his old friend, David Hartley,

"Your newspapers are filled with accounts of distresses and miseries, that these states are plunged into, since their separation from Britain. You may believe me when I tell you that there is no truth in those accounts. I find all property in land and houses, augmented vastly in value; that of houses in town at least four-fold. The crops have been plentiful; and yet the produce sells high, to the great profit of the farmer. Working people have plenty of employ, and high pay

KARTINDO PUBLISHING HOUSE (Kartindo.Com)

for their labor."

There were many imperfections attending the old Confederacy. In the year 1787, a convention met in Philadelphia, to frame a new constitution. There was strong opposition to this movement. Washington and Franklin were both delegates. Washington took the chair. The good nature and wisdom of Franklin ruled the house. The convention met in the State House. Franklin, eighty-one years of age, was regularly in his seat, five hours a day, for four months. He was thoroughly democratic in his views, and opposed every measure which had any tendency to extend aristocratic privilege. He had seen that the British government was in the hands of the nobles. And silent, as prudence rendered it necessary for him to be, in reference to the arbitrary government of France, he could not but see that the peasantry were subject to the most intolerable abuses. This led him to detest a monarchy, and to do every thing in his power to place the government of this country in the hands of the people.

Much time was occupied in deciding upon the terms of union between the smaller and the larger States. It will be remembered that this was the subject of very excited debates in the convention of 1776. The discussion was earnest, often acrimonious. Such bitterness of feeling was engendered that, for some time it was feared that no union could be effected.

It is evident that Franklin, as he approached the grave, became more devout, and that he lost all confidence in the powers of philosophical speculations to reform or regenerate fallen man. He saw that the interposition of a divine power was needed to allay the intense excitement in the convention, and to lead the impassioned members to act under the conviction that they were responsible to God. On the 28th of June, this venerable, patriarchal man offered the following memorable resolve:

"Resolved, That henceforth prayers, imploring the assistance of Heaven, and its blessings on our deliberations, be held in the Assembly every morning before we proceed to business; and that one or more of the clergy of this city be requested to officiate in that service."

The speech which accompanied this motion will forever be conspicuous in our annals. He said:

"Mr. President! The small progress we have made, after four or five weeks close attendence and continual reasonings with each other; our different sentiments on almost every question, is, methinks, a melancholy proof of the imperfection of the human understanding.

"In this situation of this Assembly groping, as it were, in the dark, to find political truth, and scarce able to distinguish it when presented to us, how has it happened, sir, that we have not yet hitherto once thought of humbly applying to the Father of Lights to illuminate our understandings?

"In the beginning of the contest with Britain, when we were sensible of danger, we had daily prayers, in this room, for divine protection! Our prayers, sir, were heard, and they were graciously answered. All of us, who were engaged in the struggle, must have observed frequent instances of a superintending Providence in our favor. To that kind Providence we owe this happy opportunity of consulting, in peace, on the means of establishing our future national felicity. And have we now forgotten that powerful friend? or do we imagine that we no longer need his assistance?

"I have lived, sir, a long time. And the longer I live, the more convincing proofs I see of this truth; *That God governs in the affairs of men.* And if a sparrow cannot fall to the ground without his notice, is it probable that an Empire can rise without his aid? We have been assured, sir, in the Sacred Writings, that 'except the Lord build the house, they labor in vain that build it.' I firmly believe this. And I also believe that, without His concurring aid, we shall succeed in this political building, no better than the building of Babel."

It is almost incomprehensible that, under the influence of such an appeal, the great majority of the Assembly should have voted against seeking divine aid. In a note appended to this speech, Franklin writes,

"The convention, except three or four persons, thought prayers unnecessary."[39]

[Footnote 39: Mr. Parton undoubtedly suggested the true reason for this strange refusal to seek divine guidance. He writes,

"I think it not improbable that the cause of this opposition to a proposal so seldom negatived in the United States, was the prevalence in the Convention of the French tone of feeling with regard to religious observances. If so, it was the more remarkable to see the aged Franklin, who was a deist at fifteen, and had just returned from France, coming back to the sentiments of his ancestors."--

Parton's Franklin Vol. 2, p. 575.]

The convention came to a triumphant close, early in September, 1787. Behind the speaker's chair there was a picture of the Rising Sun. While the members were signing, Franklin turned to Mr. Madison, and said,

"I have often, in the course of the session, and the vicissitudes of my hopes and fears as to its issue, looked at the picture behind the President, without being able to tell whether the sun were rising or setting. But now at length, I have the happiness to know that it is a rising, not a setting sun."

Washington was universally revered. Franklin was both revered and loved. It was almost the universal feeling that, next to Washington, our nation was indebted to Franklin for its Independence. Franklin occupied, in the arduous field of diplomacy, the position which Washington occupied at the head of our armies. It was certain that Franklin had, at one period of his life, entirely renounced his belief in Christianity, as a divine revelation. His Christian friends, numbering hundreds, encouraged by some of the utterances of his old age, were anxious to know if he had returned to the faith of his fathers. Dr. Ezra Stiles, President of Yale College, was a friend of Franklin's of many years standing. When the revered patriot had reached his eighty-fifth year, Dr. Stiles wrote, soliciting his portrait for the college library. In this letter, he says,

"I wish to know the opinion of my venerable friend, concerning Jesus of Nazareth. He will not impute this to impertinence; or improper curiosity in one, who, for so many years, has continued to love, esteem and reverence his abilities and literary character, with an ardor and affection bordering on adoration."

What Dr. Stiles, and the community in general, wished to know was, whether Dr. Franklin recognized the Divine, supernatural origin of Christianity. Franklin evaded the question. This evasion of course indicates that he did not recognize, in the religion of Jesus, the authority of, "Thus saith the Lord." But he wished to avoid wounding the feelings of his Christian friends by this avowal. He wrote,

"This is my creed. I believe in God, the Creator of the Universe; that he governs it by his Providence; that he ought to be worshiped; that the most acceptable service we render to him, is doing good to his other children; that the soul of man is immortal, and will be treated with justice in another life,

KARTINDO PUBLISHING HOUSE (Kartindo.Com)

respecting its conduct in this. These I take to be fundamental points in all sound religion, and I regard them as you do, in whatever sect I meet with them.

"As to Jesus of Nazareth, my opinion of whom you particularly desire, I think his system of morals and his religion, as he left them to us, the best the world ever saw, or is like to see. But I apprehend it has received various corrupting changes, and I have, with most of the Dissenters in England, some doubts as to his Divinity; though it is a question I do not dogmatize upon, having never studied it. And I think it needless to busy myself with it now, when I expect soon an opportunity of knowing the truth with less trouble.

"I see however no harm in its being believed, if that belief has the good consequence, as probably it has, of making his doctrines more respected and observed; especially as I do not perceive that the Supreme takes it amiss, by distinguishing the unbelievers in his government of this world, with any peculiar marks of his displeasure. I shall only add respecting myself, that, having experienced the goodness of that Being, in conducting me prosperously through a long life, I have no doubt of its continuance in the next, though without the smallest conceit of meriting such goodness."

He then adds the following suggestive postscript. "I confide that you will not expose me to criticism and censures, by publishing any part of this communication to you. I have ever let others enjoy their religious sentiments, without reflecting on them, for those that appeared to me unsupportable, or even absurd. All sects here, and we have a great variety, have experienced my good will, in assisting them with subscriptions for the building their new places of worship. And, as I have never opposed any of their doctrines, I hope to go out of the world in peace with them all."

Much of his time, in these hours of sickness, he employed in writing his Autobiography. The sufferings he endured were at times very severe. But when he spoke of his approaching departure, it was with composure. At one time, when his daughter expressed the wish that he might yet live many years, he replied "I hope not."

A clerical friend visited him, just as one of his paroxysms of pain came on. As his friend in consequence was about to retire, he said,

"Oh no; don't go away. These pains will soon be over. They are for my good. And besides, what are the pains of a moment in comparison with the pleasures of eternity."

There was, in one of the chambers of his house, a very beautiful painting of Christ on the Cross. He requested his nurse, a very worthy woman, of the Friends' persuasion, to bring it down, and place it directly before him. The Rev. David Ritter, a great admirer of Franklin, called to see him. He had, however, but a few moments before, breathed his last. Sarah Humphries, the nurse, invited David into the chamber, to view the remains. Mr. Ritter expressed surprise in seeing the picture of the Saviour on the cross occupying so conspicuous a position, saying, "You know, Sarah, that many people think that Dr. Franklin was not after this sort."

"Yes," she replied, "but thee knows, David, that many make a great fuss about religion, who have very little. And many, who say but little, have a good deal. He was never satisfied, if a day passed away unless he had done some one a service.[40] Benjamin Franklin was one of that sort. I will tell thee how the picture came here. Many weeks ago, as he lay, he beckoned me to him, and told me of this picture, up stairs, and begged I would bring it to him. I brought it. His face brightened up, as he looked at it, and he said,

"'Ay Sarah; there is a picture worth looking at. That is the picture of him who came into the world to teach men to love one another.'"

"After looking at it wistfully for some time, he said, 'Sarah, set this picture up over the mantel-piece, right before me as I lie. I like to look at it.'

"When I fixed it up he looked at it very much; and indeed died with his eyes fixed upon it."

[Footnote 40: This reminds us of the exclamation of the Emperor Titus, who, at the close of a day in which he could not perceive that he had done any good, exclaimed, sadly, "Perdidi Diem." *I have lost a day.* Beautifully has the sentiment been expressed in the words, which it would be well for all to treasure up,

"Count that day lost, whose low descending sun, Views at thy hand no worthy action done."]

However deeply Franklin, in these dying hours may have pondered the

KARTINDO PUBLISHING HOUSE (Kartindo.Com)

sublimities of Immortality--the Resurrection--the Judgment Throne--the Final Verdict--Heaven--Hell,--he was very reticent respecting those themes. We certainly see none of the triumph of Paul, and of thousands of others, who have in varied language, expressed the sentiment that,

"Jesus can make a dying bed Feel soft as downy pillows are."

A few hours before his death, as some one urged him to change his position, that he might breathe easier he replied, "a dying man can do nothing easy." These were his last words. He then sank into a lethargy, from which he passed into that sleep which has no earthly waking. It was eleven o'clock at night, April 17, 1790. He had lived eighty-four years, three months and eleven days.

But no candid and charitable reader can peruse this narrative, without the admission that Benjamin Franklin, notwithstanding his imperfections, was one of the wisest and best of all the fallen children of Adam. From his dying hour to the present day his memory has been justly cherished with reverence and affection, throughout the civilized world. And there is no fear that this verdict will ever be reversed.

THE END

KARTINDO PUBLISHING HOUSE (Kartindo.Com)

www.ingramcontent.com/pod-product-compliance
Lightning Source LLC
Chambersburg PA
CBHW060501290526
45791CB00001B/220